*Harnessing the Holocaust*

*Stanford Studies in Jewish History and Culture*
Edited by Aron Rodrigue and Steven J. Zipperstein

# Harnessing the Holocaust

The Politics of Memory
in France

Joan B. Wolf

Stanford University Press
*Stanford, California* 2004

Stanford University Press
Stanford, California
www.sup.org

Library of Congress Cataloging-in-Publication Data

Wolf, Joan B. (Joan Beth)
    Harnessing the Holocaust : the politics of memory in
France / Joan B. Wolf.
        p.   cm.
    ISBN 0-8047-4889-6 (alk. paper)
    1. Holocaust, Jewish (1939–1945)—France—Influence.
2. Memory—Social aspects—France.   I. Title: Politics of
memory in France.   II. Title.
D804.3.W64 2004
940.53'18'0944—dc22                                    2003019108

Printed in the United States of America on acid-free, archival-
quality paper.

Original Printing 2004

Last figure below indicates year of this printing:
13   12   11   10   09   08   07   06   05   04

Designed and typeset at Stanford University Press in 10/12
Galliard.

*For my father*
*Bob Wolf*
*in loving memory*

# Contents

# Acknowledgments

This is a well-traveled project. It has accompanied me to Germany, France, and Spain; Chicago, Wisconsin, and Texas; six apartments and one house. It has also followed me into marriage and motherhood, onto and off of the tenure track. It has wended a circuitous path, and it never would have made its way between two covers without the stewardship of several people.

*Harnessing the Holocaust* began as a dissertation written at the University of Chicago. My heartfelt thanks to my advisers, Bill Sewell, Susanne Hoeber Rudolph, Moishe Postone, and Peter Novick, for their enthusiasm, discernment, and example. Both Bill and Moishe will be pleased to know that the introduction resembles only slightly the interminable drafts to which I subjected them as a graduate student. I am grateful to my Chicago colleagues at Wilder House, the Center for the Study of Politics, History, and Culture, as well as those in the Workshops in Interdisciplinary Social Theory and Comparative Politics and Historical Sociology. Thanks also to Nathalie Hester, *professeur extraordinaire*, who prepared me for Parisian French and managed to keep a straight face the day I told her my family had exploded.

I am indebted to the thoughtful critics who commented on different chapters and who have made this book immeasurably more focused and readable: Steve Ellingson, Nancy Green, Sylvia Schafer, Ruth Schwertfeger, Katie See, and Ken Waltzer. Ivan Ermakoff read the entire manuscript with characteristic trenchancy, and an anonymous reviewer at Stanford University Press made compelling suggestions for revision. Participants at conferences sponsored by the Social Science History Association and the Association for Jewish Studies offered insight on chapters four and six.

The research, writing, and publication of this book were made possible by financial contributions from the Andrew Mellon Foundation, the Georges Lurcy Trust, the Memorial Foundation for Jewish Culture, the Fuerstenberg Foundation, and the University of Chicago Division of the Social Sciences. At the University of Wisconsin–Milwaukee I received support from Yair Mazor and the Center for Jewish Studies; Mark Tessler and the Center for International Studies; the Center for 21st Century Studies; the Department of Foreign Languages and Linguistics, and the Wisconsin Society for Jewish Learning. Mark Bradley offered wise counsel regarding publishers. At Texas A&M University, the Department of Political Science provided space and clerical support during the manuscript's final revisions. While in Paris I received invaluable assistance from Sara Halperyn, Marcel Meslati, and the Centre de Documentation Juive Contemporaine; Jean-Claude Kuperminc and the Alliance Israélite Universelle; Jean Astruc and the Institut d'Histoire du Temps Présent; the press dossier section at the Fondation Nationale des Sciences Politiques; and the Bibliothèque Nationale. I also would like to thank my editor, Norris Pope, who was a pleasure to wrok with, and Dave Toback, who listened with good humor to every word, capitalization, and punctuation mark of the manuscript during proofreading.

This book, finally, is in no small part the product of the relationships that sustained me while I wrote it. Special thanks to my sisters, Allison Wolf and Cherie Marcus, for a lifetime of support; Jen Pashup and Rachel Baum, sisters in friendship; Vivien Eisenberg, whose unwavering presence saved me in ways literal and figurative; Phyllis and Gary Toback, models of curiosity, commitment, and compassion; and Katie See, mentor and friend, without whom I would be neither the writer nor person I continue to become.

And finally, to my boys: Dave Toback, my husband, intrepid in love as in all things; and Bobby Toback-Wolf, my miracle child, who could not bring me more joy if he tried. I love you both.

*Harnessing the Holocaust*

## CHAPTER ONE

# *Introduction*
# French Identity and the Politics of Trauma

In 1967, on the eve of the Six-Day War, Claude Lanzmann told *Le Monde* that "if Israel were destroyed, it would be more serious than the Nazi Holocaust."[1] Such sentiment would seem at least slightly overwrought were it not for the fact that French Jews with widely varying social, political, and religious affiliations imagined an Israeli defeat in equally apocalyptic terms, repeatedly turning to imagery of the Holocaust and raising the specter of a second genocide. For the first time, they spoke publicly and with emotionally charged rhetoric to the rest of the French nation about the Holocaust, which they presented as a trauma: singular, incomparable, and incomprehensible. By the end of the short war, however, the Holocaust had become a theme, a symbol of persecution and victimization that could be depicted in a variety of public narratives not necessarily related to Jews, Jewish suffering under the Nazis, or even World War II. Because they insisted that the Holocaust was traumatic, that it was incommensurable, many Jews rebelled against this expansion of its meaning. In so doing, they initiated a confrontation over the Holocaust that continued into the twenty-first century. This book tracks the battle.

As I researched and spoke to American audiences about the politics of the Holocaust in France, I encountered two common responses. On the one hand were those who asked: why France? While Israel and Germany seemed logical choices, especially given the prominence of the Holocaust in recent German and Israeli public discourse, they were unfamiliar with France's anti-Semitic legislation and deportation of Jews. On the other hand were those who knew that the Vichy regime, the French government, had collaborated with the Nazis. They assumed that I was going to reveal the truth about France's persecution and deportation of Jews, its ongoing attempts to conceal these crimes, and the long-standing myth of national heroism. In fact, the Holocaust has been the subject of extensive academic research and an almost daily source of controversy in the French media for nearly two decades. The details of how the wartime government shipped Jews to their death and how later administrations cultivated a legend of un-yielding opposition to the Nazis have produced anguishing and protracted debates and are hardly the taboo that even many French critics claim them to be. Rather than an introduction to or an exposé about World War II France, therefore, this book is an inquiry into how the French have become acquainted with their past and how the meaning of this legacy has evolved since the end of the war. In it I explore how the emergence of Holocaust consciousness reflects the long history of Jews in modern France and how public discussions have both influenced and been shaped by trends in French political culture. This is not simply the saga of one nation's attempts to dodge responsibility, although there certainly has been and continues to be a fair share of what many would call denial. Nor is it merely a chronicle of a victimized group's efforts to fight continued discrimination or to have its suffering acknowledged, though again, this was and remains an impor-tant dimension of the story. The prominence of the Holocaust in French public discourse reveals a nation and an ethnic group in flux, both strug-gling to carve out new identities in rapidly shifting social contexts. It is a story about the present and future as much as the past. And it is a parable for the vicissitudes and enduring power of history.

Many Jews' insistence on the traumatic quality of the Holocaust led af-ter the Six-Day War to conflicts among and between Jews and non-Jews over a range of issues, including Jewish identity, support for Israel, the ex-tent to which the Holocaust resembled other atrocities and instances of op-pression, and ultimately, the culpability of Vichy, the Republic, and France itself. Images of the Nazi genocide were absorbed into national discourse, and the Holocaust developed from a primarily Jewish concern in 1967 to a source of diffuse identification in the 1980s and 1990s. As increasingly large numbers of non-Jews identified with the Holocaust experience, it became a metaphor for various phenomena that could be represented in terms of per-secutors and victims (though only infrequently did it encompass Gypsies or homosexuals, casualties of Hitler who were not as well represented as Jews and others in contemporary politics). By the 1987 trial of SS officer Klaus Barbie, the Holocaust had become a metaphor both for oppression in gen-eral and for the suffering of the French Resistance and nation at the hands of the Nazis. And by the end of the 1990s, the Holocaust had become a symbol of victimization on a broad scale: victimization of the French population by the Vichy regime during World War II, and victimization of the French nation by "the state" in the postwar period. As awareness of the Holocaust broadened, its meaning was dramatically expanded, and what resulted was a narrative politics: a campaign, waged with competing narratives of the genocide, for ownership of the past and control over the contemporary significance of history. If politics is generally understood as a battle for limited resources, the elusive commodity in narrative politics is meaning. And while it seemed as though virtually everyone in France was talking about the Holocaust, often using the same language, its meaning was widely contested.

In this study, I trace the evolution of French Holocaust consciousness by exploring public discourse during moments either explicitly linked to World War II and the Holocaust (i.e., crimes against humanity trials and commemorations of deportations) or tied to issues which are themselves thematically related to Jews and the genocide (i.e., Israel, anti-Semitism, and racism). I understand public discourse to be largely a mediation of experience, a medium that shapes how people think about major events and then responds to popular thinking. It is comprised primarily of news and critical commentary, reports and analyses of public reaction, and then further observations based on popular response. In France, where wars of words are common and the views of intellectuals especially prominent, it is not only an indication of what opinion-makers are thinking but also a window onto popular opinion. The latter is a rather transient phenomenon, refracted only partially through each of the various lenses through which it can be viewed, and public discourse is no exception. But to the extent that commentators both shape and are shaped by mass opinion, public discourse is an ongoing dialogue between critics and the populace, and, as such, one perspective on how the French were thinking about the past. When people turned on their televisions and radios, what did they hear about the Holocaust? As they walked past the kiosks and storefronts advertising the press, what were the most prominent headlines? While they perused their favorite newspaper or magazine (in a country where the line between news reporting and commentary is often blurred), when they spoke to their families, friends, and co-workers, what were the points of view that helped fashion their understanding of history and its meaning in the present? In turn, how did their thinking influence critical debates?

My main sources are newspapers and magazines but include pamphlets, films, television and radio programs, public conferences, and academic texts. Though they are available throughout the country, most of these media originate in Paris, thus I focus less on local debates than on those that take place on a national level. The publications I have probed most systematically are the "quality newspapers"[2] or "the big three": *Le Monde*, politically centrist and probably France's most respected newspaper; *Le Figaro*, conservative and one of France's oldest dailies; and *Libération*, a leftist paper that began in 1973, restructured in 1981, and became one of France's leading news sources. I also have examined other prominent newspapers: the communist *L'Humanité*; the Catholic *La Croix*; *Le Quotidien de Paris*, which merged with the conservative *L'Aurore* in 1980; and *Le Matin*, which ceased publication in 1988. Others, such as the Christian *Témoignage Chrétien*, the Trotskyist *Rouge*, and the monarchist *Action Française*, I have turned to only infrequently. Finally, I have investigated in-depth France's increasingly popular news magazines: *L'Express*, *Le Nouvel Observateur*, *Le Point*, and *L'Événement du Jeudi*.

I also examine debates within the Jewish community, including opinions emanating from Jewish institutions, newspapers, and magazines. The most important Jewish organizations since World War II have been the Conseil Représentatif des Juifs de France (CRIF), the consistories, and the Fonds Social Juif Unifié (FSJU). Founded in 1944 under the Nazi occupation, the CRIF serves as an umbrella organization, bringing together groups with varying orientations, and represents the political interests of French Jewry. Its leaders have intervened most frequently in public discourse having to do with the Holocaust. Established in 1808 by Napoleon, the consistories handle religious matters within the Jewish community, and the Paris Consistory represents religious concerns to the Republic. While consistory members initially dominated the leadership of the CRIF, the organizations are independent, and the increasingly ultra-orthodox orientation of the Paris Consistory beginning in the late 1980s made clear the divide between the two. The FSJU, finally, has concerned itself more with the social and cultural aspects of Jewish life. Created by the CRIF in 1949, it has raised money for the integration of North African Jewish immigrants, Israel, and the establishment of Jewish schools.

Of Jewish publications, the two most prominent throughout most of the period I examine are *L'Arche* and *Tribune Juive*. *L'Arche*, which developed from a journal begun by the FSJU in 1950, is a moderate monthly devoted less to news reporting than to reflection and analysis of Jewish politics and culture. *Tribune Juive* is a weekly magazine that grew out of *Bulletin de nos communautés*, which was established just after the war in the decimated region of Alsace-Lorraine. It reports regularly on Israel and the French Jewish community, and like its predecessor, prides itself on a certain independence from Jewish institutions. I also have looked to other publications, including the monthly *Information Juive*, published by the Association of Jews from Algeria and headquartered in Paris beginning in 1962; *Cahiers Bernard Lazare*, the respected monthly journal of the socialist-Zionist Cercle Bernard Lazare; the weekly *Actualité Juive*; and various regional publications. Exact readerships for these titles are difficult to ascertain, though most estimates suggest that a small percentage of Jews regularly read the Jewish press.[3] Where possible, and especially once the Holocaust becomes a subject of national discussion, therefore, I examine Jewish views expressed in the mainstream media. In addition to the opinions voiced therein, nonetheless, the Jewish publications are an invaluable source of information about community gatherings and events.

When I speak of a particularly "Jewish" or "non-Jewish" discourse, of "many" or "most" Jews or non-Jews, I am referring not to social subjects with the same meta-psychological structure that psychoanalytic theory attributes to individuals but to points of widespread agreement within the dominant strands of public dialogue. Whether there existed in any objective sense a collective Jewish subject in 1967 or a unified Jewish consciousness across time and space is largely irrelevant, and at times all one can find to connect disparate professions of Jewish identity are the claims themselves. The same is true for "Frenchness." These moments are themselves remarkable, however, because they demonstrate a felt shared consciousness, an experience of membership in a collective, real or imagined; and it is the expression of this sense of being Jewish or French in all of its forms that in this study constitutes Jewish and non-Jewish discourse. As a mutual dedication to being Jewish or French does not necessarily mean a shared philosophy of what that identity entails, I analyze the tensions among and between Jews and non-Jews and the meaning of various approaches as they develop.

Because in 1967 many Jews spoke of the Holocaust as traumatic, my inquiry focuses on how they might have arrived at that interpreted experience and how it shaped future debates about the Nazi genocide. I do not attempt to answer the question of whether the Holocaust was a trauma in any clinical sense or whether Jewish responses were psychologically warranted. Instead, I argue that many Jews responded to events in the Middle East as though the Holocaust were a trauma, that they verbalized their experience as one of trauma, and that understanding the significance of this trauma is essential to comprehending how it evolved as a subject of national debate. My aim is to unpack the traumatic narrative, first by analyzing its history and then by exploring its consequences in public discourse. What are the political, cultural, and historical processes that might explain Jews' heretofore unexpressed anxiety about the Nazi genocide? How can we appreciate why so many Jews described the Holocaust as trauma in 1967, and how does this help us understand the discussions that came before and followed? In exploring the dynamics of trauma in public discourse, my intention is to ascertain not which narratives come closer to some normative (and arbitrarily established) interpretation but instead what each Holocaust story means to specific actors in particular social circumstances. What determines how, when, and why an ethnic group publicly communicates an experience of trauma, and what are the politics of trauma in a diverse social context?

In the chapters that follow, I analyze public discourse during a series of controversial events in France, including the Six-Day War, the release of Marcel Ophuls's "The Sorrow and the Pity," a controversial interview with a former Vichy minister, the broadcast of the American television film "Holocaust," the attack in 1980 on Paris's rue Copernic synagogue, Robert Faurisson's Holocaust revisionist publications, the desecration of a Jewish cemetery at Carpentras, the trials of Barbie, collaborator Paul Touvier, and Vichy official Maurice Papon, and widespread controversy over President François Mitterrand's collaboration with the Vichy regime. While debates surrounding these events cannot be reduced to polemics about the Holocaust, they did serve as loci for intersecting narratives about the past and present and as points of departure for new interpretations. At these moments, Holocaust imagery and metaphors were pervasive and explicit, and in a discursive context characterized by a wide range of concerns, each of which undoubtedly informed the others, even remarks not expressly about the genocide resonated in the Holocaust register. Chapters two and three are necessarily more oriented toward the Jewish community, where the majority of discussions about the Holocaust initially took place. Later, especially after the attack on rue Copernic, the Holocaust became a subject of national public discourse, and my focus broadens considerably. My contention is that the postwar story of the Holocaust in France is rooted in the national history of Jews since the Revolution, and in particular, in the unresolved dilemmas of Jewish emancipation. I suggest that notions of trauma have collided with the dynamics of public discourse in an effort to harness the Holocaust that is as much about contemporary social transformations, especially the emergence of radically new forms of ethnic and national identity in France, as about the Nazi genocide of the Jews.

## Trauma and Narrative

Because it challenges ordinary notions of temporality, psychoanalytic reasoning can be disconcerting for those trained in the methods of historical and social scientific research. If, to use a fairly banal example, a child who is raised by thrifty parents develops into a parsimonious adult, we might say that her frugality is a result of her upbringing. If, on the other hand, she becomes wasteful and a spendthrift, we also might label her profligacy a response to the environment in which she was raised. Because it can explain both outcomes, nurture is not a terribly edifying *a priori* explanation of the adult child's spending habits. However, if we are in an analytic situation and we listen to how she narrates her past, attentive to what is said and unsaid and when, we might be able to understand why she followed a particular economic path. If, moreover, we examine her past actions in light of the narratives she constructs, we should be able to uncover the conscious and unconscious motivations behind both her behavior and commentary. What is significant, in other words, is less the family approach to financial issues than the ways in which it has been interpreted and assimilated, a process dependent on social context and often evident only in retrospect. Causality, in this case, is ongoing, or diachronic; it cannot be reduced to subjective interpretation, but neither can it be independent of experience. The conscious and unconscious practice of telling stories about the past, in other words, creates narratives that are not always apparent as they unfold. And storytelling endows certain phenomena with an extended temporality that problematizes the linear chronologies and predictive theories that historians and social scientists often seek to establish.

Trauma, an occurrence whose significance is initially inaccessible even to those who experience it, disrupts time in just such a fashion. Trauma is most often defined as a dramatic shock or rupture, "an overwhelming experience of sudden or catastrophic events." Traumatic episodes, suggests Judith Herman,

overwhelm the ordinary systems of care that give people a sense of control, connection, and meaning . . . [T]hey overwhelm the ordinary human adaptations to life. Unlike commonplace misfortunes, traumatic events generally involve threats to life or bodily integrity, or a close personal encounter with violence and death. They confront human beings with the extremities of helplessness and terror, and evoke the responses of catastrophe.[4]

Kirby Farrell similarly describes "post-traumatic culture" as "belated, epiphenomenal, the outcome of cumulative stress . . . a disturbance in the ground of collective experience: a shock to people's values, trust, and sense of purpose." But what distinguishes a trauma, such as French Jewry's experience of the Holocaust, is not only the dramatic and unexpected break with the past, the sudden collapse of what was familiar, the brutal estrangement from what was implicit and assumed. An inherent component of trauma is victims' ongoing efforts to make sense of the shock. As Farrell writes, *the injury entails interpretation of the injury.*" Analyzing what she designates as "disrupted lives," anthropologist Gay Becker suggests that "[w]hen expectations about a course of life are not met, people experience inner chaos and disruption. Such disruptions represent loss of the future. Restoring order to life necessitates reworking understandings of the self and the world, redefining the disruption and life itself." A disrupted life encompasses "the disruption itself, a period of limbo, and a period of life reorganization." Because, in the words of Cathy Caruth, trauma is "an event that is constituted, in part, by its lack of integration into consciousness," it is similarly comprised of both the initiating shock—the "disruption" or "injury"—and the expressive forms by which it is mediated.[5]

The struggle to make meaning of the entire spectrum of events in our lives, to make our current experiences congruent with our past, is an inescapable part of the human condition. This process of trying to make sense, to create coherence from the disparate pieces of everything we know and encounter, is in many ways as involuntary as breathing. With the exception of those whose reality is inaccessible to the rest of the world, such as psychotics, most of us spend our lives in a constant and often unconscious process of situated storytelling. We build bridges between moments in our past and present lives by identifying with particular events and people and by creating connections between what we perceive to be related experiences. Narrative, or the telling of these stories, is a means by which individual subjects and social groups construct coherent identities and an instinctual response to the potentially overwhelming amount of information with which we are confronted each day. It is how we create the conceptual order that enables us to function as human beings, and the analogy to breathing is apt: as physical pressure, and particularly stress to which we are unaccustomed, challenges our bodies in ways that make breathing more arduous, the strain of cognitively and emotionally trying situations renders the process of making sense or meaning more calculated and complex. Yet regardless of the intensity of the stress, the reflex to construct narratives that cohere and provide maps to understanding our lives remains potent. We are driven to order our lives cognitively in the same way we are compelled to maintain physical exertion at an optimal level. Meaning-construction is as inevitable in traumatic situations as in those that are banal or joyous.[6]

If the *process* of narration is almost instinctual, however, the form and content of the resulting stories are widely variable and dependent on social and political circumstance. As Farrell argues about trauma, victims can "symbolically transform it, compulsively re-experience it, or deny it. And those interpretations are profoundly influenced by the particular cultural context." No event, however traumatic, is inherently immune to interpretation, even if it seems never to be satisfactorily or finally explained. And how one remembers or responds to trauma depends on the events that precede and follow the traumatic shock. The stories told, writes Becker, are victims' efforts "to create coherence and provide closure to situations that are at odds with their notions of order . . . to integrate disruption and its aftermath with prevailing cultural sentiments." But after a traumatic shock, cultural norms, or the "prevailing cultural sentiments," are no longer implied. Social practice becomes more conscious and deliberate, and the constituent beliefs that structure what Jerome Bruner calls a culture's "folk psychology" are no longer taken for granted. New narratives, which specialize in "the forging of links between the exceptional and the ordinary," must be constructed to re-establish social equilibrium. "However controlled it may appear, however hedged by rules and social apparatus," Farrell contends, "trauma destabilizes the ground of experience, and therefore it is always supercharged with significance and always profoundly equivocal in its interpretive possibilities." Because trauma upsets customary modes of interpretation, in other words, its narrative integration involves reconfiguration of the cultural and linguistic conventions around which meaning was constructed in the past.[7]

A narrative frames and freezes an event such that it forgets more than it remembers; exactly which aspects of the past are included and which neglected often is clear only in the context of the current event through which the original experience is invoked. Because this representation of the past is inherently connected to the present, because the past does not appear in the present in pristine, unmodified form, "the past is necessarily violated in narrative memory and in history writing, and so the very act of remembering can seem like an act of narrative infidelity."[8] Traumatic narratives exacerbate this betrayal because the shock unsettles and can even disable existing configurations of meaning. Victims therefore confront the overwhelming force of trauma without a vocabulary or the conceptual means to make sense of it. In a social context, where a group perceives itself as the victim of a collective trauma, the attempt to articulate the shock is further complicated by the obligation that group members feel to their peers and forebears. "We are not only trying to convince ourselves with our memory reconstructions," writes Bruner. "Recalling the past also serves a dialogic function. The rememberer's interlocutor (whether present in the flesh or in the abstract form of a reference group) exerts a subtle but steady pressure."[9]

Many students of the Holocaust have pointed to victims' frustration at the impotence of existing narrative tools, and they have argued that language cannot adequately express the magnitude of the trauma. As Lawrence Langer contends, for example, labeling the Holocaust an example of "mass suffering" merges it with past models that are "meager measures" of the event. Neither victims nor sympathizers can appreciate the Holocaust, he writes, without suspending an attachment to normal notions of order and meaning—"the search for correspondences"—because "a cultural tradition and mental attitude that demand normal intellectual reactions from abnormal historical situations" prevent us from "admitting the Holocaust" into consciousness. Others have gone so far as to claim that the story of the Holocaust cannot be told and that even the attempt runs the risk of creating a false sense of comprehension, what Claude Lanzmann has called "the obscenity of understanding." For Lanzmann, the Holocaust cannot be "engendered" because "a gap, an *abyss*" separates all explanation, all description, from the reality of the horror. What is objectionable is the attempt to bridge this gap through narrative, because narrative is "a way of escaping; it is a way not to face the horror." To deny the categorical impossibility of under-standing, to suggest coherence or sense, to give in to what Michael Bern-stein has called "the pleasure of comprehension, the satisfaction of the hu-man urge to make sense out of every occurrence, no matter how terrible," is obscene. Jean-François Lyotard has even suggested that the proper response to the Holocaust is silence, a silence that stands for that which has not been determined and therefore cannot be articulated.[10]

Regardless of its purported shortcomings, however, narrative construc-tion is an unavoidable part of being human, and a massive collection of di-aries, memoirs, and historical texts suggests that survivors and a host of others have long tried to convey the Holocaust in various narrative forms. Whether these stories capture the meaning of the event or fail miserably, they demonstrate the centrality, indeed the inevitability, of the narrative im-pulse in human cognition. Lanzmann himself has been taken to task for fail-ing to acknowledge the ways in which his monumental film "Shoah" re-flects the very conventions of narrative that he abjures. That Lanzmann simultaneously condemns and produces Holocaust narrative demonstrates the fundamental aporia of trauma: the desire to convey and even master the shock and at the same time to preserve the very incomprehensibility that de-fines it as trauma. According to Herman, "[c]ertain violations of the social compact are too terrible to utter aloud: this is the meaning of the word *un-speakable.*" But because trauma refuses to be buried, "[t]he conflict between the will to deny horrible events and the will to proclaim them aloud is the central dialectic of psychological trauma." As Michael Roth writes, a trauma draws one to the original event

even as it demands acknowledgment that one can never comprehend what hap-pened there. The "need" for integration stems from the claims that the traumatic past can still make on the person in the present. But there is also a *threat* of integra-tion, stemming from the possibility that the horrific past may, after all, be distilled through "existing mental schemes." The successful integration would necessarily rel-ativize this past in relation to the rest of one's life.

This conflicting drive to both share and protect the inexpressible core of trauma explains why, in the words of Herman, "people who have survived atrocities often tell their stories in a highly emotional, contradictory, and fragmented manner which undermines their credibility and thereby serves the twin imperatives of truth-telling and secrecy." These essentially incoher-ent expressions betray the desire to tell the story and at the same time pre-serve its traumatic component: the inability to be told.[11]

But how can trauma be managed, yet alone overcome, in the absence of a communicable language? And how, as Elizabeth Bellamy asks, "can one enter into an exchange with the past that can negotiate trauma and, at the same time, locate and preserve historical specificity?" The internal contradictions of trauma can cause great stress for victims, possessed by the shock and at the same time unable to articulate it. "Denial of reality makes [survivors] feel crazy," writes Herman, "but acceptance of the full reality seems beyond what any human being can bear." In a self-consciously therapeutic dialogue, where both participants are committed to the successful integration of the trauma, the process of working through, of finding a way to express the rupture that acknowledges its unknowable, untransmittable aspects, is lengthy and excruciating. It can take place only in an environment of safety, where the victim is certain that his or her feelings will be validated and the trauma appreciated. The reconstruction of trauma, Herman emphasizes, requires that the patient and therapist "be clear in their purpose and secure in their alliance." The survivor

is not simply describing what she felt in the past but is reliving those feelings in the present. The therapist must help the patient move back and forth in time, from her protected anchorage in the present to immersion in the past, so that she can simultaneously re-experience the feelings in all their intensity while holding on to the sense of safe connection that was destroyed in the traumatic moment.[12]

But the dialectic of trauma, the simultaneous demand for and rejection of empathy, explodes in a political environment where multiple egos vie for preeminence without regard for any restorative project. The antithesis of a safe therapeutic medium, public discourse is an inherently contentious arena, fueled by competing ideologies and interests, where the antinomies of trauma are exacerbated. Victims call to question established cultural practice and reject seemingly entrenched ways of knowing that are unproblematic for others. What used to make sense, they suggest, no longer does, and the rules of social discourse must change to accommodate the trauma. In the meantime, ostensibly unaffected bystanders try in a variety of ways to make sense of the trauma on their own terms, a "mis-understanding" that victims tend to find intolerable. Whether these responses are sincere attempts at empathy or extensions of political battles already in place, victims often experience them as inadequate: as evidence of either partial or total absence of comprehension, as misguided attempts at commiseration, or at worst, as shameless appropriation.[13] Once traumatic memories are articulated in public discourse, they are *shared* with those whose previous connection to the victims might have been one of sympathy, indifference, or animosity. Even the most compassionate of these interlocutors faces the virtually impossible task of conveying an appreciation of the trauma to those who consider themselves guardians of an experience that must but can be integrated only at great cost: the erasure of the event's traumatic component. As for those whose regard is one of apathy or hostility, victims experience their refusal to recognize the trauma as an assault, and this adds a new dimension of conflict to an already antagonistic situation. What results from the public presentation of trauma is a narrative politics of the past: a debate, at times direct and unflinching and at others subtly woven into discussions about other issues, in which the event is plotted in competing stories that either confirm or deny its traumatic component.

## French Jewry and the Trauma of the Holocaust

Like Jews around the world, French Jews were stunned by the extent of Nazi persecution. European anti-Semitism, especially in Russian pogroms, had been brutal, but nothing had prepared them for the mass and systematic annihilation that was the Holocaust. What was particular to the French Jewish trauma was the apparent failure of the very principles on which modern France had been founded and on which Jews, since the Revolution, had staked their secular lives. Although Jewish emancipation had been granted in stages and only after extensive debates punctuated by anti-Semitism,[14] most Jews welcomed their new status as French citizens, expressed faith in social progress and citizenship, and pledged their allegiance to France. In the words of Berr Isaac Berr, a Nancy Jewish community representative during the Revolution, "we can be both faithful Jews and good French citizens. Indeed, we will be both, and we swear it to you!" In the century that followed, many Jews claimed that they were "happy as God in France" and that French citizenship was a sign of the Messiah's impending arrival.[15] For over 150 years, without ever abandoning their Jewishness, most had engaged in a process of assimilation that assumed a fundamental symmetry between their French and Jewish identities. And most remained convinced of this harmony even during crises when public discourse was dominated by those who explicitly denied it. During the Dreyfus Affair, for example, the majority of Jews "chose to assert their Frenchness and their devotion to the Republic." Like most French people, they believed Captain Dreyfus was guilty of treason, and once the military tribunal had announced the verdict, they considered it incumbent upon all to defer to the court's authority. Those Jews who did publicly support Dreyfus, such as human rights activist Victor Basch, writer Marcel Proust, politician Joseph Reinach, and sociologist Emile Durkheim, made clear that they were engaged in a struggle to defend not a Jew but the basic principles of the Republic. Most others, especially Jewish leaders, professed faith in French officials and believed that the best response to this moment of crisis was to demonstrate Jewish patriotism. And once Dreyfus was exonerated in 1906, it seemed that the Republic ultimately had protected the rights of Jews as citizens. "From the vantage point of French Jewry," writes Paula Hyman, "the system had worked."[16]

The Vichy regime was the most serious blow to the peaceful coexistence of Jewish and French identity. In October 1940, just over three months after the Franco-German armistice that left northern France occupied by the Nazis and most of the south under the administrative control of the Vichy regime, Vichy head Marshal Philippe Pétain signed the Jewish Statute. The law, which provided a definition of "Jew" and restricted the rights of Jews in French civil law and society, was the first in a series of legislative acts that progressively worsened conditions for Jews in France. In March 1941, Vichy created the Commissariat Général aux Questions Juives (CGQJ), which oversaw the major arrests and deportations of Jews from France. The most sweeping of these actions took place in the summer and fall of 1942. On July 16 and 17, French police initiated the Vél d'Hiv roundup: close to 13,000 Jewish men, women, and children from Paris were arrested and crowded into the Vélodrome d'hiver, a bicycle stadium on the right bank, with no provisions for food, water, or sanitation. From there those captured were transferred to Drancy, a concentration camp just north of Paris, before being deported to the east. Extensive roundups of Jews in the unoccupied zone began in earnest at the end of August, and deportations continued through August 1944. All told, approximately 76,000 Jews were deported from France. Fewer than 3,000 returned at the end of the war.

In November 1941, the Vichy government created the Union Générale des Israélites de France (UGIF). Charged with "representing Jews to the public authorities, notably for matters of public assistance, mutual aid, and social readaptation," the UGIF took the place of existing Jewish philanthropies and social agencies, and all Jews were required to join. Beholden to the Vichy regime, it extracted money and supplies from the Jewish community throughout the war, resources which ultimately facilitated deportations and aided the Nazi war effort. It also was responsible for collecting spectacular fines that the Nazis levied on the Jewish community in response to Resistance assassinations of German soldiers and officials. Old-stock Jews (*la vieille souche*) responded to the UGIF's creation and the arrests and expulsions that followed in ways that emphasized their commitment to France. They complained about being lumped together with Jewish immigrants from eastern and central Europe who either were not French citizens or had been naturalized only recently. Those who went on to serve as UGIF administrators eventually expedited the arrest and deportation of these "foreign" Jews in the hope that native-born Jews would be spared. Fearing German reprisals against the Jewish community, these officials seemed to believe that cooperation with Vichy would ensure that the regime would protect them from the worst of German atrocities. In the end, UGIF leaders in the northern and southern zones were deported and murdered at Auschwitz. The failure of most French Jews, especially UGIF functionaries, to understand that Vichy was the enemy and that their fate was ultimately tied to their Jewish identity (and thus to their fellow Jews) was perhaps the most poignant example of French Jewry's overriding confidence in assimilation and the security of citizenship. Jewish immigrant organizations, on the other hand, recognized that whatever its intentions, the UGIF furthered Nazi and Vichy objectives. They refused to join the Union board and continued to operate illegally. As Hyman argues, the UGIF acted under severe restrictions and was not responsible for the fate of Jews in France during the Holocaust. But the contrast between its actions and those of immigrant groups, such as the Amélot Committee, is one measure of how powerful was the faith of many French Jews in the country to which they had pledged their allegiance since emancipation.[17]

From the early days of the Revolution, Jews seemed to absorb and reflect the great political concerns of the day, to function as something of a discursive screen onto which competing political projects could be projected. Controversies about Jews often served as a medium for debates about the nation, as battlefields on which ideological wars about the meaning of Frenchness were waged, and this was particularly true when national identity was most in flux. Jews, therefore, seemed to be inextricably bound up in questions of national identity. Jewish emancipation, for example, was the natural extension of revolutionary logic, and citizenship was granted largely "because there was really no alternative for the makers of the Revolution."[18] The bitter dispute over Dreyfus's guilt or innocence was the latest clash in a long-standing conflict between republicans, on the one hand, and the Church, the army, and monarchists, on the other. For anti-Dreyfusards, the captain's guilt demonstrated the absurdity of universal citizenship and the impossibility of democracy; resolute anti-Semites like Edouard Drumont notwithstanding, rhetoric and violence against Jews were part of a larger project to reestablish Church power. For Dreyfusards, on the other hand, failure to provide the captain with the protections of citizenship was an abrogation of republican principles; even more troubling, they feared, were the political gains being made by his adversaries, who were also enemies of the Republic. Thus Dreyfus was an instrument in efforts either to consolidate or dismantle the Third Republic.[19] As for the Vichy regime, there is little evidence that either Pierre Laval, prime minister, or René Bousquet, chief of police, was particularly anti-Semitic. But when it became clear that anti-Jewish legislation and Jewish deportations from France were a way for

Vichy to express its willingness to cooperate with the Nazis, thereby maintaining a veneer of bureaucratic autonomy and ensuring a prominent place for France in what was assumed would be a German-dominated Europe, Jews became a means to an end: a weapon in the war against the Republic and a sacrifice for the advancement of Nazi-French relations. In all three cases, Jews served as a vessel for competing visions of France, as symbols for national identity.

As emancipation opened the doors of modernity to French Jews, it also introduced a tension between their *particular* identity as Jews and their putatively *universal* identity as citizens. The revolutionary mission was to create an unmediated civil society based on universalist principles and populated by individuals without particularist loyalties. The very notion of universalism, however, was predicated on the problematic assumption that a metaphysical France existed independent of all particularisms, and it failed to grasp that France had been and would continue to be a perpetually evolving project.[20] Thus the Jews (like all other French citizens) were required to demonstrate unadulterated loyalty to a nation that was unconscious of its own ongoing contingency, and both the birth of modern France and the political emancipation of French Jewry were bound up in the same logic that assumed a clear distinction between the universal and particular aspects of civic identity. The rhetoric of the Revolution also failed to make clear precisely what distinguished "French" from "universal." In principle, Frenchness was based not on blood or lineage but on a commitment to equality between men. National identity was indistinguishable from a certain universal identity, and what was "French" became inseparable from a normative universalism that was synonymous with humanity. That this elision in revolutionary logic was problematic would become clearest during the Vichy years, when Jewish allegiance to the nation did little to alter the course of their deportation, and in the last twenty years of the century, when public debate on the Holocaust produced sharp disagreement over the extent to which the genocide was significant for all humankind.

Once they were granted full civil and political rights, a contradiction emerged between Jews as individual citizens and Jews as a distinct collective within France, "a nation within a nation" in the famous words of Count Stanislas de Clermont-Tonnerre. Despite this tension, most Jews became *fous de la République*,[21] republican zealots who largely embraced citizenship without recognizing the incongruity between adopting universalism, on the one hand, and claiming it as consistent and harmonious with their Jewish identity, on the other. In their vision of modernity, the universalism reflected in national citizenship was not incompatible with the particularity of their Jewish identity. What they did not address was the fact that their project—the successful integration of Jewish and French identity—was not shared by the architects of the Revolution, who either opposed emancipation altogether or assumed that it would lead to the abandonment of Judaism, backward and anachronistic, and the "regeneration" of Jews as "new men." Indeed, revolutionaries who argued on their behalf indicated that "the Jews deserved freedom much more for what they promised to become than for what they were," that the logical and desired outcome of citizenship was the end of the Jews *as Jews*.[22] Certainly they were not the only group targeted by the new anti-corporatism; but the fact that Jewish rights were bestowed only secondarily, after additional debates, suggested that even proponents of the Revolution had serious doubts about Jews' ability to meet the demands of citizenship. That the largely unassimilated Jews of Alsace and Lorraine were emancipated in 1791, almost two years after the culturally and economically integrated Jews of the Southwest, further indicated that racialized thinking would not disappear with democracy, that it remained in republican consciousness despite the revolutionary logic that stipulated its obsolescence, and that the conflation of universalism and French identity was untenable from the start.[23]

Most Jews chose not to draw attention to the persistent anti-Jewish sentiment among both advocates and opponents of the Revolution. In order to become citizens—indeed, to convince reluctant republicans—Jews were forced to abandon public claims of difference despite—because of—the fact that French people across the political spectrum were still persuaded that they were immutable. As Hyman writes of the Assembly of Jewish Notables, convoked by Napoleon in 1806, which ruled that Jewish law was subordinate to French civil law, "[t]he process of emancipation into a state with little tolerance for particularist identities, especially in the public sphere, left them no other alternative short of rejection of citizenship." In a sense, Jews were not owners of their public identity because they were constrained to argue that they were unmarked citizens like everyone else, indeed that their public identity *as Jews* did not exist. Having long served as a discursive screen for others' political projects, they had little autonomous public identity with which to respond to attacks on their Frenchness. The strategy of silence they took to the Dreyfus Affair, therefore, befitted their absence *as Jews* in the Republic. Because communal institutions were linked to the state either by mandate or custom, moreover, Jews lacked a strong and independent organization to represent them *as Jews* during both the Affair and World War II. And once these institutions were dissolved into the UGIF, Jews were without either the conceptual or structural resources to react to what Vichy had in store for them *as Jews*. In a political context where universalism was dead, they continued to prioritize their French identity and to oblige a government that had abolished their civil, political, and human rights. They were committed to "legalism," Hyman writes, "almost to the point of self-delusion."[24] As long as their primary concern was to demonstrate loyalty to France, their desirability as French citizens, the particularity of their Jewishness was eclipsed by their Frenchness.

That their total loyalty to the nation had not protected them, and moreover, that the Vichy government had collaborated actively with the Nazis in Jewish deportations—this was for Jews a betrayal of monumental proportions, one that could not be reconciled with the principles the nation had professed to incarnate and around which a particular Jewish vision of modernity had been constructed. The Holocaust nullified the notion of Jews as both particular and universal citizens, and this was felt most acutely in France, where Jewish emancipation and democratic universalism had been born. In exploding the contradiction between being Jewish and French, it betrayed the lie of French Jews' most fundamental understanding of their place in the modern world. It was, in a word, a dramatic rupture, a break in what had been unquestioned expectations. The shock for the collective "French Jewry" was both mass death and the collapse of the conceptual apparatus that before the war had ordered their secular lives. The shock was that their Jewish and French identities had been irreconcilable, and this was the essence of the Holocaust trauma.

## Holocaust Trauma and French Public Discourse

Not surprisingly, Jews first publicly articulated the trauma of the Holocaust in the days surrounding the Six-Day War, when the compatibility between being Jewish and French once again seemed to be threatened. The War, in fact, was the seminal event in the development of public discourse on the Holocaust. With Israel and Egypt on the brink of war and Charles de Gaulle adopting a policy that indirectly favored the Arabs, Jews spoke with emotionally charged rhetoric to the nation as survivors of the Nazi genocide and as potential casualties of a second Holocaust, this time to be perpetrated in the Middle East. For the first time in French history, they unequivocally asserted themselves as Jews in public discourse and declared that the singular, incomprehensible horror of the Holocaust demanded a public display of their Jewishness as well as the nation's unconditional support for Israel. This unprecedented assertiveness was bolstered by the recent arrival of North African Jews, who had fled Egypt after the Suez crisis and Morocco, Tunisia, and Algeria during decolonization. Between 1956–67, roughly 235,000 Sephardi Jews immigrated to France, mostly to Paris but in large numbers to the Midi as well. The newcomers tended to be more religious and less self-conscious about their Jewishness than their Ashkenazi

counterparts. Having fought tenaciously in their countries of origin to preserve their rights as Jews, they brought with them both a pride in being
Jewish and a tendency toward militancy that was, literally, foreign to their
coreligionists. Deeply attached to Israel, the only place they were still welcome in a part of the world where they had lived for centuries, they found
the public reserve of French Jews equally alien and, especially in the current
crisis, incomprehensible.[25]

By the end of the Six-Day War, many non-Jews and Arab supporters
challenged the notion of trauma put forth by Jews by claiming their own
identification with Holocaust victims. Indeed, once Israel occupied Arab
territories, some went so far as to accuse Jews of being Nazis. As soon as
Jews spoke of the Holocaust as trauma to the nation—that is, once they expressed it publicly and repeatedly—the genocide became part of national
consciousness and available for use in contemporary discourse much like
any other event. The total guilt of Nazi perpetrators and absolute innocence
of Jewish victims became a theme that could be infinitely reconfigured and
then grafted onto a variety of narratives focused on persecutors and victims.
As long as French Jews were discrete about the Holocaust, as they largely
had been since the end of World War II, Holocaust narratives—stories
about either the past or present where an interpretation of the Holocaust is
explicitly or implicitly a central theme—were inconsequential in national
politics. But tensions were unmistakable from the Six-Day War through the
end of the 1990s, when myriad social and political subjects identified with
Holocaust victims in ways that many Jews experienced as an appropriation
of the Holocaust trauma.

That the actors within Holocaust narratives in 1967 were variable made
possible a proliferation of commentary based on an identification with Nazi
victims. What ensued was a narrative politics of the Holocaust, a conflict in
which different social groups told competing and often contradictory stories about the Holocaust in an effort to explain both past and present. At
times this politics was open and vitriolic, an all-out war over the meaning
of history. At others it was a battle over inflection, a politics of nuance in
which people used the same language to convey very different messages.
Frequently the Holocaust figured prominently in these debates; sometimes
it was an invisible presence, a subtext of discussions that seemingly had little to do with or were only marginally related to either Jews or Jewish suffering during World War II. The Six-Day War initiated a widespread effort
to harness the Holocaust to competing political and cultural agendas. What
developed in the over thirty years that followed were parallel strands of
Holocaust discourse, layers of narrative that were linked by language but
separated by a broad gulf in meaning.

From the Arab-Israeli conflict, many Jews derived three axioms that would orient their participation in the next thirty years of public debates. The first concerned Jewish identity: the Holocaust justified and even obligated Jews to claim their Jewish identity in the public sphere. For nearly two centuries they had restricted open demonstrations of their Jewishness, and in their zeal to prove themselves worthy of citizenship, they had endeavored, even when under attack, to comport in public in ways that denied even the possibility of conflict between their Jewish and French identities. The Middle East war accomplished a break with this history, a rupture initiated by the Holocaust, and in the days that followed the short war, Jews began the long and arduous process of narrating this disruption, of explaining to themselves and others when and why they might present themselves not as unalloyed French citizens but as Jews with political commitments rooted in their Jewish identity. This was a radical revision of the terms under which citizenship had been negotiated; it required dramatic new ways of thinking about how to be both Jewish and French, and many Jews labored in the decades that followed to articulate the parameters of such a hybrid identity. They struggled to reconcile the failures of their country, the promise of Israel, and their commitment nonetheless to remain French. They wrestled in multiple registers with their new dedication to being Jewish and a continued loyalty to France, a desire to be recognized as a unique collective and at the same time as the unmarked individual citizens so valorized by the Jacobin revolutionaries. Jewish leaders often found themselves at odds with North African Jews who were uncommitted to the assimilation project pursued by earlier generations. Many young Jews, especially Sephardi youth, expressed disdain for community leadership, found the rhetoric of French universalism a shibboleth, and preached Zionism as the only solution to centuries of Jewish persecution. In continuing debates about Israel, public demonstrations, and discussions of provocative films such as "The Sorrow and the Pity," "Holocaust," and "Shoah," in intensely polarized national debates about the Holocaust during the trials of Barbie, Touvier, and Papon, and in the controversies surrounding Mitterrand—Jews grappled for the rest of the century with whether and how to be Jews in public. Their only consensus was on the desirability of articulating a coherent French Jewish identity, an effort that has been and remains a hallmark of Jewish public discourse on the Holocaust.

The second axiom gleaned from the Six-Day War concerned the relationship between the Holocaust and Israel: the Holocaust was proof that a Jewish state must exist, that it must be defended at all costs, and that threats to Israel's moral and territorial integrity must be combated on all fronts, including France. Israel, in other words, was the center of many Jews' conceptual universe, and during the 1967 conflict, Jews with disparate ideological commitments invoked the Holocaust to explain their unconditional support for the young state. At the end of the war and in the years that followed, when public discourse was rife with critics who challenged Israel's legitimacy, many Jews sought to separate their unequivocal support for the Jewish state from their provisional endorsement of particular governments. This project, of distinguishing unqualified Zionism from a conditional backing of specific Israeli parties or policies, was especially pronounced on the Jewish Left, where many turned to the Holocaust to defend Israel despite what they argued were its at times egregious moral shortcomings. But this was a nuance lost in a public discourse that at times failed even to distinguish Jews from Israelis. When the French government openly supported the Arabs and the public did not rally to Israel's side during its 1973 war with Egypt; when newspaper, magazine, and television critics accused Israel of imitating Nazi Germany following its invasion of Lebanon and the massacres in the Sabra and Shatilla refugee camps in 1982; and when Barbie's defenders compared the plight of Palestinian children to the ordeal of Jewish children deported by Barbie—even Jews critical of Israel angrily rejected any comparison of Israelis and Nazis and indeed invoked Jewish suffering during the Holocaust to demonstrate that the Israeli cause was irreproachable. Praising the mission and virtues of Israel has been and continues to be a central project in Jewish public discourse.

The third axiom justified the first two: the Holocaust was a trauma whose uniqueness needed to be safeguarded. Precisely how "uniqueness" would be defined and demonstrated depended on the particulars of the political context. Some Jews were convinced of the Holocaust's categorical singularity. Thus the more that others made sense of the Holocaust on their own terms, the more these Jews felt compelled to correct the record, to explain it "better" so that its meaning could not be metaphorically extended. But the more that they pressed their case, the more they solidified its role as a theme in public discourse, where an already elusive empathy usually appears in the symbolic forms of identification that trauma victims find intolerable. This was especially true during debates surrounding Klaus Barbie, when many Jews experienced Resistance identification with Holocaust victims as disingenuous empathy that bordered on outright usurpation. For those Jews most wedded to the notion of absolute singularity, therefore, the central dialectic of trauma—the simultaneous demand for and rejection of empathy—has been aggravated since the Holocaust became part of the national discursive landscape. But as discussions of terrorism, racism, and oppression became pervasive in the late 1970s and early 1980s, other Jews found it difficult to justify a discourse that denied the Holocaust's place in a century filled with violence and mass death. They pointed to links between the Nazi genocide and other atrocities, including communist and colonialist crimes, and they acknowledged that the Holocaust was an event rooted in the horrors by which it was preceded and reflected in abominations that followed. During crimes against humanity trials and debates about the Vichy regime, they recognized that the Holocaust had taken place during a world war where suffering was ubiquitous. At the same time, they insisted, either subtly or explicitly, on those aspects of the Holocaust that distinguished it from other instances of evil.

## The Holocaust and National Identity

While Jews contemplated their political identity in light of the Holocaust, the rest of the nation wrestled with the memory of Vichy and its implications for national identity. Until the release of "The Sorrow and the Pity" in 1971, this memory had been dominated by the so-called "Gaullist myth." Mindful of the need to reconcile a people that had been bitterly divided, de Gaulle argued from 1940 until his death that Vichy had been a parenthesis in the history of France and that the Republic, embodied by the Resistance, had never ceased to exist. According to the General, the French had overwhelmingly backed the Resistance while only a handful of traitors had led the country down the path of collaboration. This narrative of national heroism was complemented by one of French suffering, captured most powerfully in the story of the 1944 massacre at Oradour-sur-Glane. Just four days after the Allied landing at Normandy, SS soldiers murdered 642 women, children, and men in a gruesome bloodbath that wiped out virtually the entire village. As Sarah Farmer has written, Oradour "provided an interesting corollary to the notion of France as a nation of resisters and bystanders: that of France as a nation of victims, martyred regardless of political choice or wartime activity." According to postwar mythology, therefore, World War II France had been a nation of heroes and victims. In the 1970s, however, the nation experienced what Henry Rousso, who has chronicled France's struggle with its Vichy past, has called a "forties revival." In films, historical texts, and politics, de Gaulle's notion of a France united in resistance collided with a new vision of a government and people willfully collaborating with the Nazis.[26]

If the national past no longer seemed clear, the present and future looked equally murky. By the end of the 1970s, new forms of political identity were emerging that challenged entrenched notions of what it meant to be French. Unlike earlier immigrants from Europe (and like North African Jews), new arrivals from Asia and Africa were reluctant to give up their cultural distinctiveness. Claims of oppression and victimization brought new credibility as various racial, ethnic, and minority groups in France spurned the principle that citizenship — more easily accessible in the early Mitterrand years—required an abandonment of particularity in the public sphere. Immigrants, women, and others declared their "right to be different" and asserted themselves as citizens with commitments beyond the nation. Though by no means unanimously endorsed, a particularly French version of multiculturalism had become a familiar part of public discourse by the 1990s. Homosexuals demanded family rights, and women called for *parité* in political representation. Muslim women declared the right to wear head scarves in public institutions and were affirmed by the Conseil d'Etat, the highest court with jurisdiction over the state. Not surprisingly, while traditional notions of Frenchness came under attack, the Far Right fulminated against immigration and the diversification of French culture. Supporters of Jean-Marie Le Pen and the National Front, which won eleven percent of the votes in the 1984 European elections and thirty-five seats in the National Assembly in 1986, argued that immigrants were taking jobs and other opportunities from French citizens and that France was in danger of losing its national distinctiveness. To the proponents of cultural pluralism Le Pen offered exclusionary nationalism, and while he never came close to attracting a majority of French voters, he made clear that the civil war over the meaning of France was still being waged.

Outside pressures also weighed on French identity. The globalization of the workforce brought new populations to France, and the Internet opened the world to anyone who had access to a computer. American movies and music were so popular that the government passed legislation protecting the French language and limiting the amount of "foreign" programming in the media. But national identity, indeed the very idea of France, was especially vulnerable in a unifying Europe. Discussions about and eventually the construction of a European Union diminished the influence of the nation-state, both in idea and practice, throughout the continent. In France, a certain disaffection from the state had been apparent as early as the protests of May 1968 and had deepened in the 1970s, especially during the presidency of Valéry Giscard d'Estaing, who was accused of using state power to protect the Far Right. Regionalist movements in Brittany and Corsica, decentralization of political power to the *départements*, and the Socialist Mitterrand's decreased intervention in the market (and apparent abandonment of the workers' cause) further diminished the stature of the state. Mitterrand, who occupied the Elysée for fifteen years, twice chose not to resign despite having lost control of the National Assembly, and the divided government that resulted dramatically weakened the state's credibility. A strong, centralized state had long been a defining feature of France, and its inevitable further weakening in a consolidated Europe added to the developing crisis in national identity.

As the diversity of the French citizenry and the certainty of a European

Union became apparent, discussions about the Holocaust, Vichy, and identity became intertwined, each informing the others and all contributing to a discourse that reflected the shifting parameters of French national identity. Jewish and non-Jewish discussions converged on the tropes of memory, and the Holocaust became the most recognizable component of World War II. If the dominant concern for most Jews was the trauma, however, non-Jews found in the genocide a metaphor, a representation of perpetrators and victims whose exact form and meaning depended on the idea of France being expressed. Favored by Left and Right, Jews and non-Jews, and supporters and detractors of Israel, the rhetoric of the Holocaust was invoked to extol the Resistance, malign Le Pen, isolate Vichy, and calumniate the state. Holocaust rhetoric, therefore, did not necessarily signify a discussion about the Nazi genocide; what for most Jews had been a shattering break was for the rest of the nation a symbol, and the Holocaust came to serve as a tool or screen in much the same way that Jews had functioned during emancipation debates, the Dreyfus Affair, and Vichy rule.

The 1980 bombing of the synagogue on Paris's rue Copernic, which followed just after the television broadcast of "Holocaust," was the catalyst in this discursive concentration on the Holocaust. For weeks after the attack, newspapers were filled with accounts of groups as disparate as homosexuals, Jews, Palestinians, and feminists turning to Holocaust imagery to protest such diverse ills as homophobia, sexism, and colonialism. The bombing revealed a nascent new approach to political identity, one in which cultural particularity and French identity were compatible, and it produced a widespread identification with Jewish victimization that made the Holocaust a metaphor for social suffering. The arrest of Klaus Barbie a few years later sparked a protracted national battle over whether the Holocaust and Nazi torture of the Resistance were comparable, a controversy in which the genocide became a source of national identification. In the trial that followed, the Holocaust served as a metaphor for Resistance (and by association, national) victimization at the hands of the Nazis. After the 1990 desecration of a Jewish cemetery at Carpentras, the nation denounced the "fascist" Le Pen in a narrative that was tantamount to a repudiation of Vichy and an identification with its Jewish victims, and the Holocaust came to stand for the suffering and innocence of the French people at the hands of the evil and guilty Vichy regime. This distinction between the wartime population and government then crystallized during the Mitterrand years as a divide between the people and the Mitterrand state, and when former Vichy functionary Maurice Papon stood accused in 1997–98 of having authorized the deportation of Jews from Bordeaux, it was the French state throughout history on trial.

After the Copernic attack, Jewish and national memory were inextricably linked in their use of Holocaust rhetoric and worlds apart in terms of the meaning they ascribed to it. Jewish memory had its own dynamic, one of trauma, where the Holocaust was conceptualized as unique, as a rupture whose singularity necessitated a reconfiguration of the relationship between Jewish and French identity. For the rest of the nation, the Holocaust was a narrative that was structurally about victims and perpetrators and substantively about anything that this frame could sustain. First as a metaphor for suffering and then as a metonym for Vichy and the French state, it was a story told in various ways about national identity. When Jewish and national memory crossed paths, their different visions of the Holocaust were clear. In the battle over Barbie's indictment, for example, most non-Jews argued that torture of the Resistance was equal to the Holocaust and should be included in the trial dossier, while most Jews contended that Barbie's crimes against the Jews were unparalleled. But even when these memories seemed to merge, as in the events of the 1990s, their meanings remained distinct. When Papon was sentenced in 1998 to ten years in prison, much of the national press rejoiced that the state was no longer an "untouchable" institution while many Jews lamented that the sentence failed to reflect the uniqueness of the Nazi genocide. Thus the argument put forth by Rousso and journalist Eric Conan, that memory of Vichy has anachronistically fixated on Jews, fails to probe beyond the rhetoric.[27] While the language of public discourse has been dominated by the Holocaust, the memory has not always been about Jews.

## CHAPTER TWO

# "*Anne Frank is Dead, Long Live Anne Frank*"
## The Six-Day War and the Origins of Holocaust Consciousness

Any attack on the state of Israel would be as intolerable as the resumption of the crematory ovens and gas chambers of Auschwitz, in front of Notre-Dame. . . .

Such was the emotion expressed by Jewish essayist Manes Sperber on the eve of the Six-Day War. Lest this appear to be the intemperate outburst of one Jew, buried in a Jewish community journal, or hysteria confined to the opinion pages of national newspapers, writer Richard Nollier's cover story in *Le Monde*'s June 3, 1967, edition made palpable the acute anxiety of many Jews and non-Jews across France. History, Nollier remarked, "seems fond of bitter repetitions."

But the repetition is only superficial. Twenty-two years ago, they massacred defenseless people. Today, the survivors have tanks, rockets, and a national flag. The difference is appreciable. It has to do essentially with the way of dying.

And further:

The fact remains that for the first time, the Jews *as Jews* have their territory, their citizenry, and their paratroopers. After centuries in the ghetto, after Auschwitz, they know what they represent. They also know that if they lose Israel, it will never return.

It is Auschwitz that will return. Because they will be defenseless once again. And because man does not change. He is partial toward attacking that which is defenseless.

That is why Israel is much more than the dwarf-like country we have trouble finding on a map. It is the insurance policy of a good thirty million people—Jews, half-Jews, spouses of Jews—who have begun again throughout the world. A policy which guarantees them that we [*on*][1] will not make fertilizer of their parents' bones and soap of their children's flesh, while the universe discreetly turns its head, as it so recently did.

For such a guarantee, what isn't one prepared to do? . . . [2]

That the nation was suddenly riveted to the Middle East was remarkable for a number of reasons, not the least of which was the scant and unexceptional coverage of Arab-Israeli friction earlier in the year. There was no crescendo, only an explosion in May 1967 of often frenzied public debate that catapulted events surrounding the Six-Day War to the front pages of virtually all major Jewish and national newspapers and magazines. While the War was yet another tense moment in the protracted conflict between Jews and Arabs in the Middle East, it was the first chapter in the post-World War II story of the Holocaust in France, or the beginning of a certain Holocaust consciousness in French public discourse.[3]

Few in France were prepared for the Six-Day War, at least by view of the nation's major press. There had been no indication through April that events in the Middle East would become a crisis in May, and few in mid-May had suspected that a full-scale war would erupt in June. Major newspapers, including *Le Monde*, *Le Figaro*, and *L'Humanité*, had reported periodic border skirmishes between Israel and Jordan and Syria in the early months of 1967, but they had devoted little interpretive attention, such as editorial space, to what they largely viewed as a continuation of the intractable Arab-Israeli conflict, or the unpleasant reality of interminable small-scale violence in the Middle East. The Jewish press seemed equally unconcerned.[4] If the explosion of war on June 5 was something of a universal surprise, even less expected was the tenor of the public discussions that preceded and followed Israel's unexpectedly sweeping victory. The Six-Day War marked the first widespread Jewish presentation of the Holocaust in French national debate, Jews' first sustained public discussion of the Nazi genocide outside of the Jewish community. What many Jews perceived to be an imminent threat to Israeli and Jewish survival, possibly a second genocide, structured a debate that was about both the Arab-Israeli conflict and the Holocaust. Motivated by the perception that Israel was in immediate danger, Jews began to search actively for new ways to make sense of both the Holocaust and their place in the Western world.

In the process of bringing the Nazi genocide to national public discourse, Jews articulated the Holocaust as trauma: a shock to taken-for-granted structures of meaning in place since France first granted Jews citizenship during the French Revolution; a rupture in Jews' confidence in the security of citizenship and the compatibility of Jewish and French identity; and a resulting bewilderment before the task of trying to make sense of the event, to comprehend the Holocaust with the conceptual tools that French Jews had employed for over 150 years. As the meaning of Jewish existence in the diaspora, and especially in France, became a pressing question in late-May and June 1967, the centrality of the Holocaust rupture in problematizing contemporary Jewish identity became apparent. By presenting their encounter with the Holocaust as traumatic, Jews identified with their ancestors and rejected the course that had led to Auschwitz. For the essence of the trauma they verbalized in 1967 had to do with differentiation and renunciation, the separation or demarcation of pre-Holocaust Jews and their subsequent abandonment. Many Jews in contemporary France articulated the trauma by empathizing with and then appropriating that historical distinction: Jews would announce and embrace their Jewish particularity before it would be thrust upon them. To avert the catastrophe that was the Holocaust, French Jews in 1967 would be Jews in public, openly and unequivocally, as their ancestors for centuries had been unwilling to be. Their identification with earlier generations and public assertion of Jewish identity betrayed an attempt to understand present and past in each other's terms, to homologize two moments in time and to reconcile the implications each held for the other. The Holocaust and the Six-Day War thus became interlinked and temporally congruent in such a way that any effort to understand or assign meaning to one event directly implicated the other.

Non-Jews were also captivated by the Arab-Israeli conflict, and those who sided with Israel did not hesitate to invoke Holocaust imagery to mobilize support for the Jewish state. The Six-Day War, therefore, was the first prolonged and truly national public discussion that addressed the Holocaust. The trauma of the Holocaust was nonetheless expressed only by Jews, who alone presented it as a shock and a challenge to historically and culturally entrenched expectations about Jewish life in France. The traumatic aspect of the Holocaust, in fact, was precisely what most non-Jews, including Israel's advocates, found difficult to understand. It was this notion of trauma, moreover, that made contentious post-1967 debates about Israel's occupation of Arab territory and that created controversy around various non-Jewish interpretations of the Holocaust. It was the trauma, in other words, that sparked a narrative politics of the Holocaust in France.

## Between the Holocaust and the Six-Day War

Little in the decades preceding the Six-Day War suggested the extent of this trauma. In addition to searching for lost relatives, caring for the enormous number of newly orphaned children, and rebuilding community institutions, most French Jews were discursively committed in the immediate postwar years to integrating their wartime ordeal into the national suffering of France. Early testimonies from Holocaust survivors, for example, focused not on the observance of Yom Kippur in the concentration camps but on the celebration of Bastille Day; they excoriated not a centuries-long anti-Semitism but an eternal and insatiable German nationalism. To wear the yellow star had been for Jews to "carry the cross" with the rest of the French nation.[5] "The Holocaust" did not exist at this time, and the Nazi genocide of the Jews was itself indistinct, or unremarkable as an event with its own boundaries and significance. *Le Monde*, for example, defined "genocide" in a December 1945 article but mentioned it only twice in 1946, once without reference to Jews.[6] And "Night and Fog," Alain Resnais' 1955 award-winning film on Nazi concentration and death camps, never spoke of Jews.

Less than a decade after the war, a controversy regarding the Holocaust gave little indication that Jews would contest the long-standing assimilationist ideal. In February 1953, a woman living in Israel tried to reclaim her two Jewish nephews who had been entrusted to nuns during the war by their parents, both of whom had died in the Holocaust. The Finaly boys were then abducted by the woman who had been taking care of them, and she claimed to have had them baptized and "turned into little Catholics." During the Finaly Affair, the tension between the dominant Jewish and non-Jewish understandings of assimilation was clear: the boys had been circumcised, one during the war, which was one indication that the parents had wanted them to remain Jewish; but the Church hierarchy and other commentators claimed that the boys' consignment to the nuns had suggested a different choice, that the parents had selected French over Jewish identity, and that many Christian organizations' risky behavior on behalf of Jewish children justified the baptism. For the Finaly parents, it had been possible to be both French and Jewish, while for many non-Jews, this dual identity made little sense. The rabbinate decried the baptism, but the majority of Jews were not inclined to press the issue publicly.[7]

After Israel's victory in 1948, many French Jews identified almost completely with the Jewish state. Jewish publications and community gatherings demonstrated a frenetic concern with developing the new nation's economy and infrastructure, resettling Jewish refugees from Eastern Europe and other Middle Eastern countries in Israel, promoting Israeli culture and politics, and raising money to finance Israel's endeavors. Strong support for Israeli independence across a broad spectrum of French opinion, France's official recognition of Israel as a sovereign state, and popular and governmental support of Israel during the 1956 Suez crisis enabled Jews to feel confident in the young nation and to look to Israel as the guarantor of a luminous Jewish future.[8] Israel represented hope, and a France friendly to Israel's interests enhanced Jewish perceptions that the new state was strong, in control of its destiny, and relatively safe from external threat, including from Arab countries that openly called for its destruction.

Jewish identification with this stable and well-supported Israel was apparent in the sheer breadth of attention the young nation garnered in Jewish conversations as well as in the content of scant Jewish Holocaust narratives that did appear before the Six-Day War.[9] Though the Nazi genocide itself was not a major focus of Jewish discussions, when it was invoked, it was as a symbol of Jewish courage and heroism, as a stage in the linear unfolding of Jewish redemption represented by the state of Israel. In particular, sporadic discussions of the Holocaust before the Six-Day War focused on the Warsaw Ghetto Uprising, "one of the most glorious epics of our history," the "war of independence" that testified to "the renaissance, courage, and will to survive among Jews."[10] A 1954 prize-winning essay in *Information Juive*, for example, projected the experience of the ghetto combatant: "In firing his last shot, he knew that his example would not be lost and . . . that his revolt, his first revolt as a Jewish Man, would bear the blood and iron that would soon unfurl the star of David on the Land of Israel. . . . " History will judge that the ghetto resister died as both a martyr and a hero. "But above all," the essay concluded, "he died as a victor, because he died for Hope, materializing in his death the words to 'Hatikvah.'"[11] Similar sentiments were expressed in an article that associated the ghetto revolt with the thirteenth anniversary of Israeli independence in April 1961:

Sometimes history links strange events. Perhaps it is to confer on them their thematic unity that history has reassembled in one month the exodus from Egypt, the Warsaw Ghetto Uprising, and the Resurrection of the State of Israel.

One only has to verbalize these three events for their relationship to be clear.

Like the heroic exodus from Egypt, the article continued, the courageous ghetto combatants confronted and triumphed over their enemies. "Like Moses, most of these ghetto heroes were unable to reach the promised land. But the renaissance of the State of Israel was in large part their victory."[12]

Jewish reaction to the Eichmann trial was further affirmation of their identification with a vigorous and vital Israel. Between 1960 and 1962 the Jewish state kidnaped Eichmann from Argentina, brought him to trial in Israel, and condemned and executed him. In its rather sparse coverage of the surrounding controversies, the French Jewish press drew more attention to the pivotal role of Israel than to Eichmann's crimes. One cover of *Cahiers Bernard Lazare* showed a sketch of Eichmann before both a youthful Israeli, seated behind a podium emblazoned with national insignia, and a "jury" of Holocaust victims, clad in striped uniforms and yellow stars. The emphasis was on the autonomy, power, and moral strength of Israel. The journal never featured more than one article per issue on Eichmann; the cover of its October 1961 issue, which directly preceded the trial, featured a small cartoon on the bottom where Eichmann claimed "I said nothing, heard nothing, saw nothing," but no articles. Coverage in *L'Arche* was equally minimal. The trial was far from ignored, but the details were relatively insignificant in a discursive context where most Jews were oriented not toward the painful Jewish past but toward Israel as a beacon for the Jewish future. Despite the centrality of the Holocaust to the trial, the Jewish press continued to devote most of its attention to the project of building and strengthening the Israeli state and society. And while some in the non-Jewish press were disgruntled about Eichmann's abduction and the fact that he was tried in Israel, national debates were characterized less by anti-Semitism than by an implicit reverence for the potency exhibited by a young state so recently built on the ashes of destruction. Israel's seemingly limitless possibility and a relatively stable social climate at home fueled French Jews' confidence in Israel and their devotion to its development.

Traces of the Holocaust in Jewish conversations suggest that the period between 1945 and 1967 was not one of repression but of disavowal.[13] Far from being absent or indirectly apparent only in some displaced form, the Holocaust was clearly a part of Jewish consciousness, even if they spoke of it only infrequently beyond the parameters of the Jewish community. But what is equally apparent from the vantage point of 1967 was a certain unwillingness among most French Jews to confront the rupture in meaning that was the Holocaust, a disinclination to wrestle with the challenge to a long-standing and unquestioned assumption: that their loyalty to France and citizenship would mean protection via inclusion in the national community. The apparent stability of Jewish life in France and Israel during this period was such that when Jews did turn to the Holocaust, they focused only on that which provided a source of contemporary hope and inspiration. Israel was a vigorous and growing state, and French Jews felt strong by virtue of their identification with the young nation. This perception of Israeli vitality, as well as broad French support for Israeli sovereignty, encouraged a Jewish narrative of the Holocaust that was not traumatic but redemptive.

In 1967, however, Jews overwhelmingly perceived Israel to be at risk, and their continued identification with the Jewish state made them feel vulnerable as well. By 1967, decolonization, the Algerian War, and other struggles for "national liberation" had allied much of the French Left with the Palestinians. In addition, de Gaulle announced a policy toward the Middle East conflict that was widely perceived to be part of his larger plan to move France away from the United States and closer to the Soviet Union and the Arab world.[14] Because the United States was a strong supporter of Israel and the Soviets and Arabs unabashed enemies, and because large segments of the Left embraced the kind of anti-colonialist rhetoric that had been adopted by the Arabs, many Jews worried that popular and governmental support for Israel was a luxury of the past. They heard Egyptian president Gamal Abdel Nasser's repeated calls in 1967 for the "destruction" and "annihilation" of Israel in a very particular way: Israel would be "destroyed" as had been the plan for biblical "Israel" during the Holocaust, and de Gaulle would abandon "Israel" (both biblical and juridical) as Pétain had abandoned the Jews during World War II.

In May 1967, as Arab countries vowed to destroy Israel and de Gaulle and the French Left allied with Israel's enemies, Jews felt the shock of the Holocaust abandonment. Fortified by Sephardi resolve, their communal identification with a seemingly invincible Jewish state and the associated redemptive account of the Nazi genocide became in discussions surrounding the Six-Day War a nationally announced identification with a defenseless Israel and a traumatic narrative of the Holocaust. Although their own sense of abandonment was more proximately linked to France's departure from North Africa than to any direct experience with genocide, Sephardi Jews relied heavily on Holocaust imagery to express their allegiance to Israel. The threat to survival—of Israel, the Jewish people, and Judaism—was at the forefront of nearly every Jewish discussion, and in widely expressed fears of a second Holocaust, the centrality of the Nazi genocide to Jewish identity became clear. A gap, however, between most Jewish and non-Jewish understandings of the Six-Day War and the Holocaust became profound even before the short war had ended. Non-Jewish responses to Israel's annexation of Jerusalem and the West Bank and de Gaulle's November 1967 press conference made the extent of this gulf clear even to the most weakly identified Jews.

## The Six-Day War

In the days surrounding the War, French Jews took to the streets of Paris and the provinces in large numbers and without reserve. In public demonstrations, Jewish newspapers and magazines, and the national press, they expressed their practically unconditional support for Israel by linking the Holocaust and the Six-Day War. The most common narratives claimed that diaspora Jews were responsible to Israel because of the Holocaust. André Neher, for example, described the diaspora as part of a broad regiment of world Jewry, as a posterior of potential and of inexhaustible reserves "where the moral and material arms of Israel's battle for life are forged." Even yesterday, lamented the well-known scholar of Jewish philosophy, "I only devoted a fraction of myself to Israel. Today, all of my thought, my action, and my self identify with Israel and its battle: body and soul, with iron resolve, available day and night." Neher suggested that the Jewish diaspora stood just behind the front lines of Israeli soldiers. He then further identified world Jewry with Jewish bystanders during the Holocaust and linked contemporary Jews to those in France in the 1930s. Today, he wrote, the diaspora's identification with Israel

is also in the proximity of Auschwitz: not the specter of Auschwitz, but the certitude that we must hold the means to reject a new Auschwitz . . . Jews who lived in free countries—the Jews of France in 1936, the Jews of the United States in 1943—did not know. The former did not know that Auschwitz was possible, the latter that Auschwitz was Auschwitz. We know. So in 1936, in 1943, the battle was defensive. Today, it is offensive.[15]

In a similar effort to merge the moral responsibility of the contemporary diaspora with that of Jews beyond Hitler's reach during World War II, René Weil, president of the Strasbourg Jewish community, wrote in the regional newsletter *UNIR* that during the Holocaust, as he watched thousands go to their deaths each day,

I naively thought that my fellow Jews in America and Switzerland and the citizens of these countries would not tolerate this genocide . . . if they knew. Since then, I have learned from Elie Wiesel that they knew, that they could have responded but failed to do so.

Fortunately, Israel is able and has a ferocious will to defend itself. But we have to understand that two and a half million of our brothers in Israel are in danger and that this time, we make up the "Americans" and "Swiss" of 1967.

On the front page of the same issue, *UNIR* made a foreboding comparison by invoking, as had many others, the Holocaust survivors who made Israel their home:

As in 1933, we have been warned; we will be forgiven no doubt: facing the world, Israel's enemies have proclaimed their will and goal to annihilate Israel in a total war . . . We will not tolerate that our brothers, survivors of the concentration camps or expelled from their native countries, Jews who have found in Israel a refuge of peace, work, and good fortune, be massacred there.

In its appeal for donations to the Israeli cause, an editorial posed an awesome question: "Is there one among you who can assume that terrible responsibility of not having fulfilled such a profound obligation?"[16]

In a context where direct links and analogies with the Holocaust pervaded public debates, *UNIR*'s challenge was the most penetrating attempt to assimilate the horror of the Holocaust with the crisis in the Middle East. It embodied the same urgency that other accounts conveyed, but it was even more so an attempt to confront French Jews individually, to place each Jew in the position of Jews before the Holocaust, so that the very claim to be a Jew rested with the critical obligation to ally oneself with Israel. This unbreakable connection between past and present Jews grouped together French Jews in much the same way that the Holocaust had collectivized European Jewry. It suggested that Jewish identity was not optional, that Jews were identified as Jews by others and were therefore obligated to act based on that association. Once a certain subjective equivalence had been established between contemporary Jews and their ancestors of the 1930s and 1940s, the alliance between Jews and Israel served as a strategy to cope with a certain guilt for not having predicted or prevented the Holocaust, for having survived or not having experienced the Holocaust, and became nothing less than the prevention of a second Holocaust.

The Six-Day War provided an opportunity to confront the Holocaust as trauma: as a breach with the nearly one and one-half centuries of citizenship that had preceded it, as a rupture that had overturned established structures of meaning and rendered inoperable the patterns by which French Jews had made sense of social and political life. The crisis in the Middle East, wrote Neher, "strikes me at my roots, shaking up the very structures of my being." I have developed other beliefs "that are more upsetting because they challenge what gave order to my world of yesterday." The Six-Day War provoked so many Jews not simply because they believed that Israel was in danger but because it was the first moment since the Vichy regime that they felt the French government was turning against them, the first time since the Holocaust that they experienced what felt like an immovable wedge between their Jewishness and Frenchness. But unlike before and during World War II, when Jews devoted to assimilation had failed to recognize the barriers created by their ineffaceable difference, contemporary French Jewry chose to embrace that difference unconditionally. Now, in 1967, Jews would assert their Jewish identity before others imposed it upon them.

Even many Jews on the Left publicly sided with Israel.[17] A regular columnist for the popular left-wing *Le Nouvel Observateur*, Jean Daniel made clear that his sympathies were with the Jewish state. "Whatever may be the faults of the Israelis—and they are multiple and serious—and even if we consider the creation of the state of Israel in 1948 to have been an error (committed also by the Russians)," the Jewish state was threatened with extinction. If this were to happen, he wrote, it would be "for each among us, whatever our political convictions, an indelible shame . . . If the young sabras, descendants of the survivors of the greatest crime in history, were one day condemned to dispersion, if Israel were destroyed, this would be to despair of mankind. We will not despair." Claude Lanzmann echoed Daniel's sentiments in *Le Monde*.

Are you [*on*] going to force me to cry "long live Johnson" if the United States is the only country to oppose the extermination of Israel? I am ready to do it. It is the result of the contradiction of the Jew. Not my contradiction [but] the contradiction of socialist countries faced with the problem of the Middle East . . . If Israel were destroyed, this would be more serious than the Nazi Holocaust. Because Israel is my liberty. Admittedly, I have no confidence. Without Israel, I feel naked and vulnerable. . . .

President of the League of the Rights of Man, former Socialist minister, and a tireless advocate of universalist principles, Daniel Mayer delivered a scathing attack on Israel's detractors.

I am ashamed to be a socialist, and that is the epithet accorded to the Soviet Union's politics which encourage aggression. I am ashamed to be French, since official policy, for the second time in thirty years, represents the abandonment at a crucial moment of a nation which is a friend and ally. I am ashamed to be human because nothing is being done by humanity to check the repetition of genocide. And to respond to others in advance, I will add that I am not ashamed to be a Jew.[18]

Mayer's categorical pronouncement of his Jewishness, not to mention his condemnation of socialism, France, and humanity, was striking, especially given his reluctance throughout his career to back initiatives that distinguished among French citizens.[19] But what did it mean to be a Jew? And what would be the long-term implications of this new Jewish assertiveness, not just for Jews on the Left but for Jewish identity in France? The leaders of the National Coordination Committee (NCC), which had been formed to consolidate Jewish efforts on behalf of Israel, were themselves divided on the issue. Guy de Rothschild, committee president, and Claude Kelman, vice-president, both understood that widespread Jewish demonstrations on behalf of Israel represented a break with the community's customary public discretion and that the war could be a turning point for Jewish identity in France. But, as their remarks in the June 1967 issue of *L'Arche* demonstrate, each envisaged the future differently.

Faced with de Gaulle's professed neutrality toward the Middle East conflict, said Rothschild, Jews feel "an irresistible need, an itch" to do something on behalf of Israel. If this conspicuous impartiality manages to resolve the crisis to everyone's satisfaction, "then bravo!"

On the other hand, if this policy does not succeed, only its unpopularity will remain, and our memory will be a bitter one, a memory of deception that neither we nor many others will be able to forget . . . This policy, and I have already said it elsewhere, is bound to succeed.

We are in a painful position, Rothschild continued, "condemned to suffer ambiguous positions and intense frustrations, not by our own fault, not by a lack of good will, not by a lack of generosity, not by a lack of loyalty." He offered the following "advice" to the Jewish community:

Let us always remember that if humanity has sympathy for those who suffer—I am thinking about all of our current friends—it takes a quick and sudden dislike to those who moan and complain. It is not fair but it is true . . . It is again in fortify-ing our internal resolutions that we will be the most prepared to face the current cri-sis, in presenting a calm face, whatever might be the passions which trouble us, in tackling other subjects in our relations with others. The real strength is in the spirit and in the heart; it is not in yelling and making noise, and if we must undertake ac-tion vis-à-vis public opinion, it will be worthwhile only in the sense that we remain moderate and in control of ourselves.

It is never easy to bear with dignity and courage, with discretion and modesty, this blessed burden, this exalted cross that has always been the Jewish condition.

That Rothschild was willing, however modestly, to suggest Jews' poten-tial disappointment in de Gaulle represented a certain radicalization even among established Jewish leaders. But any hint of criticism was eclipsed by Rothschild's faith in French leadership. If de Gaulle failed, Jews and many others would maintain a bitter memory; but if he succeeded, he would be celebrated, and he was "bound" to succeed. Jews were frustrated and the government's policies were ambiguous, although there existed goodwill, generosity, and loyalty. Jews were to be on their best behavior, to strengthen their internal resolve, and not to talk about Israel with non-Jews. Rothschild's speech in many ways affirmed the abiding notion that Jewish concerns should remain a communal affair. He was confident in the com-patibility between Jewish and French ideals, moreover, and stressed that the abandonment of Israel was unlikely because it "would be contrary to our idea of the French tradition." What he feared and sought to contain was the radicalization of young Jews, a post-Holocaust generation with roots in both France and North Africa that proclaimed its support for Israel and Jewish identity in the streets, in public. But what he failed to realize was that even many older Jews had been provoked by the Middle East crisis to demonstrate their unequivocal support for Israel and to embrace a political identity rooted in their Jewishness. Rothschild's initial ambivalence, his modest critique of the government, represented an acknowledgment of Jewish fears. Yet his advocacy of a righteous resignation to Jewish martyr-dom stood in stark contrast to large segments of French Jewry, including some of his colleagues.

NCC vice-president and Zionist activist Claude Kelman, for example, suggested on the next page of *L'Arche* that although the French Jewish com-munity had become accustomed to the volatility of the Middle East, the current situation was serious not just for Israel but for Jews in the free world. "And here I want to insist on a very important fact: what we are doing today is the effect of a clear and definite position, without ambiguities or equivocations; we are acting as *Jews*, our reactions are *Jewish* reactions." Recently we deplored French Judaism's passivity, he continued, but today it "has emerged from its lethargy. It was shaken up in its very depths, and suddenly, by its conviction, its fervor, its resolution, the definitiveness of its self-affirmation, it found itself soaring compared to its sister communities in Europe." We cannot allow this vigilance around Israel to fade, Kelman stressed. We must cultivate "the reserve of energy and faith that our great community holds, a community which in these days has assumed a Jewish dimension that we did not know existed. There is in this a lesson for us. When the moment will have come to draw the lesson."

Kelman's endorsement of the public and specifically Jewish character of the community's mobilization on behalf of Israel represented in a rhetorical sense a response to Rothschild as well as the nation, both of whom had grown accustomed to French Jewry's discretion during crises. It also was something of a rebuke to the project of assimilation that Jews had undertaken since the Revolution and that Rothschild seemed committed to upholding. Rothschild argued that politics should remain in the family, that strengthening the "internal resolve" of individual Jews and the Jewish community was the most effective way to face the current conflict, and that this kind of discipline was and always had been "the Jewish condition." For Kelman, on the other hand, Jews had presented themselves collectively and publicly for the first time, and it was precisely the politicization of Jewish identity, the public pronouncement of their presence as Jews, that he hoped to sustain. Together, their opinions illustrated the tension between being Jewish and French that the War had made apparent. And the cover of *L'Arche* depicting crowds of defiant protesters waving "Israel Will Live!" signs indicated that in the immediate moment, Rothschild's appeal to inner strength and public quiescence was less popular than Kelman's plea for an enduring Jewish militancy. National debates following the Six-Day War confirmed one's fear and the other's affirmation of a French Jewry unafraid to announce itself publicly as Jewish. Yet they also demonstrated many Jews' firm desire to remain French and not to repudiate the country that was their home.

## The Nation, the War, and Holocaust Counter-Narrative

While Jewish opinion was almost without exception pro-Israel, non-Jewish discussions during the Six-Day War ranged from unconditional support for Israel to unqualified backing for Egypt and its allies. Despite the fact that de

Gaulle's de jure neutrality and embargo on arms to the Middle East were rather candidly recognized by both sides of French debates as a de facto boost for Nasser, public opinion in favor of Israel was far stronger than support for the Arabs. According to a survey conducted by the French Institute of Public Opinion during the first two days of the war, fifty-eight percent of Parisians sympathized with Israel and only two percent with Egypt and the Arab countries, a finding reproduced almost exactly in a survey conducted throughout France between June 8–11. Similarly, only six percent of the French considered Israel to be the aggressor, as opposed to fifty-four percent who blamed the Arab countries. In terms of who was "principally responsible for starting the war," fifty-one percent pointed to the Arab states, thirty-four percent to the Soviet Union, twenty-nine percent to the United States, and seventeen percent to Israel.[20]

*Le Figaro* was by far the most pro-Israel of the widely read non-Jewish French newspapers, *L'Humanité* the most ardently pro-Arab. These parameters were due in no small part to the former's unmitigated anti-communist, anti-Soviet position and the latter's equally absolute endorsement of communist and Soviet politics. Between these two poles, other publications adopted less ideological but equally political positions regarding the rights of Israel and the Arab world. If initially less pervasive than in Jewish opinion, the rhetoric of the Holocaust was also embraced by non-Jews sympathetic to the Jewish state. Yet by the end of the war, a powerful counter-narrative of the Holocaust, one that transcended typical political and ideological divides, began to appear in various forms in non-Jewish publications. This new narrative suggested a disagreement between Jews and non-Jews over the meaning of the Holocaust, a dispute that itself became the premise from which many Jews re-narrated the Holocaust and the whole of Jewish history.

Whether they connected the Holocaust and the contemporary conflict, non-Jews who favored Israel viewed the crisis as a threat to Israeli survival. The cover of *Le Nouvel Observateur*'s May 31 issue, for example, featured under the headline "Must Israel be destroyed . . . " a circle divided into three sections: one, an old man, hunched over, as if about to fall; the second, two religious Jewish boys, smiling and arm-in-arm; and the third, armed Israeli women in fatigues. The elderly, women, and children—their suffering, particularly during war, is commonly invoked to describe brutality, immorality, and senseless violence. This picture intimated that to destroy Israel would be tantamount to slaughtering old people, women, and children. It suggested that Israel was "innocent," a word with multiple layers of meaning in the context of the Middle East crisis. It also implied that Israel was weak, that it needed to be protected. And the absence of any young male presence in the circle reinforced this image of powerlessness.

The cover can also be understood by narrating the constituent parts of the circle in their relation to each other: the elderly were dying, the children were oblivious, and even Israeli women had mobilized to protect the less able. There was something familial about the picture, as if Israel constituted a family but also as if the possibility of Israel's destruction was as deeply felt as would be a threat to one's family. Furthermore, women not only ensure the continuation of the Jewish people (Judaism is matrilineal), but they are also considered responsible for providing and maintaining Jewish life at home. Women guarantee the reproduction of Jewish people and a particular Jewish quality of their lives. According to the photo montage, then, it was Israeli women who protected the Jewish people and the state of Israel: structurally, as a sovereign state; and substantively, as a Jewish state. This cover of *Le Nouvel Observateur*, which in multiple ways juxtaposed innocence and frailty with hardened resolve, was one indication of the depth of French perceptions that Israel was facing annihilation. It both contributed to and reflected an emotional discourse that animated rallies and protests where references to the Holocaust were common.

*Le Figaro* consistently devoted editorial space to the Middle East, printing commentary that drew frequent analogies between the current conflict and the Holocaust in order to express support for Israel. On May 30, for example, former ambassador André François-Poncet argued that despite Israel's partial responsibility for the general conflict in the Middle East, Nasser was a "declared admirer and emulator of Hitler" whose goal was "to suffocate the Jews." Catholic columnist André Frossard argued on the front page of *Le Figaro*'s June 6 edition that "[o]ne side battles to reconquer a territory, the other fights against a threat of annihilation. For one it is a political affair, for the other, a question of life or death." *Le Figaro*'s reliance on both explicit and subtle Holocaust imagery stood in relative contrast to editorial positions taken up in other widely read non-Jewish organs of the press before and during the conflict. *Le Monde*, for example, maintained a tenuous neutrality through the end of the war, and its editorials were more analytic than polemical.[21] *La Croix*, the nation's leading Catholic newspaper, was mainly concerned with ensuring the safety of holy places in Israel and preventing the "Vietnamization" of the Middle East; it focused largely on great power responsibility.[22]

Neither *Témoignage Chrétien* nor *L'Humanité*, both of which sided definitively with the Arab states, spoke with any discernible frequency about the Holocaust. Yet often their opinions were punctuated by statements that resonated with the Holocaust imagery conjured by others. While *Témoignage Chrétien*, a weekly newspaper, usually sided with the Left, *L'Humanité* was the official organ of the French Communist Party and fully aligned with the Soviet Union. Thus both were inclined to understand immediate tensions, as well as the Arab-Israeli conflict in general, as a battle between the forces of Western imperialism (read: Israel and the United States) and colonial liberation (read: Arab countries). Georges Montaron, *Témoignage Chrétien*'s chief editorialist, seemed therefore to be responding to portrayals of a potential second Holocaust when he wrote: "Israel is not-the threatened lamb that they [*on*] describe to us and to the aid of which flock those who are just. And Egypt is not the 'big bad wolf' that the righteous portray with great eloquence." The same was true for *L'Humanité*, which in a front-page May 24 editorial suggested that "[n]othing is more false than the image Western propaganda tries so hard to give of the poor and innocent little state of Israel exposed before the hostility of the Arab world." Later, *L'Humanité* claimed:

We are not the ones who have forgotten, and with good reason, the suffering inflicted on Jews during Hitler's occupation. But it is precisely because we believe that all people have the same right to exist and to live in peace that we cannot approve of the manner in which Israeli leaders have chased over a million Palestinian Arabs from their territory and deprived them of their possessions.[23]

*L'Humanité*'s allusion to the Nazi genocide of the Jews represented an inchoate and somewhat nebulous version of a counter-narrative of the Holocaust, one that emerged as the war neared its end and helped set the terms for future discussions about the Holocaust. Shifting analogies to the 1938 Munich crisis, when "peace in our time" ultimately led to the Nazi invasion of Czechoslovakia, were one example of the extent to which this new narrative contrasted with earlier discussions of the Holocaust. Once Nasser had blocked the Gulf of Aqaba and ordered the withdrawal of UN troops, for example, many newspapers expressed fears of "another Munich," which they understood to be a particularly grave prospect for Israel, "refuge for tens of thousands of Holocaust survivors." Yves Cuau argued in *Le Figaro* that "it would take a miracle for nothing to happen" once Israel had lost access to the Port of Elath. "To let themselves be manipulated by the Arabs would be much more serious than to renounce a port. There are too many survivors from the death camps in this country for Israelis not to remember what happened in Europe between 1934 and 1939." Certain voices say that the Gulf of Aqaba is not important, reported Roger Massip, but we cannot forget the advice given to the Czechs in 1938. Six months after taking the Sudetenland, Hitler invaded Czechoslovakia. Israelis fear that "another Munich" would condemn them, and who can blame them? A letter to *Le Monde* from French writers and intellectuals expressed opposition to a "new Munich," which would seriously threaten the existence of Israel. And playwright Eugène Ionesco argued that Jews were

the only people who authentically believe in morality in politics . . . A quarter of a century ago, Czechoslovakia was also not aggressive. Hitler, that ignoble tyrant who is Nasser's model, accused Czechoslovakia of being aggressive only so he could overrun it . . . The moderate reactions of the world's moral conscience are appalling.[24]

The Jewish press also made use of the Munich analogy. An editorial entitled "Current News and Historical Constants" in *Bulletin de nos communautés* argued that the contemporary context was "eerily reminiscent of Hitler's diplomatic tactics between 1935 and 1939. Are we not on the eve of Munich?" *Information Juive* similarly connected 1938 and 1967. "Israel's very existence is directly threatened, and it is its most basic right, its obligation, to defend that existence by every means. One does not choose between Munich and war because in the end one has them both. We paid a very high price to know that forever." And several associations of French rabbis united Munich, the Holocaust, and the present in a frank appeal that ended with the following benediction: "May the Great Powers not repeat the irreparable error committed a quarter of a century ago when they allowed Hitler's monstrous genocide to be perpetrated."[25]

Before and during the war, the Munich analogy was employed in public discourse exclusively to bolster support for Israel. These discussions established an explicit continuity between Jews as victims of the Holocaust and survivors as potential victims once again in 1967. Giving up the Gulf of Aqaba was tantamount to appeasement. Munich, however, appeared at the end of the war in a radically different image of the contemporary conflict. On June 13, *L'Humanité's* front-page headline read "Israel Blocks the Exodus of Dozens of Thousands of Arab Families," while the front-page editorial was entitled "No Munich!" Unlike before the war, when the communist newspaper had largely avoided the Holocaust theme in general and analogies to Munich in particular, *L'Humanité* turned to Munich at the end of the Six-Day War in a narrative that reversed the meaning established in the pre-war period. The communist paper viewed Arab countries as partners in a global struggle against Western imperialism, as combatants against Israel, which represented an American outpost artificially implanted in the Middle East. The 1967 war, therefore, was only indirectly linked to the Holocaust and World War II. Analogies with Munich, and specifically the meaning of the Czech crisis in the unfolding of the Holocaust, were before the Six-Day War neither rhetorically nor historically compelling for French communists.

But by the end of the war, after countless public debates saturated with Holocaust imagery and in light of Israel's occupation of Jerusalem and the West Bank, Munich became a comprehensible narrative strategy to argue against those who had invoked it only a few days earlier. The front page of *L'Humanité*, in fact, suggested that Arabs were the victims and Israelis the perpetrators in the Middle East. It was Israel that blocked the exodus of tens of thousands of Arab families just as Germany had blocked the departure of Czechs in the Sudetenland and eventually Jews in Nazi-controlled Europe. Arabs, not Jews, were the refugees and Jews, not Germans, wielded repressive power. The editorial headline "No Munich!" which in 1938 would have meant "No Nazis!" and in pre-Six-Day-War discussions "No Arab Nazis!"[26] here became "No Jewish Nazis!" For communist Arab supporters, the Munich crisis related to both the Holocaust and the Middle East only to the extent that Jews could be likened to Germans. The structure of the Holocaust analogy remained operative while its content was displaced. Those who had in some way endorsed an identification between Jews in the present and past, such as writers in *Le Figaro*, continued after the war to support Israel, but largely without alluding to the Holocaust, which no longer could be employed self-evidently or hegemonically to support Israel. Those who sided with the Arabs, however, as well as those who had refrained from invoking the Nazi genocide in their analyses of the Six-Day War, began to refer directly to the Holocaust in expressing their support for the Arabs.

In one of two pro-Arab opinions published in *Le Monde* before the end of the war, for example, Vincent Monteil, director of the Fundamental Institute of Black Africa, first decried the idea that Israel was a bastion of democracy by pointing to what he called the "Oradour of Deir Yassin."

Regarding the persistent confusion between the imperialist and colonialist bridgehead that Israel represents, on the one hand, and the martyrdom inflicted by Hitler on millions of European Jews, on the other: this does not justify that Zionists make themselves the exterminating angels of the Arabs, who have nothing to do with Auschwitz or Treblinka.[27]

By the end of the war, others in favor of the Arabs were frequently employing variations on this new narrative that identified Jews with Nazis. "Why," demanded one reader in *Le Nouvel Observateur*, "must the tortured become the torturers? Why must the humble and the annihilated of one day become these enraged dogs who think only of biting?" To start a war and then claim to have been attacked, argued another reader, "is irritatingly reminiscent of the methods employed by a certain Goebbels."[28]

The most radical Arabs charged that Israel, and at times "the Jewish people," had transformed themselves into Nazis and that Europe had sacrificed the Arabs to assuage its own guilt for the Holocaust. A group known as the Committee for the Support of the Arab Revolution wove these two accusations into a formal announcement of its position: "Is not the white breast of ideological purity accorded to Israel the symmetrical and inverse operation of the 'purifying' act which made the Jews the scapegoats of our society?" The Nazi genocide, where the Jewish people suffered the greatest and most massive persecution of its history, "weighs on our consciences as

much as on the destiny of the Jewish people. But in the violence that justifies *a priori* anything that an Israel threatened with death would be able to
do, we recognize again the mark and the inverse of that guilt," where the
former victim is allowed all the passion of the persecution originally exercised against it.

We are, therefore, far enough from Auschwitz. But on the other hand, the second
Auschwitz—which the Arabs, it seems, would have liked very much to perpetrate—
was rendered impossible because the Israelis seized the same values from which
Auschwitz itself was able to arise so that these values could never again be turned
against them. Who could not see that in pursuing this type of reasoning, one would
logically come to recognize in Israel the virtual capacity to unleash a genocide on
others. . . . [29]

The argument that massive support for Israel was a measure of European
guilt for centuries of anti-Semitism, including the Holocaust, and that Israel had adopted Nazi values vis-à-vis the Arabs, was not confined to radical or Marxist Arabs in France, even if other remarks were less directly accu-
satory. *La Croix*, for example, which had refrained from clearly supporting
either the Arabs or Israel before and during the war, argued at the end of
the war that the danger of anti-Semitism had turned into a potential "reverse racism." Jews have suffered enormously at the hands of Christians,
wrote Antoine Wegner, "but that does not mean we should fall from one
excess into another."[30] The following day, arguing that Israel needed to
"master its victory," Jacques Duquesne undertook a front-page analysis of
Europe's "bad conscience."

The credit which Israel enjoys is proportional to European self-reproach for its own
attitude toward the Jewish people. If the Jews left en masse for Palestine in 1945, was
this not to find at last a haven of peace and security that Europe—far from it, unfortunately—did not know how to provide? And Europe watched them leave with
cowardly relief. Let them deal with the Arabs? And let the Arabs deal with them!
 In the bloody conflict in the Middle East, we bear a heavy responsibility.
 But is it necessary, because we did not know how to do justice to the Israelis
when they lived among us, that we not do justice to the Arabs?

For Duquesne, European guilt was the motivating force behind Europe's
contemporary support for Israel, though neither he nor *La Croix* directly
accused Israel of harboring genocidal aspirations.

 Yet if Duquesne did not openly suggest a congruence between Israel and
Nazis, he drew more subtle parallels which reverberated with that analogy.
Having posited a continental guilt, Duquesne claimed that "we are not do-
ing justice to the Arabs," who find themselves in the same situation as
France in 1871 and 1940.

Each new humiliation, each amputation of territory, can only arouse in them a desire for revenge. It is always dangerous to humiliate a people. Those who demonstrated so much passion in support of Israel during the war should now devote themselves to convincing the Israelis that to do justice to the Arabs is the best way to build peace.[31]

When Duquesne associated the Arabs with France in 1871 and 1940, two of the most devastating moments in French national history,[32] he created a direct bond between France and the Arabs, on the one hand, and an implied association of Israel and Germany, on the other. In a discursive context where accusations of Nazism and images of the Holocaust were widespread, these analogies reinforced a perception of Israelis as Nazis and Arabs as victims. When Duquesne merged 1871, and in particular, 1940 France with the 1967 Arab world, furthermore, he suggested an additional narrative alliance between France and the Arabs against Israel. While his comments did not directly invoke the Holocaust, their meaning both shaped and was shaped by analyses of the present that assimilated either Jews or Israel with anti-Semitism and Nazi persecution—narratives, in short, that made Jews and Israel the persecutors and Arabs the victims.

Like *La Croix*, *Le Monde* had avoided supporting either side during the early stages of the conflict; and like the Catholic paper, *Le Monde* argued repeatedly that Israelis should "master their victory" and "show that they are capable of generosity" in order to "open the heart of their neighbors, whom they have humiliated enough, even if only by their success." On June 13, a front-page editorial implored Israeli leaders to "master their victory and demonstrate a generosity spectacular enough to convince Arab hearts that vengeance is not the only route open to them." And the following day, *Le Monde* called the situation of Arab soldiers trapped without food and water in Israeli-occupied territories

a tragedy without precedent. Would not every solidarity movement in the world which demonstrated in favor of Israel when it seemed threatened now continue in favor of the defeated soldiers and civilians in distress? A man can be reproached for nothing more serious than to have abandoned his brother to despair.

As was true in *La Croix*, *Le Monde*'s first analysis that clearly supported one side in the conflict was a compassionate plea to pity the Arabs, an appeal that those who had supported Israel when it "seemed" threatened now turn to the Arabs "in distress." At a time when the unparalleled evil of the Nazi genocide of the Jews was a common assertion, *Le Monde*'s lament that the situation for Arab soldiers was "a tragedy without precedent" implied that the Holocaust had not been an outstanding case of evil, indeed that the contemporary Arab plight was a greater tragedy. The ways in which both *Le*

*Monde* and *La Croix* narrated a strong identification with the Arabs, combined with multiple calls for Israel to "master its victory," further turned on its head earlier stories of the Holocaust that depicted Arabs as Nazis and Jews, once again, as victims.

Le Monde and *La Croix* read as subtle challenges to the identification of Israel as a potential victim of a second Holocaust. Pierre Déméron's *Contre Israël* (*Against Israel*), however, was both a direct attack on Israel and an explicit accusation that Israelis were acting like "little Hitlers." "The Jewish state," wrote Déméron, "wants to be as purely Jewish as Nazi Germany wanted to be pure of Jews." During World War II, Jews were victims of their Nazi overseers. "Those who look most like [the Jews and Nazis] today are Arabs and Israeli soldiers, their guardians."

This shameless exploitation of the dead from Dachau, Auschwitz, and Treblinka by the survivors is nothing but a moral swindle. The victims of Nazi barbarism are in this way not only martyrized by their living, who do further violence to their memory. From their cadavers the Nazis extracted bars of soap; the Zionists got alibis.

For the Oradour carnage, argued Déméron, "the SS took the assassination of a German officer as pretext, while the SS of the Irgun carry out their massacre coldly and by pure political calculation."[33] If Déméron's views were typical of the most extreme reader letters and opinion columns in left-wing journals, they also were a crude representation of what more moderate opinions either directly or inadvertently had intimated.

Published along with *Contre Israël*, Jacques Givet's *La gauche contre Israël* (*The left Against Israel*) presented an emotionally charged defense of the Jewish state and a refutation of the Israel-as-persecutor image by affirming the narrative continuity established by Jews before the war. Each one of the six million Holocaust victims "could have been, should *normally*—I dare to say it—have been me," he wrote. He reiterated the Arab-Nazi analogy that so many Jews and other supporters of Israel first had drawn in the days leading up to and during the short war.

[W]hen Nasser talked about "the destruction of Israel," he was thinking about the state, not the people. A nuance. Undoubtedly, we do not have a good sense of nuance. We could have learned it from Hitler: when he predicted "the elimination of Judaism" in 1939, he obviously did not foresee the extermination of the Jews. The Jews were the aggressors for him as well.

Jordanian textbooks, Givet accused, demanded of Arab students: "'If you kill seven of ten Jews, how many are left to kill?' We could pose the same problem on another level: 'There were sixteen million Jews. We killed six million. How many . . . ?'" The Jewish people feel discouraged, wrote

Givet, and to try to justify themselves "would be as futile as it would have been for a resister or a Jew, arrested under the occupation, to have attempted to convince a Gestapo captain."[34]

Givet captured most vividly the spirit of Jewish responses to postwar narratives of the Holocaust. Having posited an existential link to European Jews of the Holocaust era, most French Jews in the aftermath of the Six-Day War refused to accept any challenge to this connection. Confronted by their critics, many felt like Jews during the Holocaust, faced with the Gestapo. They appeared to be fundamentally incapable of understanding how they could be perceived as racist or how the state of Israel could be conceptualized as a perpetrator, even as it occupied Arab land. Jews were the victims of the Holocaust trauma, and the diffuse accusation that both they and Israel were somehow morally culpable was an idea that they simply could not comprehend. They viewed the Holocaust, and therefore their current position, as morally unambiguous. The Arabs could not be victims of Israeli Nazis because Israel and the Jews were victims of the German Nazis and because the Holocaust was not a symbol of anything. It was a trauma, singular and incomprehensible. The Arabs were humiliated? For what? For not having annihilated Israel, or worse?[35]

## Strong Jews, Weak Jews

For Givet, the lesson for Jews was clear: "Israel will be vulnerable, or Israel will not be . . . Israel, if it is not vulnerable, is guilty . . . Israel must be alienated because there can be no Jew but the alienated one." He concluded: "As long as we are alive, we embarrass them; once we are dead, they feel sorry for us. Anne Frank is dead, long live Anne Frank. But only if she is truly dead."[36]

Givet's perception, that a strong Israel was by definition guilty, was echoed by Jews from across the religious and political spectrum. Novelist Arnold Mandel, a frequent contributor in the Jewish press, suggested that "those who no longer want to hate us cling tightly to their capacity to feel sorry for us. And if they cannot, they complain about us." Everyone asserts Israel's "right to exist," he noted, "but this has to be a weak Israel . . . [W]hat is significantly Jewish must be maintained within the limits of debility and precariousness." Philosopher and critic Eliane Amado Lévy-Valensi challenged the logic of those who accused Israel of persecution:

*If they are* survivors of the death camps we cannot allow them to be massacred a *second* time. If they are not survivors from the camps, we can obligingly let them be exterminated, as were some of their direct or indirect ancestors.

And further:

We have said it, we repeat it, and we need to say it again: the world was ready to cry for two and one-half million Jews added to the six million of the last war and to the innumerable victims of a more distant past. Israel victorious confuses the world and takes its breath away.

"Sympathy" for Israel, mused Jewish activist and *Information Juive* contributor Emile Touati, existed only in the etymological sense. "It was limited to a certain *compassion* before persecution or the threat of persecution. Israel victorious (at one against ten or twenty, and whatever de Gaulle says, despite an enormous disadvantage in armaments), Israel victorious antagonizes, irritates, worries."[37]

De Gaulle's November 1967 press conference provoked the most vituperative rebuttal from Jews. Among other remarks, the general stated that the Jews "remained what they had always been: that is to say an elite people, sure of itself and domineering . . . " and that Israel had been since 1956 "a warlike state resolved to self-aggrandize."[38] De Gaulle, it seemed, was angry at having been undermined during the Middle East conflict. In the events surrounding the Six-Day War, Jean Daniel pointed out, Israeli Foreign Minister Abba Eban had disregarded de Gaulle by starting the war; the Soviet Union had flouted him by rejecting his proposal for a conference of the world's major powers; and the French nation had defied him by openly and overwhelmingly expressing sympathy for Israel. De Gaulle, according to Daniel, believed that France was his "oeuvre" and simply would never pardon these transgressions. "Is de Gaulle an anti-Semite? No. Not especially. If he estimates one day that it would reinforce the idea he has constructed of himself and of France, he will be anti-Arab, anti-Armenian, or anti-anything. So it goes with nationalism. . . . " Daniel Mayer resigned from his post as a columnist at *Témoignage Chrétien* when editorialist Georges Montaron, a staunch opponent of de Gaulle, endorsed the president's statements on Jews and the Middle East. "The definition of aggression provided by the chief of state means that in 1939, the aggressor was France," Mayer noted. "Are resisters ready to admit how and by whom Hitler's Germany is thus rehabilitated?" De Gaulle's characterization of the Jews, he lamented, "which will be used by anti-Semites, justifies, after all, if not the crematory ovens, at least the ghettos; who would want to prevent a domineering and conquering people from being harmed?"[39]

Of all the emotion provoked by de Gaulle's press conference, the most stunning expression of outrage came from Raymond Aron, the conservative Jewish philosopher and respected columnist in *Le Figaro* who in the past had been candid about his discomfort with the purportedly primordial links among Jews and between diasporic Jews and Israel. Aron attacked the president with a passion he never before had expressed—and had repeatedly denied[40]—on behalf of Israel. Anti-Semites, argued Aron, had just received from the chief of state "the solemn authorization to start afresh and to use the same language as before the horrible massacre." With "some half a dozen words, loaded with resonance," de Gaulle had "rehabilitated" an "always latent anti-Semitism" and "scientifically and voluntarily ushered in a new period of Jewish history, and perhaps of anti-Semitism."

I feel less removed from an anti-Semitic French person than from a southern Moroccan Jew who speaks only Arabic and who has scarcely emerged from what appears to me to be the Middle Ages, from the impenetrable obscurity of a radically foreign culture. But the day when a sovereign power declares that Jews around the world constitute "a people sure of themselves and domineering," I do not have any choice. Only children defend themselves by accusing others: "it's not me, it's him."

We have returned to a time, Aron continued, when what goes without saying is better when said. And although I still refuse to support the Israeli government unconditionally, he added,

I also know, more clearly than yesterday, that even the possibility of the destruction of the state of Israel (which would be accompanied by the massacre of part of the population) strikes me in the depths my soul. In that sense, I have just confessed that a Jew could never achieve perfect objectivity when it is a question of Israel.

For Aron, de Gaulle seemed to have lent legitimacy to a narrative in which Jews were no longer victims but Nazis. "On the persecuted," he wrote, "falls the responsibility for persecution."[41]

Aron's sense that he had "no choice" but to rebuke de Gaulle exemplified the twists in political allegiance and identity surrounding the Six-Day War. His remarks took on special meaning in light of past claims that he considered himself somewhat more Catholic than Jewish and that French-Jewish support for Israel would lead to understandable accusations of "double loyalty."[42] They also served, in a purely rhetorical sense, to seal the war as an event in public discourse. Public conversations after Aron's riposte and other responses to de Gaulle were more focused on Arab-Israeli negotiations, the Israeli occupation of the West Bank and Jerusalem, and the dynamics of the cold war in the Middle East. Although allusions to and images of the Holocaust appeared from time to time in both Jewish and non-Jewish debates in 1968, the qualitative and quantitative force with which the Holocaust had appeared in 1967 discussions was not nearly as strong.

## The Six-Day War and French Holocaust Discourse after 1967

The Six-Day War is instructive about how the Holocaust would develop in French public discourse over the next thirty years. Shifting analogies with the 1938 Munich crisis, for example, suggested that no image is private in a public conversation, that once the Holocaust moved from Jewish to national debate, it became part of the "public domain" and could be narrated in theoretically limitless ways. Moreover, although anyone could assume the position of perpetrator or victim—and in 1967, Jews and Arabs were both—what was remarkable was the almost complete absence of traditional anti-Semitic rhetoric, or of any positive identification with Hitler or the Nazis. While the relationship between anti-Semitism and anti-Zionism became the subject of intense debate after the war,[43] no respectable organ of opinion argued for the moral acceptability of whoever was the Nazi in Holocaust narratives. Debates in 1967 equated contemporary perpetrators and Nazis and constructed a positive identification between the currently oppressed and the victims of Nazism. This identification with Jewish victims, with the *idea* of Jewish victimization, stipulated the absolute guilt of perpetrators and the total innocence of victims. It became widespread in discussions after the 1980 bombing on rue Copernic, when the Holocaust once again assumed a central place in public discourse, and in fact was the defining characteristic of debates that continued through the 1990s.

Tensions that were subtle in discussions regarding the Middle East conflict became problematic in later debates. Jewish unity, for example, was more precarious than it might have seemed, especially around the issue of Jewish identity in France. While most believed that the June war was a question of survival for "Israel" in the biblical sense of the word and that Jews must respond publicly and definitively on behalf of the Jewish state, there was less agreement on the form of this response and its longer-term implications for Jewish identity. While NCC president Rothschild counseled against public demonstrations and reminded Jews of their allegiance to France, vice-president Kelman insisted that they act *"as Jews"* and that they not "revert to the euphoria of yesteryear." Solidarity with Israel was so strong in the days surrounding the war that differences of opinion about Jewish identity were barely visible. But in discussions of the Holocaust in the decades that followed, Jews argued among themselves about how to articulate a public Jewish identity compatible with the obligations of citizenship. In 1967, moreover, when Jews and many others believed that Israel's existence was imminently threatened, Jewish insistence on the innate righteousness of Israel and the unbreakable bond between the diaspora and the Jewish state had a certain emotional and rhetorical appeal. But as the extent of both Palestinian suffering and Israeli intransigence became clear, many Jews (especially on the Left) struggled to express their unconditional support for the state of Israel and at the same time to distance themselves from specific Israeli policies. Narratives that linked French Jewry, Israel, and Jewish victims of the Nazis became less tenable and the sense of the Holocaust as trauma even more difficult to convey.

Finally, discussions of the Holocaust surrounding the Six-Day War indicated that the meaning of the Nazi genocide was widely variable among those who employed its imagery. When the Left assimilated the Holocaust into various narratives of its own suffering, for example, a clear cognitive divide separated Jews and non-Jews. This was most evident in Montaron's response to Mayer's resignation from *Témoignage Chrétien* in December 1967.

[Israel] monopolizes the enormous Holocaust of the Jews persecuted by Hitler for its unique profit. As if most of these Jews had not been free citizens of the countries that they loyally served. As if these martyrs had died for certain exclusive heirs. As if their seed could only bear fruit on the banks of Jordan. Let us not shut away their ashes in a ghetto, behind the frontiers of a state, whichever it might be, because their sacrifices have a universal value.[44]

From the perspective of many Jews, the salient point was that "loyally serving" their countries had not saved European Jews from genocide. Montaron's remarks were an attempt to universalize an experience that was singular, to create a metaphoric source of identification from an incommensurable event, and to deny the Holocaust trauma. While Jews in 1967 experienced themselves as victims of the Holocaust, others perceived the Jewish link to the genocide as no less figurative than their own. Many Jews believed that they were traumatically and therefore existentially connected to the Holocaust. But from the vantage point of numerous others, Jews failed to recognize that their relationship to the genocide was also a symbolic one. In public discourse, the Holocaust trauma was impossible to maintain because for most non-Jews, including defenders of Israel, the traumatic narrative was just another metaphor.[45]

Many Jews did argue in 1967 that the Holocaust concerned others primarily to the extent that it obligated them to support Israel. Yet despite their particularistic understanding of the Holocaust, they invited broader associations when they claimed that "the battle for Israel is today the human battle par excellence," that Auschwitz and Treblinka had been "the negation of the rights of man," that Israel was "the outpost for the defense of a certain international morality," and that "the Jewish experience of persecution teaches all people that when Jews are struck as individuals or as a people, soon it is every person and the whole world which are struck."[46]

Jewish opinions in 1967 reflected an attempt to honor the specificity of their experience and at the same time to locate it in a more comprehensive narrative of universal suffering, to create a particularly Jewish identity and at the same time to claim their place in the non-Jewish world. The tension between the universal and particular significance of the Holocaust was one to which French Jews contributed and was a constant theme in public discussions of the Holocaust. For the ability of Holocaust narratives to accommodate various perpetrators and victims made possible the expansion of Holocaust discourse simultaneous with its fracture along the lines of meaning.

## CHAPTER THREE

# Jewish Identity and the Banality of the Holocaust

The Holocaust trauma had upset the long-standing equilibrium between Jewish identity and loyalty to France, and the aftermath of the Six-Day War made clear that Jews' new consciousness of the genocide would have lasting effects on both communal and national debate. As they struggled with how to be Jewish and French, to make Jewish suffering during World War II both distinct from and part of French national suffering, many Jewish thinkers sought to establish a correspondence between the particular and the universal that could accommodate the values of Judaism, Israel, France, and humanity. In the meantime, as the nation began in the early 1970s to speak more critically about World War II and the Vichy regime, Jews and non-Jews argued over the extent to which the Holocaust was a specific event, with its own structural and temporal parameters, and whether it could be likened to other instances of oppression. In discussions surrounding the so-called Darquier Affair and the subsequent telecast of the American film "Holocaust" in the late 1970s, Jews tended to emphasize the Holocaust's distinctiveness while others focused on its comparability. As the contours of a narrative map of the Holocaust began to form, it became clear that many Jews and non-Jews would travel different paths.

## Israel, the Holocaust, and Jewish Identity in France

During the Six-Day War, for the first time, Jews had openly acknowledged their allegiance to Israel. Now, in the war's aftermath, they were publicly confronted with the contradictions of a divided identity. Though there was without doubt debate among them, at times anguished and vituperative and most often provoked by Jews on the Left critical of Israel's continued occupation of Palestinian territories, there was also widespread accord among Jewish writers and intellectuals, who spoke plainly and without caveat about their devotion to Israel and the dilemma that this created for them as French citizens. Jacquot Grunewald, editor of *Bulletin de nos communautés*, was one of the first to address this new challenge directly. And the title of his article, "Nous, Juifs de France (We, Jews of France)," was itself indicative of Jewish resolve on behalf of Israel, as custom had been for Jews to refer to themselves as French citizens who were Jewish (*français israélites*) and not, conversely, as Jews who were French (*Juifs français*).[1] Grunewald devoted the text to explaining how it was possible, indeed necessary, for French Jews to speak out against de Gaulle's Middle East policy.

It is not only by virtue of the right of a citizen of a free country to express his disagreement with the official position of his government that we ask for the justness of Israel's cause to be recognized, *but it is because our obligation as French citizens requires that we, Jews of France, should campaign for Israel.*

We have the right to ask for such an acknowledgment not only as French citizens, he contended, "but simply as Jews, who, from a particular perspective, that of their spiritual mission in the world, have the obligation to proclaim the biblical ideas of peace and justice. . . . "

If, as many would like to assert, this clear and direct course should evoke in France an anti-Semitism all too happy to find support thanks even to some Jews, the repugnant accusation of double loyalty or lack of French patriotism: may that anti-Semitism rise and show its face! Let us assume our responsibilities with conscience so that the cowardice that would make us dread a lack of security in our country will never be a pretext for cowardice toward Israel.

Grunewald's plea was an attempt to narrate a continued compatibility between French and Jewish identity. Jews were just like other French citizens, such as those with ties to Quebec, and what distinguished them was not loyalty to two nations or betrayal of France but a spiritual obligation to spread peace. Whereas since the Revolution Jews had fulfilled the obligations of citizenship by addressing their interests within the confines of the Jewish community, now, in 1967, it was not only Jews' right as citizens of a free country to speak their minds and criticize the French government but indeed their *obligation as French citizens* to share their intimate knowledge and campaign on behalf of Israel. This was a dramatic reconceptualization of the meaning of national citizenship, a practical about-face on Jews' revolutionary pledge to avoid pressing their community interests in the public sphere. If the citizenship contract was not being renegotiated, its terms were beginning to be redefined by the descendants of its signatories.

This revised interpretation of citizenship, however, did not go uncontested by non-Jews, many of whom found Jews' outspoken commitment to Israel tantamount to a betrayal of France, the very "double loyalty" that Grunewald had denied.[2] Nor was his confidence that Jewish and French identities were compatible necessarily shared by fellow Jewish thinkers, most of whom agreed that in practice their bonds to Israel were unbreakable but that in principle these ties were difficult to explain. Here, as after de Gaulle's 1967 press conference, Raymond Aron attempted to convey both the certainty and ambivalence of many Jews. "What degree of sympathy [for Israel] are we allowed without facing the accusation of double loyalty?" he asked. Certainly each Jew is entitled to choose to be exclusively French, Gaullist, or communist, but only on one condition: "that he not push his concern for intellectual comfort so far as to deny the evidence in the eyes of others: he, too, belongs to this 'elite people, sure of itself and domineering' . . . I, for one, do not share this detachment, and I do not want to share it, despite what I have written at other moments."[3] Writer Jean Bloch-Michel echoed Aron's sentiments in the same issue of *L'Arche*.

We know what Israel's defeat would have been: the resumption of genocide and a massacre of "the Jews." Israel's victory, curiously, is only one of a friendly country to which French Jews and non-Jews are linked by particular ties that I will not analyze here. Which leads me to conclude that if my "Jewish conscience" is unaffected by Israel's victory, it would have been deeply shattered by Israel's defeat. Because the victory was Israeli, while the defeat, given the explicit intentions of the Arab countries, would have been a Jewish defeat. That there is some ambiguity in this attitude, ambiguity which is my own, I acknowledge.

Bloch-Michel and Aron were struggling with the apparent illogicality of their joint allegiance to France and Israel: each was a committed French citizen with a personal sense of responsibility for the security and future of Israel; neither considered himself culturally or religiously Jewish, but each expressed an almost organic connection to fellow Jews. Both were aware that these contradictions challenged the persuasiveness of their claims to be committed to both nations, yet neither could do more than acknowledge the tensions and embrace them.[4]

It was perhaps writer Edgar Morin who explained the situation most succinctly in an opinion entitled "Double Loyalty and Double Non-Loyalty." "There has been a return to *the Image of Auschwitz* in the Jewish conscience . . . Until now seen as only in the past, Auschwitz looms like an eventual future." The debates surrounding the Six-Day War "reopened healed wounds," he wrote. "They made contradictory what had seemed only to be juxtaposed and in equilibrium, and all found themselves confronted in a new way with their old Jewish conscience, where loyalty to Israel had captured the terrain." Morin understood that one of the legacies bequeathed to Jews by the Six-Day War was the reintroduction of Auschwitz, the Jewish past, as Auschwitz, the possible Jewish future. And deeply embedded in this contentious narrative of the Holocaust was a new appreciation for the politics of being a Jewish citizen in France. What before had seemed "juxtaposed and in equilibrium" were Jewish and French identity, and they had been made "contradictory" by the perceived threat to Israeli survival, on the one hand, and by non-Jews' detachment from the Holocaust trauma that for many Jews justified a public commitment to the Israeli state.[5]

As Jewish thinkers began to reflect openly on what it meant to be a Jew in France, they faced the difficult task of condemning France, especially the Vichy regime and de Gaulle's putative neutrality in the Middle East, and at the same time praising a France worthy of continued Jewish allegiance. In opinions that celebrated Israel, how could they finesse their devotion to a nation they condemned? Their response was to distinguish "true" France from "official" France and to portray Israel and the real France as representing the same values. Historic links among Jews and between them and the land of Israel then made it possible to be passionate about the Jewish state while remaining in France. As Emile Touati wrote,

We have always constructed for ourselves a certain "idea of France." And that idea is composed of justice, truth, loyalty, generosity, good sense, and moderation. That image was tarnished at times, in particular from 1940–1944, but we distinguish between official France and true France, and we put our misfortunes on the account of the foreign occupation. . . .

In the same issue of *Information Juive*, writer André Neher chastised de Gaulle for having instituted an embargo on arms for which Israel already had paid. We Jews believed in France, he wrote, that Jewish and French traditions were two faces of the same dream, and we believed this through Bismarck, Wilhelm II, Mussolini, Hitler, and Stalin. We believed it until today:

Cynically provoked by de Gaulle, who so recently rescued the Marseillaise to London, launching in one tidal motion the history of Vichy onto the side of the anti-France, this rupture, of course, fills us with sadness . . . And it is of the moribund Weimar Republic that many think today, faced with this spectacle offered by the government and parliament of France . . . .

The Vichy government, or official France, was in fact the anti-France. That Neher wrote of the "moribund" Weimar Republic and not of the democratically elected parliament that abdicated power to Pétain revealed most Jews' reluctance at this time to emphasize France's role in Jewish deportations. By September 1969, the Jewish press was celebrating the twenty-fifth anniversary of the Liberation by recalling the contributions of Jews, most of whom, it claimed, had been Zionists. Real France, triumphant, was represented by the Liberation, whose ideals had been shared by those who fought for the creation of a Jewish state.[6]

The omnipresence of a purely benevolent Israel in post-1967 Jewish thought did not go unchallenged, even among Jews. Ever the iconoclast, the well-known Jewish writer Wladimir Rabi protested what he called many Jews' "irrational" thinking since the Six-Day War.[7] These days, he complained in spring 1972, the only consideration of the Jewish press seems to be "is this good for the Jews?" The Jewish world "was always on the defensive," considered itself to be "ontologically threatened by all the forces of the universe," and dangerously equated "threats against the state of Israel with the permanent threat against Jews." The "idolatry" of Israel, he continued, was "an intellectual heresy" and "a spiritual imperialism," and the assimilation of anti-Zionism ("perfectly acceptable") and anti-Semitism ("perfectly shameful") was "intellectually dishonest, blackmail, and an intimidation unbecoming of us." Jewish survival, in Israel as well as the diaspora, enriches humanity, Rabi wrote. "But all means are not good. I refuse amalgam, verbal delirium, passionate nonsense, extortion and intimidation. . . . " No stranger to controversy, Rabi had many critics, including the Strasbourg professor Freddy Raphael, who argued that all Jews were survivors of Auschwitz and contemporaries of Israel's resurrection and that "interrogation of the meaning of genocide and resurrection" was an obligation. All of Rabi's opinion, argued another detractor, "reflects a denial of change and of the authentic, clings desperately to humanism in the face of Auschwitz, a humanism which lamentably failed and which we could call 'the idolatry of intellectualism.'" In his rejoinder, Rabi was unmoved.

Because I want to be one man, with only one ethic, one truth, one political conviction, without equivocation, such that what I say in a certain role and a certain context I want to be able to say in similar roles and in any other milieu in which I am likely to participate, I refuse the dichotomy which [my critics] impose on me . . . The refusal of this unity is precisely what constitutes schizophrenia. . . .

The conflict between Rabi and his critics demonstrated both the particularist and universalist impulses that shaped Jewish debates after the Six-Day War. Rabi's challengers failed to acknowledge that despite his provocative presentation, his concerns were infinitely demonstrable. The Holocaust and the Israeli state constituted a lens of vulnerability through which many Jews viewed the world. At best, this perspective was skewed; at worst, it could lead to a sense of Jewish identity based only on fear of another Holocaust and unconditional support for Israel. In its most extreme form, it could lead to an identity where Jews' only concerns were their own advancement and protection and the military strength of the Israeli state. Rabi, on the other hand, would not accept that French and Jewish convictions might not always be the same, that "dichotomous" thinking might, at times, be unavoidable. He caricatured the perplexity felt by Jews themselves, many of whom had chosen to admit the confusion they felt and to live with what they recognized to be contradictions rather than to endorse the absolutism of Rabi's humanist logic. And he refused to acknowledge if not the primacy at least the salience of Auschwitz in pondering the dilemmas of contemporary Jewish life in France and Israel's place in the world.

The prominence of Israel and the Holocaust in Jewish life posed specific challenges to Jews on the Left who, regardless of ideological orientation, struggled to make sense of their Jewish identity in a universalist framework. In 1968, for example, a group of left-wing university students and professors, led by Richard Marienstras, established the Cercle Gaston Crémieux. According to the group's manifesto, "a certain diffuse and residual consciousness of the historical and cultural dimensions of their situation" had provoked Jews to rally fervently around Israel in 1967. This reaction was badly received by many non-Jewish Leftists, who argued that all appeals to the particularity of Jews "played into the hands" of those who believed that Jews were foreigners in France and that the French nation would not tolerate "double loyalties." These Leftists, the manifesto continued, presented French Jewish solidarity with Israel as an absolute acceptance of the Jewish state's current political and ideological agenda.

It therefore appears to us necessary to affirm that all claims to difference are not necessarily racism; that problems of individual, national, and cultural identity are complex and cannot be resolved dogmatically; that it is a misinterpretation of the facts to constrain Jews who proclaim themselves as such to choose between the synagogue and Zionism; that the diasporas constitute for Jews a unique mode of existence that a long past has rendered natural, advantageous, and venerable and which has maintained the best of the Jewish universalist tradition; and that the diasporas, like other minorities, must be among those encouraged by a recent declaration of UNESCO to "preserve their cultural values"—or in some cases, to rediscover them—in order to be in a better position "to contribute to the enrichment of the total culture of humanity."[8]

The Cercle, which included such participants as film-maker Claude Lanzmann and historians Léon Poliakov, Rita Thalman, and Pierre Vidal-Naquet, disbanded after three years but reorganized in 1973, this time addressing itself to "those who reject all conformism—even Left conformism; to those who want to work for a Jewish cultural renaissance wherever there are Jews."[9]

The group's agenda was to locate Jewish concerns within the putative universalism of the French Left. It sought to situate Jewish politics and left-wing support for Israel within a broader Left endorsement of decentralization and national liberation. Auschwitz, Marienstras had written in the wake of the Six-Day War, had preceded Israel, and Jewish national liberation was justified not by the birthplace of its ideology or the origins of its first partisans but by "the individuals or human groups that it liberates." In later outlining a cultural politics for the diaspora, he lamented that some Jews and non-Jews believed that "exile" was less a metaphor than a fact, the reality for Jews in diaspora. But if asked whether they felt exiled in France, the United States, England, or elsewhere, he contended, few Jews would respond in the affirmative. The principal originality of Jewish existence, according to Marienstras, was "a way of life that assumes participation in a double culture, and far from being an anomaly, a Diaspora is a model that other minorities across the world are in the process of adopting." It is time, he pleaded,

to realize that we are not alone in the world: this will help us recover that "universality" to which we constantly refer but from which we constantly separate ourselves by provincialism, ideological routine, and conformism pure and simple. . . .

For this we will have to abandon that siege mentality which in recent years has too often animated our cultural and political debates. It is precisely the notion of dialogue and *plural* or pluralist community that is at stake: if we demand, in effect, that cultural and ethnic pluralism be admitted by all nations, the least we could do would be to put it into practice ourselves.[10]

What Marienstras attempted to delineate were the parameters of a diasporic culture, distinct from the state of Israel, as well as a greater Jewish culture that included Israel, distinct from the non-Jewish world. And what he sought in the process was to reconcile his commitment to Jewish culture as a Frenchman and to legitimate diasporic existence before Israel and the world. For Marienstras, the tension between particularism and universalism marked all Jews, not just those in France.

The identification of a broad-based Jewish cultural politics and its location in a global trend of proliferating minority cultures was one strategy of those on the Left to integrate the multiple demands on their identity. Those on the Far Left, on the other hand, rooted themselves in the ideological battles of World War II. Developed capitalism was "a new fascism"; French "cops" were the "SS"; the revolution was to build "a new popular Resistance"; and communist leaders were "the new collaborators." As for the capitalist exploiter: "He is like the Nazi occupant. He is stimulating a new Resistance, continuing the old." It was an identification with this Resistance that divided the Far Left between those who eschewed violence and those who believed that the justice to which the revolution aspired justified terrorism. As Henri Weber, a former Trotskyist leader, noted, leftist terrorism had been unleashed in Germany, Italy, and Japan, three countries that had been fascist. Our fathers had most often been resisters or deportees, he said, and this is why we refused such violence. "We were not ashamed of our parents. The militant Germans, Italians, and Japanese, they were ashamed." To be sure, there were non-Jews on the Far Left who identified with the Resistance and also shunned violence. But Weber and former Maoist leader Benny Lévy argued that Jews' refusal of terrorism was an expression of Jewish identity.

Those who united resistance and liberty could not tolerate, especially in the country of Jean Moulin, that one tortured and killed in accordance with ideas that fifteen years earlier had led to the crematory ovens. They don't wear their Judaism on their sleeves. They are revolutionaries above all, but they know, even if they don't talk about it at all, that Jewish identity determines their engagement.[11]

For Lévy, these Jews were obsessed with their parents' war, the fight against Nazism, but were condemned to peace. "Lovers of a history that hides from embrace, frustrated, they have to content themselves with mimicking a war that will never take place." Born of Polish Jewish parents who had fought in the French Jewish Resistance, Pierre Goldman personified this generation that had been born too late. He was an equally paradigmatic and enigmatic figure in French leftism: paradigmatic, in that his Jewish identity and deep sense of connection to the Resistance and the Holocaust drove both his thirst for action and his ultimate inability to act; and enigmatic, in that he articulated this paradox in ways that were often directly critical of the Left, with which he was formally unaffiliated but inescapably bound. Imprisoned for murders he claimed not to have committed (and of which he was later acquitted), Goldman became something of a cause célèbre on the Left and was often compared to Dreyfus. In his memoirs, composed while he was in prison, Goldman turned to imagery of the Holocaust to describe Jews as permanently and irreducibly strangers, and he presented himself both as the eternal Jewish nomad and as the modern Jew try[12] He recounted having grown up in the memory of the Resistance, especially the Jewish communist Resistance, though his father had spoken to him only of Robespierre and Danton. "(To be or not be French had never been, for me, a question: I never asked myself. I think I always knew that I was simply a Polish Jew born in France.)"(p. 33) I am constantly "in another place," he wrote, "but I am not disoriented because I am a stranger in every place. . . . "

[P]rofoundly, I had never been French. I was only an exiled Jew without a promised land. Exiled indefinitely, infinitely, and definitively . . . [I]n Israel as in every land, I was a stranger. I was too Jewish to be or to feel Israeli. I was too Jewish, in a word, to root myself. In my mind, in my flesh, Israel was only another place in the Jewish Diaspora, another exile.

I dreamt of civil war, of anti-fascist war, of a true return of time, of history . . . In Poland, I was seized by the taste for action, invaded by the dream and desire for history, and I wanted for that history to be one of violence, to liberate me from the scar of being Jewish.

On a trip to West Germany, where he found the possibility for violent action "intoxicating," Goldman experienced a "petrifying pleasure . . . On every German face I searched for the SS gaze. . . . " Of a man he encountered who claimed to have fought in France but not killed Jews or resisters, Goldman said, "I committed the crime of not killing him." He criticized the militants of May 1968 for having substituted speech for action and for having pretended that their battle was as significant as the one they had missed during World War II. " 'CRS-SS,' they said. I found this neurotic cry ridiculous. The CRS were not the SS, and they were not partisans. . . . " The protesters' cry of solidarity with German-Jewish dissident Daniel Cohn-Bendit, "We are all German Jews," inspired an equally "profound disgust." While awaiting trial, having admitted to committing armed robbery but maintaining his innocence in the murders of which he was accused, Goldman reached the conclusion that the latter were but a simulacrum of his true transgressions.

I inflicted on myself a pain, an implacable punishment. I judged myself and executed a verdict of rigorous severity. I emerged delivered from that experience. I understood that the sentence of the judges, whatever it should be, could never touch me. A tribunal sat in me, governed by an unpitying law, and I was struck there in the face of my dreams, my ideals. Justice could never punish me because for my crimes I had *already* punished myself. These crimes were not to have committed armed robberies. I had instead punished myself for not having been my father, a partisan, for not having been Marcel Rayman, for not having battled alongside Che, de Marighella, for not having searched for Bormann and killed him.[12]

## Jewish Identity and National Politics

The struggle to define the terms of French Jewish identity took place in mainstream politics as well. President Pompidou's adherence to de Gaulle's policy of allying France more closely with the Arab world—indeed, what many Jews and others believed to be a hardening of de Gaulle's position—drew hostile reactions from the Jewish community, which in turn provoked further accusations of "double loyalty."[13] Disagreement with various Elysée policies, which continued through the presidency of Valéry Giscard d'Estaing, stimulated Jews across the political spectrum to redouble their public efforts on behalf of Israel. During the October 1973 Arab-Israeli war, when public opinion was far more equivocal than it had been in 1967, Jews sponsored an intense public campaign to raise money for Israel, largely under the auspices of the French United Jewish Appeal, and in Paris held public demonstrations in such "national" places as the Republic. In 1976, approximately 100,000 Jews participated in the first "Twelve Hours for Israel" celebration, a public festival that included films, folk dancing, and music, as well as forums with the most well-known religious, community, and political leaders. And in 1977, the CRIF revised its charter for the first time since its creation in 1944 by pledging unconditional support for the state of Israel.

Most notably, and in what many observers acknowledged to be a startling move, some Jews began to flirt with the idea of a "Jewish vote." Nearly two centuries of Jewish citizenship and assimilation in French politics had mandated that Jews maintain their Jewish interests within the community and that they vote as non-corporate "citizens of France." Submission to the state and political impartiality, according to Rabi, had been

a constant of political behavior that no ordeal was ever able to shake: not the Dreyfus Affair, not even Vichy, because the Jews of France (or in France) were unconditionally rooted in this country that had emancipated them for the first time in modern history. Luck had it that for nearly 180 years, French Judaism never imagined for one moment that their Jewish and French values could be contradictory.[14]

But the conflicts between Jewish and French loyalties were precisely what Jews had openly acknowledged during the Six-Day War. And as early as 1969, they were suggesting that Jews might have a reason to vote *as Jews*. On the eve of the presidential elections, for example, *Information Juive* tried to reconcile the long Jewish tradition of public neutrality with Jews' new outspoken commitment to Israel. "Breaking with the shocking politics of the nation's elected, whoever he might be, and with the government that he chooses, we hope that we will avoid in the future that lamentable suspicion of double loyalty under the pretext of our fidelity to another country. . . . "[15] Ensuing presidential and legislative elections provoked more pronounced debate in the Jewish press. If a "Jewish vote" were a reality, wrote *L'Arche* editor Jacques Sabbath, "[i]t would in every case be a new and significant aspect of the Jewish community still in search of itself . . . Because it could extend beyond the March elections and become a lasting political strategy." It is difficult to know whether there will be a Jewish vote in 1973, wrote Rabi in *L'Arche*. But there will be a voting trend in favor of those candidates who have "the least suspect attitude regarding the *specific interests* of the Jewish community" (italics added).[16] Drawing public attention to the political interests of French Jews in a national election was in itself notable, but alluding to a possible Jewish vote signaled an unmistakable radicalization of Jewish participation in national politics.

French Jewry's relationship with Giscard was tumultuous on many fronts. Giscard was the first French president to publicly endorse the right of Palestinians to their own homeland, and when angry Jews openly rebuked him, he reportedly told one of his closest advisers: "If the French of Israelite origin put the interests of Israel before those of their own country, this is bound to create difficulties."[17] Like Pompidou and others since the Six-Day War, Giscard implied that Jews' dual loyalties were interfering with their obligation as citizens. But the extent to which Giscard failed to measure the impact of the Holocaust trauma and the changing nature of Jewish identity in France was perhaps best exemplified by his handling of the 1974 abortion controversy. Giscard had charged Simone Veil, Auschwitz survivor and newly appointed minister of health, with sponsoring the passage of a liberalized abortion law. The assignment of Veil to this task—a Jew to formally present a law sure to incur the wrath of the Church, a former deportee to represent the government on an issue destined to raise issues about humanity and the moral uses of technology—this selection seemed overdetermined.

Françoise Gaspard, at the time a Socialist deputy, later said she had thought Veil would be "unattackable largely because of the deportation." But far from being protected, Veil was subjected to vitriolic attacks from French parliamentarians opposed to the Giscard plan. René Feit, for example, a Giscardian deputy from the Jura, delivered a scathing attack on the proposed liberalization. After abortion, he fulminated, we will have laws against the physically or mentally handicapped, the "extra mouths to feed," the terminally ill, and the "deadweights" of society, laws which will lead us "to the worst Nazi racism. Abortion is legal genocide." Jean-Marie Daillet, reform deputy from the Manche: "Suppose that we come across one of those Nazi doctors who has escaped punishment, one of those men who practiced torture and human vivisection. Is there a difference in nature between what he did and what will be officially practiced in the hospitals and clinics of France?" he asked. "We have gone as far as to claim that a human embryo is an aggressor. Well, well!" he mocked. Apparently madam is prepared to see these aggressors "thrown to the crematory ovens or filling trash cans, as happened somewhere else." At this point, Veil broke down, her head practically resting on the podium. After suffering days of personal attacks, she later said, the image of the ovens and the insinuation that as a Jew she was behaving like a Nazi "brought back the smell of burning flesh."[18]

Holocaust imagery infused the abortion controversy.[19] Veil's aides claim to have heard her repeatedly vilified in the halls reserved for deputies. "It's not surprising that she is defending this, she's a Jew . . . Bitch, Jew, how did she come back from Auschwitz?" Among the thousands of letters Veil received, many invoked her deportation in disparaging the proposed legislation. A letter, for example, from Nîmes, November 20, 1974:

> When the President of the Republic named you to the government, I learned that you had survived Auschwitz. I rejoiced for you, your family, your husband and your children. Now, I regret it. Indeed, I am sorry about it.
>
> If the deputies and senators adopt your proposed law, you will have your turn to become one of the greatest criminals of this century, the next in a long line of assassins. You are going to kill our children, you are going to destroy our country, its values, its youth . . . .
>
> A fervent Catholic, I have always opposed all anti-Semitism. I am nonetheless forced now to argue that this satanic law, Madam, is the work of a Jew [ . . . ].[20]

Like Israel after the Six-Day War, Veil, the Holocaust victim, had become a Nazi perpetrator. Throughout the ordeal, according to Veil, Giscard offered not the smallest sign or word of support. "I tried to speak with him several times," Veil recalled. "I did not succeed. I had the painful feeling that he was unavailable, that I was speaking a foreign language." Giscard's ruptures with other prominent French Jews, such as Raymond Aron and Lionel Stoléru, and his consistent bumbling of the interpersonal aspects of both Middle East policy and his relationship with French Jewry, revealed a disaccord so profound, according to historian Pierre Vidal-Naquet, that it had two serious and immediate consequences: "every day the Jews supported the politics of the Israeli government more unconditionally, [and] every day they criticized the French government more systematically."[21]

## *Occupation, Collaboration, and World War II France*

As Jews ruminated over Israel, Jewish identity, and the Holocaust, French national interest in World War II and the Vichy regime began to ferment. The Goethe Institute of Paris, for example, was pressed in February 1970 to schedule a second showing of Joachim Fest's film "Adolf Hitler" in response to increased demand; newspaper articles on the war began to appear more frequently; and in 1971, Marcel Ophuls' "The Sorrow and the Pity" was released, an event many now look upon as a watershed in the story of France's renewed interest in World War II.[22] Set in Clermont-Ferrand, composed partially of archival footage from World War II but dominated by eyewitness accounts from those who had lived through the period, the film presented testimony from collaborators and resisters; prominent political figures and lesser or unknown "locals"; Pétainists, communists, and Gaullists; and French, English, and German witnesses. It inspired widely varied reactions, from those who lavishly praised its honesty to those who excoriated its misrepresentation of the Resistance. If the Six-Day War was the first chapter in the story of French Jewry's public engagement with the Holocaust, "The Sorrow and the Pity" provoked the nation's first sustained confrontation with World War II.

The power of "The Sorrow and the Pity," its capacity to provoke such passionate responses, owed predominantly to the fact that it appeared to displace the Gaullist myth that had reigned in France since de Gaulle's triumphant march through Paris in August 1944: the notion that with the exception of very few collaborators, France had been united with the Resistance throughout the war and had been fully engaged in its own liberation and the defeat of Nazi Germany. This myth had been an important part of France's postwar reconstruction because it had enabled the nation to focus on the heroic ties that bound them together rather than the shameful wedges that drove them apart. Merely challenging this myth would have been controversial. But by presenting the nation as having been deeply divided between 1940–1944, and by implying that inaction was a form of passive collaboration, the film became "a kind of countermyth to the official Gaullist myth." The movie, wrote Stanley Hoffmann, was "both a revelation and a weapon in the painful domestic battle that the French [were] waging with their past."[23]

"The Sorrow and the Pity," in other words, was at once both liberating and frightening. On the one hand, it presented an opportunity for national reflection on "the dark years," on a national heritage that had produced both the Resistance and collaboration; on the other, the very reminder of a bitterly divided France could be experienced as divisive and ran the risk of provoking a "civil war" reminiscent of what the nation had endured directly following the Liberation. Worse, some feared, a new myth would supplant the old, one which argued that the Resistance had been a sham and that most French people had been either active or passive collaborators.[24] The prospect of returning to that epoch was both emotionally painful and politically volatile: emotionally so for those who wanted neither for themselves nor their children to be reminded of the difficult choices of that era, of what might be construed as cowardice; and politically so because current political divisions had begun to emerge between 1940 and 1944, and key political groups, especially Gaullists and communists, had based their postwar credibility on their wartime heroism. Indeed, discussions surrounding the film focused largely on the extent of participation in the Resistance and collaboration, the role of communists in the Resistance before and during the war, and the behavior of "the average French person" under Vichy and the occupation.

In a *Le Monde* discussion, writer and former Pétain supporter Alfred Fabre-Luce and his critics took up the question of Jewish deportations from

France. Fabre-Luce argued that the Vichy regime, "without experiencing any sympathy for the Jews, nonetheless set itself the task of protecting all French citizens, including Jewish citizens, from the worst of the occupant's cruelty." Pétain enjoyed only a "half liberty," while the government of Prime Minister Pierre Laval, "which consented to odious deliveries of foreign Jews, is also the one which, at the most dangerous hour, saved the ensemble of the French Jewish community, also threatened by massive deportation." Pétain was a savior, Fabre-Luce lectured, and "it is always embarrassing to see survivors condemn a man to whom they owe their lives."[25] Resister Claude Lévy, an Ophuls interviewee, was among the many Jews deeply offended by Fabre-Luce's remarks. "In no way do I owe my life to Laval or Pétain, or to their accomplices," he wrote. "On the contrary. . . . " It was only for tactical and political reasons that the Germans first deported foreign Jews, he argued, and it was only as it became less clear that the Nazis would win the war that many at Vichy became less zealous collaborators. "In any case, it was an ignominy and an illusion if some people, including certain French Jewish notables, thought that the sacrifice of their foreign human brothers which they were either offering or consenting to could spare the French Israelites." Jews who managed to escape deportation, wrote Auschwitz survivor and Jewish community activist Henry Bulawko, did so thanks only to the Resistance and "the solidarity of a part of the non-Jewish French population who helped to hide children and adults, to feed them and furnish them with false papers, and to help them cross the border. Homage must be paid to those courageous and patriotic railway workers and country dwellers, to those Christians loyal to their faith, to all those who took risks to save a Jew."[26]

The conflict between Fabre-Luce and his Jewish critics was based not just on a general disagreement over the centrality of the Holocaust to World War II. It also had to do with differences of opinion over the relative salience of Jews' particular nightmare and the more general suffering of the nation, and it demonstrated how wide the gulf could be between Jewish and non-Jewish understandings of the Holocaust. As the esteemed philosopher Vladimir Jankelevitch wrote, "One must understand the Jews. They do not experience, with their compatriots, only the legitimate resentment one nourishes toward the murderers of France: they are otherwise specially concerned, intimately offended, personally humiliated. . . . "[27] Jews, according to Jankelevitch, had endured the humiliation of France with their fellow citizens but had suffered genocide alone. They hated the Nazis because they were French but especially because they were Jewish. For Fabre-Luce, Pétain had done what was necessary to save France. Severely constrained by the Nazis, with only a "half liberty," Pétain had shielded the nation, including the French Jewish community, from the worst Nazi cruelty. Without Pétain, Fabre-Luce implied, it would have been much worse. For Bulawko, on the other hand, it was not Pétain but the "loyal Christians" and French people who had opposed Vichy and reached out to Jews who were courageous and "patriotic." These people had represented "true France" versus "official France" and in the process were the real saviors of the nation.

Yet, although both Bulawko and Lévy were clear in their condemnation of the Vichy government and its involvement in the deportation of Jews from France, they did not demand apologies or that the nation or government be held accountable. Just what had been Vichy's role, who in the government had been involved, and what had been the attitude of the French population at large were questions that remained largely unasked. While opinions like those of Fabre-Luce provoked a hostile response from Jews, there was little discussion of the film itself in *Tribune Juive* or *L'Arche*, the two most popular Jewish newspapers. In the one set of articles devoted to the film and published in *L'Arche*, Jean Blot argued that "The Sorrow and the Pity" was at least to some extent a "betrayal." No, he wrote, "it was not like that, not like that at all. It was worse. Atrocious and massive." At the time of the film's release, *Tribune Juive*'s "France" section was most often devoted to the French government's attitude toward the conflict in the Middle East, which Jews perceived to be increasingly hostile. In the Jewish media, the contemporary significance of the Holocaust had to do primarily with Israel.[28]

New controversies developed following news that Pompidou had pardoned Frenchman Paul Touvier in November 1971 and that Klaus Barbie, chief of the Gestapo in Lyon during the war, was alive in Bolivia. Touvier, who had been responsible for hunting enemies of the Vichy regime, had been sentenced to death twice, in 1946 and 1947, but had gone into hiding at the end of the war. The Touvier pardon passed unnoticed until *L'Express* published an exposé over six months later, after which the press exploded with a wave of articles on Vichy and the occupation that totaled over 5,000 through 1976.[29] Attention was fixed on Touvier as well as Barbie, who also had been sentenced to death twice, in 1952 and 1954, and who had lived most of his exile in Bolivia. Barbie's whereabouts had not been a well-guarded secret, but it was only in light of recent controversies about the past that his contempt for French justice elicited public consternation. National debates continued to focus on the wartime divisions in France, using evidence marshaled from the Touvier and Barbie stories to bolster competing assessments of Vichy and the occupation. Jewish commentators devoted scant attention to either Barbie or Touvier, and the tone of these stories contrasted sharply with the energy and sense of urgency that characterized discussion about Israel. We cannot expect Pompidou to reverse his decision, wrote Daniel Mayer, reflecting on the pardon. "We can only claim our indignation and sadness."[30]

Debates about World War II intensified following the publication of

American historian Robert Paxton's *La France de Vichy* (*Vichy France*) in January 1973. Based on research in German archives, Paxton painted a portrait of the Vichy regime as a willing co-conspirator of the Nazis, as a government run by willful and enthusiastic collaborators who met and at times surpassed the demands of the occupant. The book marked a turning point in the French historical profession, which until then had been dominated by the understanding that Pétain had been a "shield" and de Gaulle a "sword," that Pétain had staved off the worst Nazi demands while de Gaulle led the armed resistance. Paxton presented anti-Semitic legislation and the deportation of Jews from France as part of the larger project of collaboration, and as had been true in discussions surrounding "The Sorrow and the Pity," the public continued to debate the nature and extent of collaboration and resistance. Critics accused Paxton of underestimating the constraints imposed by the German occupier while others questioned why such research had not been conducted by a French scholar.[31] Jewish reviews were supportive, but the book did not attract substantial attention in the Jewish press.[32]

During the "return of the repressed," as historian Henry Rousso has characterized the return of Vichy and the occupation to French consciousness in the 1970s, the Holocaust was neither ignored nor invisible. But, in the national press, it was only rarely discussed as an independent event, one with boundaries distinct from the war within which it took place. The centrality of "The Sorrow and the Pity" and *Vichy France* in initiating France's struggle with its past has long been recognized. But debates over the film and book and controversies surrounding Touvier and Barbie also marked the beginning of two divergent strands of World War II narrative: one, expressly Jewish, devoted to the Holocaust; and the other, more national, focused on collaboration and the Resistance.

## The Darquier Affair

In October 1978, the popular magazine *L'Express* published a controversial interview with Louis Darquier de Pellepoix, former Vichy minister for Jewish affairs. By then, national discussion of World War II was structured rather firmly around a Resistance-collaboration antinomy, and Jewish conversations about the Holocaust revealed a continued tension between the particular and universal dimensions of Jewish identity in France. But the public discourse following the Darquier interview and then the telecast of "Holocaust"—the first debates to take the Holocaust as their point of departure—revealed once again what divided many Jews and non-Jews: the trauma, which was grounded in the singularity of the Holocaust itself. Darquier's comments about Jews and their deportation from France stimulated a universalization of the Holocaust, an extension of its significance to the broadest swaths of humanity, which reflected and then exacerbated this crucial misunderstanding. The result was a discourse in which Jews and non-Jews constructed parallel interpretations of the genocide, narratives whose structure was similar but whose contents and meaning were widely divergent.

The *L'Express* interview focused on the fact that from May 1942, Darquier had overseen the major deportations of Jews from France, including the July 1942 Paris roundups and the autumn deportations from the unoccupied zone that followed. Sentenced to death at the Liberation, Darquier had taken refuge in Spain, where he continued to reside at the time of the interview. Asked about the "disappearance of six million Jews," Darquier claimed "[t]his number is an invention, pure and simple. A Jewish invention, of course. The Jews are like this. They are ready to do anything to draw attention to themselves." Of the yellow star Jews were forced to wear in the occupied zone, Darquier pleaded ignorance. "It must again be a question of your Jewish propaganda." Darquier contended that he had been at the Office for Jewish Affairs only a few weeks at the time of the Vél d'Hiv roundup and that the deportation had been orchestrated totally by René Bousquet, chief of Vichy police.[33] As for the gassing of Jews at Auschwitz, Darquier was dismissive.

Darquier: At Auschwitz, they gassed only the lice.
*L'Express*: What do you mean?
Darquier: I mean that when the Jews arrived at the camp, they made them get undressed, as was normal, before taking them to the showers. During this time, they disinfected their clothes. After the war, the Jews circulated photographs showing laundry piled up or hanging from lines. And they moaned . . . "Look," they said, "it's the laundry of our brothers whom they exterminated!" That was false, of course. But what do you want, the Jews are like that. They always have to lie.

Do you find yourself at times having regrets, asked *L'Express*. "Regrets for what?" Darquier responded. "I don't understand your question."[34]

An explosion of public discussion followed the interview's publication. "Never in recent history," remarked Jean Daniel, "have so few words decidedly provoked so much commentary."[35] Many questioned whether France was "adult" enough to "confront" the Vichy past and whether *L'Express*, by giving a tribune to Darquier, had violated "a social taboo" and paved the way for "the liberation of long-repressed feelings."[36] "This is the first time since the end of the war that someone has openly dared to go this far," said Veil, who feared the "banalization" of the Holocaust. Jankelevitch warned that "dormant instincts are awakening." *L'Express* claimed to be "stupefied" by the public's reaction, especially by those who had confounded Darquier's opinions with those of the journal. "This proves that French society is not yet mature enough to assume and critique its own past. . . . "

[T]he French have not always wanted to admit that there was a French Nazism, purely French. Their fear of knowing themselves explains their refusal to assume the anti-Semitic French past, to acknowledge that here, in France, anti-Semitism was not purely an import. This quasi-psychoanalytic "censure" exists even among some Jews, who fear that the danger can be reborn. It explains, after thirty-five years, the incapacity to face the text we published as an historical document.

"Have the French people repressed their memories of the occupation to this extent?" asked an incredulous Aron, now a columnist at *L'Express*. "And are they only now discovering with consternation that there were not only collaborators but Nazis born in Cahors and lost in their delirium?" Inasmuch as the Darquier interview turned attention toward the past, public discourse centered on the "obvious" fact that France had been divided, that there had been both a Resistance and a collaboration.[37]

To the extent that the interview focused attention on the present, on the other hand, public discussion turned to the question of prejudice and repression around the world, to the various arenas within and outside of France where people had been and continued to be persecuted because of their race or ethnicity. From Left to Right, critics spoke of African despotism, European terrorism, and communist repression and warned against focusing too much attention on the Holocaust. Analyzing the "ignoble beast" of dictatorship, writer René-Victor Pilhes demanded:

What does this "never again" clamor mean? That from now on we will maintain our sanity and we will never again kill Jews? But then would a "beast" who no longer devours Jews die like a lamb? Does Hitler become honorable without Auschwitz? Why would six million assassinated Jews overshadow the political regimes, the fascist dictators who engendered the murders? . . . Because one is always someone's "Jew."

Readers in *L'Express* pointed to communist and colonial crimes as proof that Hitler's defeat was only a partial victory. "The flames from the giant crematory ovens at Birkenau and Treblinka have indeed been extinguished. But the ideology which illuminated them is not dead." In *Témoignage Chrétien*, Georges Montaron pointed to the massacres of Kurds, Armenians, and Gypsies and criticized the exclusive focus on the Holocaust. "Are there racisms that we [*on*] can accept and others that we must condemn?" Even if "anti-Jewish racism" still exists, he argued, "anti-Black and anti-Arab racism are more developed and more virulent today. This is what the Darquier de Pellepoix affair should not conceal."[38]

For many Jews, the Holocaust trauma, and therefore its uniqueness, was axiomatic. Darquier's remarks, in other words, revealed not the dangers of prejudice broadly defined but the specificity of the Holocaust and the on-going peril of anti-Semitism. At the same time, certain Jewish thinkers, such as *Le Nouvel Observateur*'s Daniel and *L'Express*'s Aron, endeavored to identify what was distinct about the Holocaust as well as its implications for a wide range of contemporary social and political problems. They sought, in other words, to underscore the specificity of anti-Semitism and the Holocaust while at the same time linking them to racism and repression around the world. On opposite sides of the mainstream political spec-trum—Daniel on the Left, Aron on the Right—each tried to articulate both the singularity of the Holocaust and its place in the pantheon of modern terror. The twentieth century, wrote Daniel, has witnessed the systematic massacre of the Armenians, Tasmanians, Tartars of Crimea, Ibos, Bengalis, and Khmers. And if it is true that Stalinism produced as many victims as Nazism, "why make Hitler's genocide of the Jews exceptional?"

The reason is simple. What was particular or specific about the Holocaust, its essence, was not the unbelievable number of victims, it was the decision made coldly and solemnly, in the name of a faith and also of a science, to justify, prepare, codify, and systematize the extermination of an entire race. Not for what it is ac-cused of doing. Nor for what it is suspected of thinking. Simply because it is . . . The regrouping of the damned, their transportation, the organization of the camps, the selection for extermination: nothing is left to improvisation. Nothing will leave a trace. It is the infernal process of the perfect crime. Its specificity is its perfection, its essence its radicalness, its magical horror its aptitude to evoke nothingness and infinity.

Aron agreed that massacres, tortures, and concentration camps had become so commonplace in the world that "the Nazi crimes unfortunately cease to seem outside the bounds of humanity." Stalin, after all, "killed millions more human beings than Hitler himself."

To ward off the risk of banalization, it is necessary to highlight what belongs to Nazism alone: the Holocaust, the deliberate, industrial extermination of an entire people, the Jews, the Gypsies. What is banal, unfortunately, is racism, the scorn or hostility that members of one ethnic group feel toward members of another group, whether the color of their skin is different or not. Far from bringing us back to ba-nal racism, Darquier's remarks shine a harsh light on the singularity of Nazism, the desire to kill those we hate and whose humanity we do not acknowledge. When Darquier asserts that they [*on*] gassed only lice, he reveals his true colors: he makes no distinction between lice and Jews.[39]

For Jews who believed profoundly in the Holocaust's singularity, the fact that Darquier's comments were often classified under the rubric of "racism" was itself an affront. The universalization of the Holocaust—the presenta-

tion of the genocide as analogous to myriad other experiences—was tantamount to its trivialization. The very attempt to understand the genocide on
terms other than its own, in the context of other suffering, was experienced
as an assault, as misguided empathy. For others, such as Aron and Daniel,
it was nonsensical not to situate the Holocaust in the recent history of mass
atrocity. While they, like Veil, feared the "banalization" of the Holocaust,
they recognized that certain links served to connect it to other examples of
oppression. What they disputed were analyses that seemed to make the
Holocaust parallel with or the same as these other forms. And often only a
very fine line separated connection from assimilation.

Regardless of the analytic distinctions some Jews tried to draw between
the Holocaust and other examples of repression, their point about the singularity of the trauma was lost in a national discourse where the Nazi genocide was not perceived as unique and where some observers deliberately
emphasized its triteness. Aron's attempt to establish the "singularity of
Nazism," for example, served as the basis for writer and conservative columnist Louis Pauwels's excoriation of communism. "Nazism has been extinguished. Absolutely extinguished, everywhere in the world," he wrote. And
as Aron has argued, "a still-blazing communism 'killed millions more human beings than Hitler himself.'" Why, Pauwels asked, have the stammer-
ings of an anti-Semitic dinosaur in *L'Express* provoked thousands of commentaries while *Figaro Magazine*'s dossier on Marxism's 150 million victims
has been ignored by the humanitarian intelligentsia? "On the paths of history, one terrorism can conceal another."[40] Aron certainly would have
agreed that history, especially in the twentieth century, was replete with
mass death and tragedy. He himself had raised the issue of agricultural col-
lectivization and the purges in Stalin's Soviet Union. But his point was to
"avoid the banalization" of Nazism by identifying what was exceptional
about the Holocaust. Pauwels, on the other hand, quoted part of Aron's
analysis in an effort to neutralize the Holocaust's specificity and to avoid the
normalization of "the terrors of today." This kind of "misunderstanding,"
where the language was the same but the meaning quite different, was at
the root of a gnawing uneasiness among those Jews most concerned with
the Holocaust trauma.

Yet Jews at times also were unclear about what, exactly, was unique, such
as *Tribune Juive* editor Grunewald's reaction to the Darquier interview.

Since Hannah Arendt, and more recently, Simone Veil, we [*on*] have spoken at
length about the "banalization" of Nazism. It is true: the minute we compare it to
other aberrations, Nazism loses its monstrosity. But there is no worse banalization
than to condemn Nazism while at the same time permitting tortures and murders
to take place today, under whatever meridian and on the order of states. For the

man, woman, and child who suffer and die, this kind of banalization is the worst of them all.[41]

The non-Jew, or someone outside the boundaries of the subjective community distinguished by the Holocaust trauma, would find little in Grunewald's remarks that would help identify the precise ways in which the singularity of the Holocaust trauma could be upheld at the same time as its links to contemporary forms of violent repression. Grunewald argued that simply comparing the Nazi Holocaust to other "aberrations" implicitly diminished its uniqueness. Yet he also wrote that the worst form of denial was to allow other tortures and killings to continue to take place, a statement which itself betrayed a comparison between contemporary torture and the Holocaust. At times Jewish opinion that sought to stress the trauma of the Holocaust actually encouraged its universalization, or broadened the range of its direct implications, and therefore exacerbated what many Jews perceived to be its routinization.

## *"Holocaust" in France*

Since the 1978 telecast of "Holocaust" in the United States, all of the major French television stations had argued that the film was too expensive to purchase and broadcast in France. Spurred by outrage over the Darquier interview, Jewish writer, activist, and Warsaw Ghetto survivor Marek Halter initiated a successful fund-raising campaign, and French television presented the American film in four parts during February-March 1979. Despite biting criticism of American television, endorsement of the film's broadcast and praise for its evocative powers were virtually unanimous.[42] Critics argued that because it could be a weapon against prejudice, "the political purpose of the series is more important that its artistic 'value.'" "Bad or good, faithful or remiss in the details, simplistic in the eyes of the refined or touching by its dramatic vigor," the film was "an event" in that millions of young people would see for the first time "what we lived through almost forty years ago." "Holocaust" is going to show us what we would have much preferred never to see again, wrote Dominique Jamet in *L'Aurore*. "And, frankly, who could this bother?"[43]

It bothered people concerned about relations with Germany. Controversy broke out between members of Giscard's UDF (Union for French Democracy) Party, seeking to build stronger ties with Germany, and the Jacques Chirac–led RPR Rally for the Republic), opposed to Giscard's plan. In a letter in *Le Monde*, the UDF expressed its concern that the film, "a spectacular story of the extermination of the Jews by the Nazis," might encourage "the anti-German campaign hatched a few weeks ago by several anti-Europeanists." The response from the film's proponents was charged with Holocaust rhetoric. When I read the UDF's letter, wrote Pierre Charpy in the RPR's *La Lettre de la Nation*, "I end up thinking that the intellectual mechanism that culminated in the crematory ovens still exists." *L'Humanité* agreed. Just as when Giscard had decided in 1975 to cancel France's commemoration of victory over Nazism, the UDF was once again "ready to cheerfully sacrifice the memory of millions of victims of Hitlerism."[44] This fear of provoking anti-Germanism was apparent outside the bounds of party politics as well. Many parents of schoolchildren in Alsace, for example, refused to allow their children to watch beyond the first night. "If young Alsatians see this," said a school principal, "more than anyone else they could react with anti-Germanism."[45]

But the results of a poll published in *Le Point* suggested that the anti-German risk was minimal. Given the crimes committed by the Nazis, the poll asked, is it necessary to consider the Germans today as "distinct" or as people like everyone else? Only ten percent responded that Germans should be considered different while eighty-three percent believed that Germans were like everyone else. What is most comforting, wrote *Le Point*, is that "four of five French people refuse to outlaw the German people from Europe or humanity." Time and wisdom have done their work, the magazine continued, as has "the discovery, during the maelstrom of decolonization, that to varying degrees, each people has powerfully somber episodes in its history."[46] The poll and commentary published in *Le Point* were significant for several reasons. First, they both reflected and oriented attention toward the Holocaust as an event that had happened in Germany. All of the questions focused on the Nazi concentration camps, Nazi criminals, or "the German people," and the analysis itself highlighted contemporary attitudes toward Germany, thereby implying that the primary concern in projecting the film was, indeed, future Franco-German relations. As history, the Holocaust became an event between Jews and Germans, and questions from a contemporary perspective were about its impact on European alliances. What is more, *Le Point*'s final observations about every country's dark history jumped almost directly from the German crime of the Holocaust to the more widespread crime of colonialism without stopping even briefly on Vichy's participation in the Holocaust. From time to time debates did take up the question of Vichy's role in the deportation of Jews from France, but this was most often en route to a broader universalization of the Holocaust, one that criticized national "good conscience" in general and which pointed to "all the holocausts of yesterday and today."[47] The distinctiveness that many Jews assigned to the Holocaust was therefore de-emphasized in the *Le Point* article in two ways: its singularity in relation to racism, colonialism, and other forms of violence; and the particularity of Jewish victimization in France, because France was largely portrayed as the perpetrator of racist and colonial crimes.

Colonialism and racism, Armenians and Kurds, Cambodians and Cubans—the broadcast of "Holocaust" stimulated a discourse suffused with imagery of violent repression in the twentieth century. It also inspired criticism of Israel and Zionism. Egyptian journalist Lotfallah Soliman took issue in *Le Matin* with one professor's fear of "a new massacre" in the Middle East, where Arab countries opposed showing the film. "I must honestly say," remarked Soliman,

that I have rarely seen such moral terrorism in the commercialization of a television series . . . [I]f the massacre of Israelis would be a matter of the "final solution," because the Israelis are Jews, what would be the massacre of Arabs? Nothing is more dangerous than to sow the seeds of racism while pretending to obliterate it.

According to the Trotskyist paper *Rouge*,

The Jews of today include the Latin American opposition to dictators in power. They are the Kurds oppressed by Arab regimes. They are the Palestinians under Israeli bombs. They were the Vietnamese under American bombs, the blacks of South Africa. . . .

Fascism is presented in "Holocaust" only in its most terrible manifestation, the massacre of the Jews . . . The Jews are alone against the SS. In this way, the film told the truth. But this truth is twisted into a very subtle justification for Jewish nationalism, incarnated by Zionism . . . There is at the end of the film this kind of making-up-for-one's-losses that is characteristic of all history invoked for the benefit of Zionism as it exists today. A nice little contradiction peculiar to this film.

Moroccan writer Tahar Ben Jelloun recalled his first encounter with the Holocaust, a lycée viewing of "Night and Fog." We knew early, he wrote, "that history can contain irony, bloody irony. Because we learned, at about the same age, that an Arab village had been decimated, a village in Palestine, Deir Yassin." Directly across from this letter in *Le Monde* was an article claiming Israel's victories to belong to Holocaust victims. In this way, Zionist activist Paul Giniewski wrote, "they are less atrociously, less uselessly, and less truly dead . . . One has to believe in the resurrection of the dead. Israel is one of its forms."[48]

This juxtaposition was a subtle reflection of the gulf in meaning between many Jewish and non-Jewish understandings of the Holocaust. Almost everyone acknowledged, either explicitly or implicitly, that the Holocaust and Israel were intimately connected. *Rouge*, for example, argued that the Holocaust served as a justification for Jewish nationalism and Israel, while Jews, too, often spoke about Israel as a haven arising directly from the Holocaust. But while the Holocaust trauma was central to much Jewish support for Israel, for critics, this recourse to the Holocaust shielded the fact that Israel, too, could be unjust. Any narrative that turned to the Holocaust to justify Israel was for most Arab supporters merely a coverup for Israeli injustice; and any argument that invoked the genocide and the Middle East other than to justify Israel was unacceptable for many Jews. When Jelloun and others suggested a relationship between Nazis and Israelis, all possible dialogue broke down. For even those Jews most critical of Israel would not tolerate any implication that Israelis were Nazis. When speaking about the Holocaust, then, Jews and non-Jews often shared a vocabulary, but their understandings of the Holocaust were distinct, and at times, radically so.

In the days surrounding the first episode's broadcast, amidst a flurry of discussion about the Holocaust in history and the pedagogical function of the film, *L'Agence Télégraphique Juive* strongly criticized Education Minister Christian Beullac for suggesting that "there has not been only one genocide, Hitler's, only one totalitarianism, Nazi, in only one region of the world, Europe. Perspective, analysis, references, critique, comparison, and explanation are necessary." How, asked the Jewish press organ, "is it possible not to see in this part of Beullac's analysis the risk of banalizing the genocide of European Jews?"[49] Actually, Jews quoted in national and communal papers indicated that they found the film rather fatuous. But for some, such as Jankelevitch and Claude Lanzmann, anything that called to question the irreducible specificity of the Holocaust was not simply banal but unbearable. In an interview with *Le Nouvel Observateur*, Jankelevitch vehemently criticized French reactions to both the Darquier interview and "Holocaust."

We are witnessing a formidable hypocrisy, a veritable cabal of sophists who, in complete ignorance, declare that of course the massacre of the Jewish people was horrible, intolerable, but that in the end it was not *worse* than other crimes forever being committed—and more specifically by Hitlerites—against humanity. That this genocide was, after all, of the same nature as those which preceded it.

The Nazis burned Jewish bodies, then their ashes. They destroyed molecules and atoms of Jews.

How can we pretend that this hatred is from an ordinary racism? To inscribe Hitler's genocide in the long series of crimes against humanity, to pretend that torture or—what do I know—the bombings of Sétif come from the same hate, that is serious. And the banalization of evil also passes through this type of confusion.[50]

Lanzmann, who at the time was filming "Shoah," claimed that the Holocaust could be repressed in two ways: one, by saying that it was the act of a handful of crazy people, and the other, by comparing it to massacres like the

Turkish slaughter of Armenians. Turkish leaders, said Lanzmann, "were absolutely primitive people. This was not the country of Kant, Goethe, and Hegel. They did not construct an entire ideology to justify their crime." The Holocaust, he stressed, is "inexpressible . . . there is an absolute singularity, an absolute uniqueness, in the extermination of the Jews which is comparable to nothing, which has no precedent in the history of the world and which will have no successor. . . . " For Lanzmann, the Holocaust was a trauma.

Between the conditions which enabled the extermination and the extermination itself—the *fact* of extermination—there is the solution of continuity, there is an hiatus, a jump, an abyss. The extermination does not create itself, and to want to portray that is in a certain sense to deny its reality, to refuse the sudden rise of violence is to want to clothe its implacable nudity, to dress it and therefore to refuse to see it, to stare into the face of what is most arid and incomparable about it.[51]

Neither Lanzmann's distinction between Germany and the "absolutely primitive people" who massacred the Armenians nor Jankelevitch's rationalization of "ordinary racism" were likely to generate empathy beyond certain segments of the Jewish community. The idea of uniqueness that they embraced, moreover, seemed implicitly to diminish the suffering of others. It was not surprising, therefore, that some non-Jews were as committed to the Holocaust's comparability as some Jews were to its singularity.

But even regarding the one issue on which most people agreed—the perniciousness of Holocaust denial—Jews and non-Jews seemed to have different concerns. In December 1978, capitalizing on Darquier's statements, Lyon professor Robert Faurisson published an article in *Le Monde* that denied the existence of gas chambers, and therefore the systematic extermination of the Jews, during World War II. In "'The Problem of the Gas Chambers,' or 'the Auschwitz Rumor,'" Faurisson argued that the method of killing by gas was scientifically and technically impossible and that the story of the Holocaust was therefore a lie. This position became known as Holocaust revisionism. Several scholars immediately denounced the Faurisson thesis, including survivor Georges Wellers and historian Olga Wurmser, and in February 1979, a declaration stating that the existence of the Holocaust was not a legitimate intellectual question was signed by some of France's most eminent historians and printed in *Le Monde*. When Faurisson later published a book prefaced by Noam Chomsky, the distinguished American linguist, the controversy intensified.[52] But apprehension expressed in public discourse had less to do with the Holocaust per se than with the parameters of acceptable academic inquiry and the limits of free speech. While many Jews saw the Faurisson text as evidence of an increase in anti-Semitism, most public debate focused on Chomsky and his politics.

In particular, critics berated him for refusing his responsibilities as a public intellectual and for stretching the principle of free speech to its logical absurdity. Missing from the "Chomsky-Faurisson Affair," as it was characterized in the French press, was much discussion of Jews, anti-Semitism, or the Holocaust.

## Trauma and Jewish Identity after "Holocaust"

In the aftermath of the Darquier and "Holocaust" controversies, many Jews showed a new willingness to be critical of the France to which their ancestors had for centuries sworn unadulterated allegiance. They continued, as many had throughout the 1970s, to reflect on the Holocaust and its implications for both their French identity and the meaning of Jewish identity in the diaspora. There is a myth, wrote Pierre Goldman, that Jews belong fully to the French community. And Giscard amplified its falsity when, in the middle of the Darquier controversy, he made a pilgrimage to place flowers on Pétain's grave. This gesture shows that our highest leadership would like for the Marshal to regain his place in the national pantheon.

It signifies that the Jews are not important enough for one to consider that to have collaborated in their massive assassination is an entirely infamous crime [and] that we are not perceived by this France as fully French. Is it necessary to be Jewish to believe that the sufferings imposed upon the Jewish people are fundamental?

Anti-Semites tell Jews not to be too loud, Goldman continued, that they are "guests" in this country.

No. The Jews after Drancy do not accept this kind of politeness and reserve. They refuse the decency that their fathers wanted to pass on to them. They think that a fundamental contract was forever broken in 1940. They no longer believe in these universalist impostors who intend to abolish or dissolve our identity. They do not reclaim but assume the right to be different French citizens. They assert that their integration into the French nation will never be obligatory; they say that their assumption of French nationality passes through their belonging to the Jewish people. . . .

They do not care if this is scandalous: what can they be afraid of? The Gauls dreaded only one thing: that the sky would fall on their head. That never happened to those proud and enthusiastic warriors. It happened to us. We are still there.[53]

We are still there, argued the Sephardi professor of Jewish thought Shmuel Trigano, because we remain in the Occident, and "Auschwitz signified without caveat the impossible normalization of the Jews in the diaspora." If communism made the Gulag, "democracy and capitalism produced Auschwitz. Both in the Occident." To forbid Nazi pamphlets is hindsight, he wrote, because the negation of Auschwitz is only a symptom of western civilization, not "a foundational act of a separate anti-Semitism." We constantly lay claim to the deposit on our diasporic lives left by the six million who died, he chided. We justify ourselves, make proclamations, experience indignation, and even brandish "proof" of the genocide. "What moral weakness, not to mention cowardice, is in this for us. We are trapped ahead of time by legitimating and acknowledging that anti-Semitism in the Occident has jurisdiction over us. In fact, we seek to persuade ourselves even rather than respond to the reality of the situation. It is the path of *suicide*." But at the same time, he lamented, Israel has become a nation-state like all others: as Jews in the desert turned first to the golden calf, Israel, too, looked to existing state models. Zionism "came from the Occident, in exteriority but not in interiority," and that Zionists continue to want to be like everyone else shows the power of diaspora mentality. Thus both the Occident and Israel—modern Jewish life—are a continuation of exile, and Jewish "alterity" is perceived as "confounded and desperately empty of authenticity." But as the Jews emerged from the experience of the golden calf, so, too, will they return from contemporary Zionism.

We must think about Auschwitz today and leave from the Occident where we (cannot) find ourselves . . . The world is for us no more than the malefic trapdoor that it was in 1939. Other horizons are opening themselves to us, beyond the meager fenced-in ghettos—symbolic and practical—of the old Europe. Provided only that we have the audacity to be who we will be.[54]

For Trigano, a positive diasporic identity was impossible. Only when Zionism shed its desire to create a state like all others and turned to Jewish values could Jews leave from exile and return to Israel to discover their true identity. But the vast majority of French Jews wanted neither to leave France nor to construct a Jewish state that was radically different from all others. For Goldman, the Darquier Affair had nailed shut the coffin of the myth that the Revolution permitted Jews to be citizens like the rest of the French; whereas Jews had been excluded until 1789 and then had battled to be citizens through 1945, contemporary Jews were resolute and unapologetic in boldly proclaiming their rights as citizens. Yet what Goldman and Trigano failed to appreciate was that most Jews were committed to both national citizenship and the integrity of their Jewish identity. They wanted to be members of the nation and at the same time Jews, to contextualize the Holocaust, argue for its contemporary implications, and still honor the singularity of its trauma. Their Jewish identity, in other words, was inextricably tangled with their French identity in ways that neither Goldman nor Trigano would countenance.

Public discourse during the Darquier and "Holocaust" controversies was, for the most part, not overtly conflicted. Most commentators, regardless of their social or political convictions, found Darquier's comments reprehensible and potentially dangerous and were in favor of broadcasting the film. Most, both Jews and non-Jews, argued that the Holocaust had been a horrible genocide, and they took the opportunity to speak out against racism and to recall other episodes of horror in the twentieth century. And almost everyone seemed to agree on certain fundamental rules grounding Holocaust discourse, including discussion of the genocide in terms of perpetrators and victims and guilt and innocence. Where they disagreed was emphasis, nuance, and the overall meaning of the Holocaust in history and contemporary context. Following the last episode of "Holocaust," for example, Philippe Boucher argued that anti-Semitism had become "a screen before other manifestations of racism."[55] Jews were not a screen where an array of political and cultural concerns were projected, but Hitler and anti-Semitism served as a screen that concealed analogous repression and suffering. What many Jews experienced as a failure to appreciate the singularity of the Holocaust, in other words, Boucher and many others perceived as a one-sided emphasis of its distinguishing features. But aside from the commentary of men like Jankelevitch and Lanzmann, this tension remained largely implied throughout the two controversies. It was events in the 1980s, beginning with the bombing on Paris's rue Copernic, that made the conflict front-page news.

## CHAPTER FOUR

# The Holocaust as Metaphor
## From the Bombing of Rue Copernic to the Bombing of Lebanon

On October 3, 1980, in Paris's posh sixteenth district, a bomb exploded out-side the synagogue on rue Copernic. Apparently slated to detonate as con-gregants left the Friday evening Sabbath prayer, the bomb exploded before the service ended, thereby killing four passers-by but sparing the majority of its targeted victims. The outcome of the explosion, at least in terms of people killed, was far less disastrous than had been the "intended massacre," but it is on the latter that public discourse remained fixated in the ensuing controversy. Hundreds of thousands of people marched to protest the bombing in cities all over France, and for weeks newspapers wrestled with its causes and consequences in a highly charged discursive atmosphere laced with Holocaust imagery.

The attack was a watershed in French Jewish identity. As had been true during the Six-Day War, solidarity with Israel was an integral part of Jewish responses, especially among Sephardi Jews and radical Zionist organiza-tions such as Betar and Renouveau Juif (Jewish Renewal). Violence in the streets of Paris, however, made Jews feel vulnerable at home, and many complained about the quality of Jewish life in France. Militant Sephardi Jews and Ashkenazi youth proudly brandished their Jewish identity, de-manded recognition of their rights as Jews within France, and vowed to de-fend themselves against a new Holocaust. Notoriously quiescent Jewish leaders also showed a new inclination to criticize public officials in the name of the Jewish community. For the first time in modern history, large num-bers of Jews publicly rebuked the government and challenged the project of assimilation to which so many French Jews had devoted themselves for centuries. If the Six-Day War had marked the first noteworthy declaration of Jewish identity in France, the Copernic violence brought about the first significant assertion of French-Jewish identity.

The bombing was also a pivotal moment in the development of French public discourse on the Holocaust. It took place in a Europe incontestably vulnerable to terrorism and in a French society that myriad observers had labeled anxious and discontent. This malaise stimulated both a fascination with and a fear of what had plagued the nation at moments of much more profound agitation, during the *guerres franco-françaises* (French civil wars) that had been waged most recently during the Vichy era and the protracted imbroglio in Algeria. In the weeks following the bombing, various politically marginalized and oppressed groups invoked the Nazi genocide to underscore their own sense of victimization in France. People with varying ideological motivations united to point a collective finger at "fascism" and "fascist terrorism" and then confronted this enemy by identifying with Jewish victims of the Holocaust. The genocide thus became "present" on a number of discursive levels, serving at once as a symbol of the uniqueness of Jewish persecution and as a metaphor for oppression, as the epitome of Jewish particularity and as the locus for a universal identification with Jewish victimization. In the public's response to the bombing, Holocaust imagery conveyed two uneasily coexistent messages: the singularity of past and continuing Jewish suffering, and the omnipresence of social and political victimization. By summer 1982, in the wake of Israel's invasion of Lebanon, many Jews' insistence on the uniqueness of the Holocaust and a continued national preoccupation with a ubiquitous fascist enemy led to further diffusion of the Holocaust metaphor, this time in a way that directly challenged the notion of Jewish innocence. In the debates that ensued, antagonisms that had been largely stifled in the post-Copernic unanimity exploded into open hostility.

## The Bombing on Rue Copernic

In the months preceding the bombing, several prominent Jewish thinkers chided Jews for overreacting to a recent spate of attacks on Jewish institutions. Léon Poliakov, the eminent historian of anti-Semitism, argued that anti-Jewish violence was an historical constant and that he saw no "outburst" at present.[1] Intellectual Alain Finkielkraut, whose recently published *Le juif imaginaire* (*The Imaginary Jew*)suggested that Jews were overly identified with Holocaust victims, acknowledged in *Libération* that a certain taboo had been lifted. But, he stressed, "vigilance" should not mean "amnesia."

The contemporary period has nothing in common with the repugnant violence of the 1930s, the anti-Semitic leagues and parties, the laws presaging the withdrawal of French citizenship from foreigners who were already naturalized . . . Let us defend ourselves, but let us not use the pretext of their attacks to forget that we inhabit a Europe preserved from totalitarian danger and that apocalypse is not our lot.[2]

Finkielkraut proved remarkably prescient. The bomb exploded on rue Copernic less than a week after his remarks, and popular response—both Jewish and non-Jewish—was based on precisely the 1930s script that he and others had argued was outdated.

   The French public was virtually unanimous in its denunciation of the attack. Non-Jews gathered with Jews in front of the synagogue the next morning, they marched collectively down the Champs-Elysées that afternoon, and protests were held throughout the night. These groups joined together again three days later, when mass demonstrations were held throughout the nation, including a Paris parade that marched from the Bastille to the Nation. Public commentary was marked by a widespread repudiation of President Valéry Giscard d'Estaing and the ruling UDF government, which had failed to identify the authors of a series of terrorist acts perpetrated in France since 1977. Giscard, who waited four days before issuing an official response to the bombing, was accused of treating the issue of terrorism with "total impertinence" and of initiating a "return to Vichy." For two years, wrote Serge July in *Libération*, "fascist attacks have killed and claimed the murders of thirteen people. Not one guilty person sits in a French prison. If this is not impunity, it is at least indifference, if not complaisance." Said journalist Jean-François Kahn, "We are simply witnessing a new and absolutely predictable phase of the fascist offensive that has been developing in France since 1974 and which feeds at once on the resignation of the authorities, the complicity of certain elements in the police, and the muteness of the major media." Various political parties and activist groups called for the resignation of Interior Minister Georges Bonnet and Prime Minister Raymond Barre, and even those less inclined to critique the UDF could retort only that things were "a bit more complicated" than was being portrayed.[3]

   The greatest criticism was leveled at the police, accused of harboring in their ranks members of the Fédération d'Action Nationaliste Européenne (FANE), a fascist organization that had been disbanded in September 1980 by the French government.[4] Two officers of the Syndicat National des Policiers en Civil claimed that Bonnet was in possession of a list of 150 FANE members, "among whom one of five is a police officer," while the Confédération Générale du Travail (CGT) maintained that the estimate was too low. The young philosopher Bernard-Henri Lévy charged that these officers, alleged in parliamentary debates by parties on the Left to have been hired to help the police root out left-wing terrorism, had been infiltrated by the neo-Nazis they were supposed to combat. Fifty-seven percent of French people polled on October 7 and 8 agreed that the police "had not done all that was necessary," while only nineteen percent disagreed. Too many signs, concluded Jacquot Grunewald, suggest that what appears to be police incompetence is in fact complicity. Save for supporters of the UDF or the Far Right, public discourse reflected a widespread belief that the police were indulgent toward terrorism.[5]

The failure to apprehend the perpetrators was seen as a reflection of French "melancholy," "a general malaise," "a phenomenon of social pathology," and, in the words of sociologist Alain Touraine, epidemic "social decay." While *Le Quotidien de Paris*'s Dominique Jamet lamented "the state of ruin, demoralization, and decomposition" of the country, *Libération*'s Olivier Rollin called on the French to "attack the intellectual and moral degradation that characterizes French society." It was not so long ago, he noted, "that the French were blamed in extremis by those who had the courage to slap them in the face. May we call to them, let us reclaim from them the title, the anti-France."[6] Rollin's remarks recalled the post–World War II purges, a virtual civil war in which many of those who allegedly had collaborated with the Nazi regime were tortured, brought to trial, and at times executed by French people who claimed to have been partisans of the Resistance. The cultural despair about which he and others wrote following the Copernic violence brought to mind the social and political confusion of the 1930s. A period of generalized xenophobia, formalized in anti-Semitic leagues and in nativistic newspapers and magazines, the 1930s were perceived to have been the heyday of fascism in France, a decade that had led almost inexorably to the end of the Third Republic and the installation of the Vichy regime. Parallels between contemporary and pre–World War II France were drawn repeatedly in early commentaries after the Copernic attack. That the target had been a synagogue, furthermore, recalled the particularly Jewish aspects of 1930s fascism, the anti-Semitism that had preceded the Holocaust. In a France where morale was low and divisions deep, the fascism of the 1930s and Vichy France and the "racism" of the Nazi genocide became the guideposts by which the Copernic explosion was analyzed.

In the days following the attack, the Holocaust was "present" on a number of discursive levels. The bombing, wrote July, had "the shock effect of the Holocaust in reduction." It demonstrated "a progressive Vichyization of French society via the transgression of all taboos . . . as if scenes from the past were being replayed before our eyes." Giscard declared that the Copernic tragedy recalled "the deportations and massacres perpetrated by Hitler," while at the other end of the political spectrum, Socialist leader François

Mitterrand spoke of Anne Frank, "that young girl who continues to brighten our night . . . [T]hey have assassinated her brothers."[7] The Holocaust was also present visually, or in the sense that it had "presence." This was clearest in the widespread demonstrations throughout France, where hundreds of thousands marched against the attack. Protests were called for Bordeaux, Cherbourg, Grenoble, Nîmes, Annecy, Mulhouse, Colmar, Saint-Alvold, Hayange, and Le Havre. Massive marches took place in the provinces: 20,000 in Marseille, 7,000 in Lyon, 1,000 in Belfort, 10,000 in Nice, between 5–8,000 in Nancy, and 4,000 in both Metz and Rouen. From 3,000 to 15,000 marched in Lille, Vichy, Forbach, Sarcelles, Strasbourg, Toulouse, and Montpellier. The largest protest was in Paris, where over 100,000 rallied around signs declaring *Plus jamais ça!* (Never Again!). This visual presence continued into the 1980s in public commemoration ceremonies and memorials of the Holocaust and in plaques marking key sites in the deportation of Jews from France. These events were largely sponsored by Jews, although public officials, such as Paris Mayor Jacques Chirac, were among those who attended.[8]

## The Bombing and Jewish Identity in France

The attack solidified the link between the Holocaust and modern Jewish identity and provoked a surprisingly bold proclamation of Jewish rights within France. In 1967, Jews had invoked the Holocaust largely in connection to Israel. This was in itself remarkable, as it marked the first time that they collectively and with little reservation had articulated a public Jewish identity in France. The Copernic bombing, however, provoked Jews' first sweeping public reproach of the French government and the viability of old notions of assimilation. In the weeks of debate that followed, the Holocaust became "present" in that it framed Jewish discussions about their political identity in France as well as their right to national protection. Although important differences among Jews remained, even those most devoted to assimilation moved substantially in the direction of criticizing the government and of asserting their right to live in France not simply as citizens but as Jewish citizens. In public protests, written commentaries, and letters to the government, Jews with a wide range of political and religious convictions voiced outrage over the Copernic bombing and the more than 100 unsolved attacks by which it had been preceded.

Much of what Jews had to say explicitly recalled the Holocaust. For a while, commented Rabi, we basically believed that every twenty or thirty years we would face a new tyrant. "We thought, however, that after Auschwitz, we had the right to believe (to have the illusion to believe) that this was finished forever."[9] Jews turned repeatedly to images of the Holocaust during a rally at the Copernic synagogue the morning following the attack. With a child in his arms, one man cried to a police officer: "How long will this go on? We have paid enough like this! Six million Jews in 1940, this isn't enough for you? It is your uniform that sent our fathers and mothers to the crematory ovens!" *Libération* noted that many Jews at the gathering were wearing badges marked *Juif de France* (French Jew), an obvious reference to the yellow star Jews in the occupied zone had been forced to wear beginning June 1942. "My family departed in gas," said photojournalist Elie Kagan. "When they [*on*] attack the Jews, the fourteen-year-old boy Elie Kagan remembers the yellow star that the French state of Pétain imposed on him, when I didn't even know that I was Jewish." Someone in the crowd asked Kagan if he was afraid. "What could be worse than the gas chambers and six million dead?" he answered.[10]

Jewish frustration was exacerbated after Prime Minister Barre claimed on French television to regret "an attack that targeted Jews at the synagogue and which struck innocent French people." Jewish and non-Jewish commentators alike decried what they perceived to be Barre's implication that Jews either were not innocent or not French, or both. "Will they [*on*] never leave us alone?" asked one young Jew. "When I hear Raymond Barre declare that the Jews are not French, that really hurts. They are forcing us to be Zionists." Said Georges Kiejman, a prominent lawyer and Socialist politician whose father had perished in the Holocaust,

I understand very well that Mr. Barre had no intention of opposing Jews and French people. Only the unconscious spoke. The significance is there, at the moment where there is perhaps less to dread from Nazi commandos than from the speed with which the sentiment can be born that Jews are "the others" and that it is important from now on not to be confused with them.

As if to make up for his "blunder," continued Kiejman, Barre said that the Jews belong to a respected community. For all other communities, this would go without saying. Kiejman called on Barre to resign.[11]

Both Jews and non-Jews recognized that the Copernic bombing marked a break in French Jewish history. "There is the community of 'before Copernic' and the community of 'after Copernic,'" declared Grunewald. "Almost all observers . . . from Paris to the provinces have arrived at this conclusion."

We [*on*] can only say that before Copernic was a carefree time . . . Whether we celebrate or deplore it, the Jewish collective in France has in some sense withdrawn into itself since the events on rue Copernic, even if, on the other hand, those who have been oriented in a rather specific way toward the Middle East are themselves even more determined to settle in Israel. There has therefore been something of a double radicalization.

Maurice Grynfogel, president of the World Jewish Congress, told the twenty-first colloquium of French-speaking Jewish intellectuals in December that "[w]e are the generation of Copernic," succeeding the generation of Auschwitz. In over ten pages of coverage the Monday following the attack, *Libération* announced that the Jewish community had "divorced the institutions of the Republic after years and years of support without major problem, even if it was not without weakness." "The reserve of the Jewish establishment has disappeared," remarked a reporter at the Saturday-morning protest that culminated in a march of 15,000 on the Champs-Elysées. "Finished the usual confidence that they [*on*] have exhibited with regard to French institutions. It is divorce. Rupture . . . The skullcaps, beards, hats, the banners of Jewish movements, chief rabbi at the helm, on the avenue of political power in France. The emergence."[12]

The image overwhelmingly conveyed in the national press was of a united Jewish community unafraid either of criticizing the government or of publicly asserting itself as Jewish. And to a large extent, Jews were united across ethnic, religious, and generational lines in a way reminiscent of the Six-Day War. The crucial difference in 1980 was the degree to which they presented themselves as Jews within France, as a particular group with needs and rights that were distinct from the rest of the French nation. Certain commentators even worried that Jews, then a community of over 500,000, would withdraw into "mental ghettos" to defend their right to be Jewish.[13] As had been true during the 1967 war, the reactions of the Rothschild family, long leaders in the Jewish community, revealed the increase in Jewish militancy as well as the dilemma of trying to uphold both an assimilationist ideal and a commitment to affirming the specificity of the Jewish experience. On October 3, the evening of the Copernic bomb, CRIF president Alain de Rothschild addressed the following official statement to Giscard:

The French Jewish community bows with profound emotion before the victims of an act of blind terrorism, one without precedent in France.

It addresses itself to the President of the Republic to deplore that the passivity of the authorities before international terrorism and attacks which have struck Jews for several years has finished in the drama of the rue Copernic synagogue.

The indifference of our governments at the time of attacks touching the Jewish community and Israel has left terrorists to believe that they benefit from total impunity.

After the liberation of Abou Daoud, after the failed inquest that followed the bloody explosion of the Foyer Médici,[14] after the absence of the least reaction to the assassination at Antwerp of a Jewish child from Paris, and after the inexplicable impotence of the police before the multiple attacks whose victims were from several associations for the defense of the rights of man, one need not be surprised to have seen the neo-Nazis raise their heads, parade their doctrine in the open, and now set themselves on innocent lives.

Mr. President of the Republic, you who are responsible for the security of citizens and guarantor of liberties, it is urgent that you inform us of the exceptional measures that you are going to ask the government to take.

As for us, those responsible for the Jewish community of France, having in our memory the recent tragedy the community suffered owing to the Nazi occupant and its accomplices, we will not rest without reacting.

Also, as of today, we are taking protective measures within the Jewish community to attempt at our level to prevent new crimes.[15]

During the Six-Day War, Alain's cousin, Guy de Rothschild, had been president of the NCC, formed to organize Jewish activity surrounding the war. In 1980, Alain was continuing the family's service in the Jewish community by presiding over the CRIF. His statement to Giscard indicated just how affronted Jews felt by what they perceived to be the anti-Semitic terrorism that had culminated in the Copernic bombing. In 1967, Guy had cautioned Jews against responding to the "itch" to do something;[16] in 1980, Alain put the government on notice that Jews were already taking measures on their own behalf. Unlike during the Six-Day War, when Guy had refrained from criticizing de Gaulle and his dubious neutrality in the conflict, Alain directly confronted the French president and demanded to know the "exceptional measures" Giscard would take on behalf of French Jewry. In 1967, Guy had implored Jews to join him in not discussing their concerns for Israel beyond the confines of the Jewish community; in 1980, Alain said that the memory of the Holocaust made it impossible for Jews to remain passive before the violence of anti-Jewish terrorism and that they would take "protective measures within the Jewish community" to prevent further attacks. This shift from a public statement of alliance with Israel in 1967 to an open demand for recognition of Jewish needs within France in 1980 demonstrated the willingness of even Jews most committed to assimilation, including those who held official positions and were most open to public scrutiny, to mark out a specific place for Jews on the French political landscape. In this sense, Jews were indeed united during the Copernic crisis.

But Rothschild's candor about Jews' dissatisfaction with the government and their plans to initiate "protective measures" on their own appears far less dramatic when contrasted with the reactions of members of the community itself, especially Jewish youth. Many of these young Jews expressed a new desire simply to proclaim their Jewish identity, such as the secular young protester who surprised a friend by arriving at the Champs-Elysées protest wearing a yarmulke, or traditional Jewish skullcap. "I want them [*on*] to know that I am a Jew," he stated.[17] Protesters criticized the interior minister's "audacity" after Bonnet claimed that he felt in the wake of the bombing "like a Jew." A crowd of over forty Jews on the rue des Rosiers in the Marais, the Jewish district in Paris, swore to strike back.

The guilty will be punished. Trust us. If they are punished by official justice, all the better for them, because our justice will not involve the same methods. Ours is less gentle . . . If our religion forbids us to cause death, it does not prevent us from either defending or avenging ourselves . . . If they [*on*] seek to kill us, we will kill! The community is ready to match blow for blow, without exception and without pity. An eye for an eye; a tooth for a tooth.[18]

Members of the militant group Jewish Renewal attacked a young man they mistakenly assumed to be a skinhead; a group calling itself Jewish Resistance claimed responsibility for a violent assault on the fascist agitator Mark Frederiksen; and in an unattributed act of violence, acid was thrown in the face of a man named Charles Bousquet, whom extremists had mistaken for Pierre Bousquet, founder of the far-right journal *Militant*. In a two-part, front-page *Le Monde* series entitled "Young Jews in France," journalist Dominique Pouchin wrote of the new "Jewish brigades" who felt the militancy of Israeli Jews and pledged to "fight the Paris front." "What good is it to demand protection when all anyone does is collect the dead?" asked a young member of the Jewish Defense Organization. "It's better for us to count on ourselves, and the Nazis of all shapes won't dare to show themselves."[19]

About six months before the Copernic attack, Henri Hajdenberg, leader of Jewish Renewal, had ignited the crowd at the third "Twelve Hours for Israel" rally in Paris. Before over 150,000 people, he called on Jews to "sanction" the Giscard government for its pro-Arab/anti-Israel policies. While Jewish thinkers in the 1970s had discussed the prospect of a Jewish vote and its potential repercussions, Hajdenberg seemed to call openly for a Jewish voting block. Many prominent Jews, including Raymond Aron and former government minister Leo Hamon, came forth quickly to oppose the so-called American-style lobby group they accused Hajdenberg of advocating. Annie Kriegel, the formerly Stalinist intellectual who had turned fiercely anti-communist and was now a *Le Figaro* columnist, even deemed Hajdenberg's appeal to be dangerous.

Dangerous: because such a suggestion, contrary to the history and the French sociopolitical tradition, can only create contestation and division, external and internal. Dangerous again: because to reduce a community whose life sources are as multiple as those of the French Jewish community only to its political dimension (not even: to its intermittent dimension as a pile of votes) is to condemn it to degenerate and wither away.[20]

At the same time, however, an increasing number of Sephardi and younger Ashkenazi Jews were beginning to identify with Hajdenberg's message that "French Jews must get over their Ashkenazi fears that they won't be French if they proclaim their Jewishness."[21] For many young Ashkenazis, the very idea of France that had molded public Jewish life since the Revolution simply did not have the same currency after the Holocaust. Raised in the aftermath of World War II, they had trouble reconciling the contradiction between the ideal of France and the horror of their parents' encounter with the Nazi genocide. The world, according to Finkielkraut, was "bipolar": Jewish at home, where young people were drawn into discussions of "our pain" and "our suffering," and French everywhere else, where they were encouraged by their parents to assimilate and live as unmarked French citizens.[22] But unlike before the Holocaust, when a belief in the compatibility of Jewish and French identity was pervasive, postwar generations of Jews had every reason to doubt it. The world had not existed without the Holocaust for these young Ashkenazi Jews. Cultivated politically either during or after France's bloody colonial wars, they were far less persuaded by the rhetoric of universalism and assimilation.

Most Sephardi Jews, moreover, had arrived in France only recently, following the Suez crisis and decolonization in Morocco, Tunisia, and Algeria, and they did not share the political culture stemming from Ashkenazi Jews' nearly 200-year history as French citizens. As one observer wrote:

The Sephardis who lived the modern national project as something a bit imposed do not have at all the exalted experience of the Ashkenazis for nationalism. The Jews of North Africa did not choose to be French, and therefore their adherence to a French project is not lived in the same way. With respect to French nationalism, like Israeli chauvinism, they experience a profound mistrust, untheorized but enduring, a vibrant skepticism.

Sentimentally attached to Israel as both the source of their Jewish identity and their only tie to a region they had been forced to leave, Sephardi Jews propelled Zionism from the community issue it had been since 1948 into the political issue it had become since 1967. They brought with them to France a more assertive political style and a pride in being Jewish that contrasted sharply with the Ashkenazi sense of "historic fatality." Unrestrained by western notions of assimilation and exultant in their Jewish identity, having fought for centuries to have their rights as Jews recognized in North Africa, they refused to compromise their Jewishness for the sake of communal discretion.[23]

In a poignant letter to *Le Monde*, a young Algerian Jew described his frustration at the failure of those responsible for the safety of French Jews.

For several days, I and many of my friends have had the impression that history is starting over again, that for the second time, France is abandoning us. For several days, I and my friends have been asking ourselves the question: must I *really* cling to what is *really* my country if every eighteen years it scornfully or offhandedly casts me to the margins history? For several days I've been asking myself if the choice is not confined to the suitcase or the coffin, and if the Zionist student directors of CLESS [Socialist-Zionist Student Committee], who cried the other night from the Opera to Copernic that departure for Israel is the only response to anti-Semitism, are not right in the end.[24]

The disillusion expressed by this man and others demonstrated the convergence of Ashkenazi and Sephardi youth on perceptions of both French Jewish identity and Israel. Linked on the one hand by common origins, separated on the other by vastly different cultural and historical experiences, these young Jews conveyed distinct but somehow shared experiences of abandonment. Those from North Africa experienced official laxity before anti-Semitic terrorism as an abandonment that recalled French withdrawal from the colonies: in the young Algerian's case, France's departure from Algeria in 1962. Post-Holocaust Ashkenazi youth encountered contemporary terrorism and France's failure to apprehend the perpetrators of anti-Semitic violence as an ominous prelude to another collective massacre in which Jews, once again, would be forsaken by the French government. In each case, young Jews confronted the attack on rue Copernic as a call to respond in a way that their parents and grandparents had not, as a challenge to subvert an historical course. The distinctive experiences of Ashkenazi and Sephardi Jews were thus joined by an overarching sensation of fear, an awareness of a looming and palpable threat that stimulated a new form of political activism. As Grunewald wrote in *Tribune Juive*, all currents of Jewish thinking

converged on a new sentiment of insecurity. The Jews of France realized that they were not protected. And when they are protected today in such a visible way, by men in uniform who, in the cold of a precocious winter, stomp their feet to keep warm in front of synagogues and Jewish schools, they nevertheless fail to experience any feeling of security. On the contrary, they have the very irritating impression of being on the margins of the nation since these are their religious places, their collective children who need specific protection. . . . [25]

It was this mutual feeling of insecurity that made the public pugnacity of French Jews, and especially Jewish youth, a joint Sephardi-Ashkenazi project.

But in debates following the bombing, a divide hardened between Jewish militants and Jewish leadership. And in a discursive context where the fascist menace lurked behind every corner, the Holocaust was an especially charged trope for many Jews to express a sense of abandonment not only by the French government but also by moderate Jewish leaders, whom they accused of being reluctant to press for Jewish rights. A CLESS pamphlet made the case boldly: "By their constitution and rhetoric, community organizations have already led a part of our people to the worst. Let us no longer allow them to take our destiny in hand . . . Our ancestors were not the Gauls. Assimilation destroys our identity. . . . "[26] In its reference to the UGIF, the French Jewish council created by Vichy to facilitate the expropriation of Jewish property and deportations, the CLESS pamphlet employed a brutally contemptuous narrative of the Holocaust to distinguish itself from contemporary Jewish leadership. An equally clear repudiation of the Gaullist lineage that served as something of a national myth,[27] the pamphlet also chastised Jewish leaders during the Holocaust as a way to denounce a long-standing Jewish vision of "France" and the credibility of an assimilationist Jewish identity. I would not say that Jewish Renewal represents "the base against the nobles," said Hajdenberg in *Le Monde*, but the Jewish establishment must take account of the changes in the community. "Le Renouveau is a CRIF that yells while the other one murmurs," said one Hajdenberg follower. "That's good, because today we have to yell."[28]

If Alain de Rothschild's official statement addressed to Giscard demonstrated an increased militancy across all segments of the Jewish population, his appeal to the Jewish community the following day betrayed the division between young activists and Jewish leaders. The national press's pervasive commentary on the "divorce" between a united French Jewry and the Republic and on young Jews poised to resort to violent means in order to guarantee Jewish safety seemed to have alarmed the Jewish leadership. With "firmness and resolution," Rothschild implored Jews not to separate themselves from the national community.

(1) It is imperative to make public opinion understand the will of the Jewish community not to let itself be isolated by withdrawing into itself. On the contrary, the community intends to contribute to the deployment of national solidarity. Because only that solidary action is likely to foil the calculations of criminals who hope to break French society by an intensification of violence: today the Jews, tomorrow the others, until fear penetrates and dissolves all national life.

(2) It is important that the Jewish community demonstrate an exemplary self-control and that it guard itself against every excess of speech or action.

We must find comfort and confidence in the unanimity of indignation and condemnation that has been expressed from all parts since the recent attacks . . .

It is important, in particular, that youth movements investigate and take responsibility for collective protection measures, specific to local situations, in liaison with the CRIF.

The French Jewish community is called to rise to the challenge it has been issued.

By its unity around the CRIF, its calm and determination, it must take part in ensuring that the cancer all of terrorism is eradicated, not only in France but everywhere it has set roots.[29]

While Rothschild's statement to Giscard had been a departure from earlier family reticence even to criticize the French government, the follow-up indicated a refusal to adopt the radical posture so many others had assumed. The appeal to the Jewish community, in fact, was reminiscent of Guy de Rothschild's 1967 address, and Alain's two 1980 statements were emblematic of the continued tension between the particular and universal aspects of Jewish identity. Whereas his address to Giscard had been comprised of statements and demands on behalf of the Jewish community, written in terms of "we," "our," and "us," his appeal to French Jewry was predominantly a call for Jews to locate themselves within the nation. Whereas the former had been replete with imagery about violence against the Jewish community and Israel, the latter spoke of "terrorism and racism" and terrorists' hope to break "French society": Jews were only the first victims in a process of national dissolution. As during the Six-Day War, when a large and vocal segment of the nation had supported Israel, French Jews should be confident in "the unanimity of indignation and condemnation" that followed the Copernic attack. And also as in 1967, when Jews had been asked not to undertake any initiative without the prior accord of the NCC, Alain de Rothschild stressed the urgency in 1980 that young Jews take action only in liaison with the CRIF. Jews should participate in a force of "national solidarity" so that "the cancer of all terrorism" would be eradicated.

On a trip to the United States later that year, Rothschild defended the French government against charges of anti-Semitism and anti-Israel politics in the Middle East. Meanwhile, at the Paris protest, he followed a "CRIF against fascism" banner while CLESS and Jewish Renewal marched behind Israeli flags and other Jewish-marked signs. Jewish leadership allied with the nation against the national fascist enemy while militant Jews separated themselves by proclaiming their Jewish identity. Rothschild's original willingness to issue a direct statement to the French president marked a notable shift in tone among Jewish leaders, but his subsequent address to French Jewry showed that the tension between speaking in the particular voice of the Jewish community and that of the putatively universal French citizen continued to be a dilemma for Jewish leadership and other assimilated Jews.

## Victimization and the Holocaust as Metaphor

While the Copernic bombing exacerbated strains in Jewish identity, it also magnified a discursive conflict between the universal and particular aspects of the Holocaust that had begun to emerge in 1967, when the defeated Arabs were identified with Jewish victims of the Nazis. For the Holocaust was "present" in still another way. In taking to the streets, in aggressively and publicly invoking the Holocaust to proclaim their rights and plans for self-defense within France, in vacillating between claims to a specifically Jewish disposition and the shared identity of French citizenship, the diverse collective "French Jewry" in a sense "presented" the Holocaust to the nation as an image that could be narrated both particularly and universally. At the same time that outspoken Jews continued to insist on the uniqueness of the Holocaust trauma and the singularity of their current vulnerability, the Holocaust developed into a metaphor for widespread victimization and oppression. The Copernic bombing became a national controversy as its implications were narrated to reach all segments of French society.

The marches protesting the attack, wrote Guy Hermier in the communist newspaper *Révolution*, were a measure of the nation's refusal of all racism. "Yes, I mean all racism. Without doubt anti-Semitic acts provoke a particular emotion as long as the millions of martyrs of Nazism are still painfully present in memory . . . [but] contrary to others, we refuse to select among the victims. We fight against all forms of racism with the same vigor." Yves Ledure, a professor at the Catholic Institute of Paris, warned that it would be "a serious mistake to shut away anti-Semitism in a specificity that today encounters universal reprobation."

Anti-Semitism is one racism among others. The Nazism that perpetrated the Jewish holocaust and the Gypsy genocide is proof. But racism is fought taken as a whole, that is to say in challenging it radically, without distinction. Because all racism is odious, whether it be anti-Arab, anti-Jewish, anti-Black, anti-Third World, anti-youth . . . , etc. To classify racism in order to establish some scale of magnitude that sought to attenuate the evil is to enter into the racist problematic.[30]

For Ledure, to focus on the particularly Jewish aspects of the crime would be to become entangled in the very logic of racism that was ostensibly to be combated. Racism could be denied only on universal grounds, or on the refusal of differences among those deemed to be different. That Hitler had targeted groups other than Jews, such as the Gypsies, was in this case proof that the attack on Copernic was an assault not specifically on Jews but on anyone who had been or was a potential victim of "racism," indeed on the very idea of universality. Some believed that France had been the target. "More than the Jews, it is France itself which is struck by this criminal attack," wrote Pierre Pujo in the monarchist *Aspects de la France*. By attacking Jews, the terrorists created an "act of psychological war of which our country was the victim." The massive demonstrations that we witness today, said Socialist leader Mitterrand, are "the defensive reflex of a community that feels threatened. What community? France. . . . "[31]

In an opinion entitled "I Will Be There," Bernard Stasi, president of the National Assembly's committee on human rights, spoke of a "national conscience" and said that he would attend the Paris march not behind any political banner but as a French citizen.[32] He was in the minority. Mobilized to protest the bombing of the rue Copernic synagogue, most of the over 100,000 participants marched proudly behind any one of a number of placards denouncing racism and proclaiming the rights of various minority groups in France. By far the most visible and pervasive banners were those reading *Plus jamais ça!*, a slogan popularized by the Zionist extremist Meir Kahane to demonstrate that Jews would "never again" allow a holocaust to be perpetrated against them. Amidst a sea of non-Jewish groups speaking out against all forms of political oppression, these signs underscored the Holocaust not as trauma but as metaphor. It was during the march, in fact, that multiple social groups on the Left rallied together in what might be called a diffuse identification with the Holocaust. In political banderoles and commentary, these groups condemned all forms of social and political oppression via various narrative identifications with victims of the Copernic attack, and by metaphoric extension, with the victims of the Holocaust itself.

The long list of groups that joined in the Paris march encompassed political and ideological projects so disparate that they at times were at crosspurposes. In addition to representatives from all of the major political parties, virtually every major left-wing social organization was present, including several unions, MRAP, LICRA,[33] the League of the Rights of Man, the ecological movement Friends of the Earth, the National Federation of Resistant and Patriotic Deportees and Internees (FNDIRP), several Palestinian organizations, regional movements from Brittany and Corsica, the Center for Anti-Imperialist Studies, and several feminist movements. There were also participants from the Federation of Councils of Parents of Public School Children, the Association of Muslim Students, the Anarchist Federation, and even from some right-wing groups, albeit far less visible and rather discreetly hidden, such as the New Royalist Action. The march was a response to an attack on Jews, and many participants, non-Jews included, carried anti-Holocaust, "Never Again!" banners. But each group spoke directly about its own suffering, about its own political oppression, about racism, sexism, nationalism, colonialism—rarely about anti-Semitism or the Holocaust.

Identification with an idea of the Jewish Holocaust victim was wide-spread. *Tribune Juive* printed four pages of official statements from organizations that either had participated in or associated themselves with the demonstrations throughout France. An editorial in an Algerian newspaper argued that violence by Europeans against North Africans was linked to bombs in synagogues. "Resolute adversaries of all forms of racist persecution and religious intolerance, we can only join this general condemnation without equivocation and express our solidarity with the victims of this racist attack." The General Union of Palestinian Students denounced "the development of racism which strikes the Arab community just as often." And the Movement for the Liberation of Women declared "Long live difference! The women's movement, every day the victim of misogyny, is more than ever in a battle against all racism when the Jewish community is attacked."[34]

The Jewish victim became the symbol for universal victimhood. To take a stand against the Copernic bombing was to combat national, political, cultural, sexual, ethnic, religious, and all other forms of collective vulnerability. "Jews have fought against Nazism at our sides and they are active citizens of the French nation," wrote Georges Montaron. "That is to say that all aggression against them is an aggression against each one of us . . . We are all Jews, Blacks, Arabs." "Jews" in France are more politically evocative than Arabs, argued psychologist Robert Pagès, with the word "Jew" consistently in quotes. The bombing "targeted 'the Jews' and indissolubly all of us who live together in France." Expressing solidarity with French Jews, Father Jean Pihan wrote in *La Croix* that neo-Nazis will spare Christianity and Christians no more than Judaism and Jews. "More and more frequently, their threatening letters end with the slogan: 'Only one God, Hitler.' But the God of the Jews is also the God of the Christians."[35] As fellow combatants in a war against Nazism, as an emotionally evocative target for terrorists seeking to destabilize the French nation, as co-bearers of the Judeo-Christian tradition, Jews evoked the empathy of their non-Jewish compatriots. To the extent that it was symbolic of a more generalized threat, the Copernic attack aroused the mass indignation of the French population; to the degree that it could be emptied of specifically Jewish content, Jewish suffering became a source of identification. In its proffering of an iconic victim, the Holocaust became a compelling metaphor in public discourse.

But the march from the Nation to the Opera was fraught with barely muted conflicts. One critic called it a veritable war of banners in which the battle was to be at the head of the procession. The march was a mélange that clashed, wrote Pierre Feydal in *Le Matin*.

As if, from one end to the other, they [*on*] felt embarrassed by the presence of their neighbor. Indeed, they did not count, they counted themselves, for history to show without doubt that the anti-racism of the other was "worth" less than their own; that the promiscuity of one evening, all evidence to the contrary, effaced nothing of the quarrels of yesterday or those of tomorrow; that they shared the same boulevard but surely not the same condition and even less so the same project; that they had perhaps a common enemy but so many different friends. . . . [36]

The banner reading "All together and everyone for oneself" encapsulated the drama. Communists denounced racism and Jews rebuked communists for supporting the USSR, an anti-Semitic state. Palestinians condemned both racism and Zionism, while Jewish Renewal and other Zionist groups were the most numerous and visible during the march. Signs reading "Down with Racism!", "Racism = Zionism!", and "Israel Will Live!" mixed together in a curious jumble. Certain aspects of the post-Copernic protests were tinged with an element of the ridiculous, such as the banner stating "Anti-Communism = Racism!", or the young man arrested for putting up graffiti stating "cops, fascists" and "yes to neo-Nazis." Many Jews marched away from the parade's front, refusing to mix with Palestinian Liberation Organization leader Yasser Arafat's "henchmen," noted one commentator, "but also refusing to follow their ancient leaders, these notables surrounding the rabbis and Monsieur Rothschild, this 'establishment' that they today judge to be too timid, too implicated with a power that is an 'enemy of Israel.'" In two compact groups, the Jewish community had clearly attempted to mark itself off, leaving a "no man's land" between Jews and the rest of the crowd. As one reporter described a young Jewish protester, "she needed to say something else and to say it in her own way."[37]

Though many Jews in the mainstream and Jewish press expressed a certain relief at the scale of public outrage, others were critical. "A generation now says 'Hitler, never heard of him!'" lamented writer and Warsaw Ghetto survivor Marek Halter. "They also proclaim, 'Auschwitz, we're sick of it!'" Essayist Arnold Mandel offered a blistering appraisal. Today's anti-Semites are "truly loyal to Hitler," he wrote in *Le Quotidien de Paris*. "The exclusive identification of anti-Semitism with fascism, historically and currently false, too easily clears the consciences of all those who know or believe themselves to be inoculated against the fascist virus: 'We are not fascists, therefore we are not anti-Semites'. . . . " We have to join those who are truly righteous, he concluded, "and no doubt this will be elsewhere than on the route leading from the Bastille to the Nation, with another conscience and with voices other than those of the simple-minded and routine catchphrases of the political comedy punctuating the drama."[38] For many Jews, the fascist epithet concealed the particular contents of the ideology behind both Vichy and Copernic: anti-Semitism. They experienced the "psychological war" Pujo claimed that terrorists were waging against France as part of the physical war led for centuries against them, a war that had reached its climax during the Holocaust. They did not feel part of a threatened French community, as Mitterrand suggested, but vulnerable as members of an eternally oppressed Jewish community. As Alain Goldman, chief rabbi of Paris, said a week after the attack, Giscard's statement following the nationwide day of marches had made no mention of anti-Semitism, and "by consequence, he had not condemned it explicitly."[39]

For most non-Jews, empathy with Jews took the form of a united front against what Mandel called the "container" of both Vichy and Copernic anti-Semitism: fascism. The bombing was meaningful to the degree that it could be narrated as a fascist attack, and castigations against a "return to Vichy" reflected an understanding of contemporary terrorism as a resurgence of Vichy-like fascism. To the extent that the nemesis was discernable, it was as a state, or in the form of the Giscard government and the national police. In targeting "the authorities," the fascist charge externalized the enemy, or enabled a frustrated French population to draw a clear boundary between itself and the state, thereby exonerating the people from a sense of responsibility in either the current or historical context. This self-exculpation both reflected and reinforced a perception of Vichy as exterior to the population, or the French nation, and it recalled the demonstrations of May 1968. Intoning "CRS = SS," students and workers had protested government repression by comparing the police to the Nazi SS, and they had chanted "We are all German Jews!" after student leader Daniel Cohn-Bendit, a German Jew, had been expelled from France. In 1968, they had rebelled against the government by identifying with Cohn-Bendit/Holocaust victims against the police and government. After the rue Copernic bombing, protestors accused police officers of being directly involved in neo-Nazi organizations and denounced Giscard for complicity with the police and neo-Nazism.[40] Both demonstrations employed Holocaust imagery to protest political oppression broadly defined, and in both cases, the people were victims of the state. Following the post-Copernic march in Paris, *Le Monde* ran a photograph of a man wearing a striped uniform like those worn in the concentration camps. Behind him was a banner reading "We are all French Jews!"

In the weeks following the bombing, perpetrator-victim scenarios were so common that the principles underlying right and wrong, other than one group's claims to have been victimized by another, became increasingly difficult to establish. The elusive and amorphous fascist enemy drove a discourse in which all racist and "fascist" crimes could be narrated as evil, and the Holocaust metaphor lent unquestionable moral credibility to victims, whether they be Jews, feminists, or members of the immigrant-phobic National Front. We are all responsible for this, wrote critic Jean-Pierre Enard in *Le Monde*, even those of us who are fundamentally anti-fascist, for we have tolerated an almost nostalgic resurgence of interest in the collaboration and a gross misappropriation of "fascism." "The whatever has become the doctrine of the intellectual class in power. . . . " But it does not mean the same thing to have been a resister or a collaborator, an anti-colonialist or a CRS supporter. "To believe that everything has the same value is to make way for a dark plague to move in." In the same issue of *Le Monde*, a front-page editorial entitled "The Virtues of Anxiety" asserted that although the motivations of participating groups were discordant and conflicted, and even if some people were conspicuously absent, the demonstrations had "pedagogical value."[41] Just as commentators had found the film "Holocaust" worthwhile despite what they identified as its myriad weaknesses, so, too, did the press endorse the general message of the marchers, despite the contradictions in their intentions. And as many Jews had experienced the film's shortcomings as a failure to capture the trauma the Holocaust entailed, so did many experience the protests and commentary surrounding the Copernic bombing as inappropriately focused on an enemy not specific to Jews. In the united front against fascism, the Holocaust bore no particular meaning.

## Jewish Identity After Copernic

The mass outpouring of support after the bombing affirmed for Jews the nation's refusal to tolerate anti-Semitism. At the same time, the public's widespread identification with the Nazi genocide called to question both the singularity of the Holocaust and Jewish identity, at the core of which was the trauma. If before the attack Jews' particularity had been refused by a nation reluctant to engage with individual experiences, now it was lost in the rush to commiserate, in the universalization of suffering. Far from being resolved, therefore, the tension between being Jewish and French continued to pose a challenge, albeit in a different form, for Jewish thinkers. For some, such as Mandel, this pseudo-empathy needed to be unmasked for what it was: an appropriation of Jewish suffering, the conflation of fascism and anti-Semitism in an effort to deny the latter. For others, including Alain Finkielkraut and Shmuel Trigano, the public's misguided identification with the Holocaust should alert Jews to the imperative of rethinking Jewish identity. Yet if Finkielkraut and Trigano agreed that this identity could not be sustained in its present form, they disagreed on both the diagnosis of the problem and the course of action necessary to ameliorate it.

Even before the Copernic bombing, in *The Imaginary Jew*, Finkielkraut had expressed concern about Jews' newfound need to separate themselves from the rest of the nation. In proudly brandishing the badge of their particularity, he argued, Jews confound assimilation with anti-Semitism, and the former becomes "the modern face" of the latter.

Jew inside, man outside: that, we remember, was the dictate of the first assimilation. Without ever admitting it, we are applying the inverse principle: we are Jews outside, for the entourage, for the public, for the external world, and inside, in the intimacy of our ordinary existence, we are men like the rest, governed by the same forms, prey to the same passions, and illustrating no cultural specificity.

Jews were not the only ones emphasizing their differences. "The need for roots," Finkielkraut argued, "has become the evil of this last quarter century." These days Jews are perceived to possess the origins that before were the outrage of anti-Semites but now are a talisman for philo-Semites who imagine that Jewish life has meaning, that the life of victimization has meaning. Far removed from the practical experience of being victimized, he wrote, Jews narcissistically embrace their fetishized role in national culture. Finkielkraut was equally disturbed by Jews' identification with Holocaust victims, especially when they had the quasi-certitude of never experiencing such horror. He accused both himself and his fellow Jews of living "in the security of anachronism" when a chasm separated them from the Nazi genocide. By behaving as if they were under constant attack, by vicariously participating in the suffering of Holocaust victims, Jews denied the real "rupture" of the Holocaust: their amputation from their ancestors. They clung to a false identification with a pre-Holocaust culture that they neither shared nor understood and thus participated in a "second murder" of Holocaust victims. Jewish identity, he concluded, was a "pathetic affirmation, ostentatious and empty . . . the ostentation of nothingness."[42]

For Finkielkraut, contemporary Jews were separated by culture and context from the victims of the Holocaust, and a Jewishness grounded in the trauma of the Holocaust was no less metaphoric (or meaningless) than any other identification with the genocide. To embrace the mantle of the eternal victim as a way to celebrate one's Jewishness was to revel in a pyrrhic identity. Instead, he argued, Jews should cease to pretend that they lived in 1930s Europe and that a new Hitler was behind every act of anti-Semitism. They should acknowledge their comfortable assimilation into the secular and non-Jewish world and forfeit the monopoly that the Holocaust and Israel claimed on their lives. It was time, wrote Finkielkraut, for Jews to recognize that "with the human collective defeated in the catastrophe [they] have no common homeland." The imperative of Jewishness today was not identity but memory, he concluded, and that memory was predicated on a conscious separation from the past.[43]

Trigano, a Sephardi professor of Jewish thought, also suggested that Jewish identity in its present form was illusory. But in *La République et les Juifs après Copernic* (*The Republic and the Jews After Copernic*), which reiterated his earlier criticism of both France and Israel, he arrived at a different conclusion, one that radically distinguished Jews from the rest of the French nation. The mass condemnation in Paris after the Copernic attack, he wrote, shut away Jews in a "universal ghetto."

It was a sacramental collective act that unfolded. People, delegations, and parties were there to run alongside their banners, but without any contact between them, neither exchange nor dialogue. An entire people was in pursuit of its national myth, a sort of collective release to exorcise the demons they sensed. But what was most surprising in this great demonstration was the erasure of the Jew. Everybody looked to the sky, their eyes practically transfixed, but the horizon had no profile: it was empty. An homage had been feverishly rendered to the image of France, but the Jews could just as well not have been there, not existed. Copernic was totally overshadowed, engulfed, evaded. The march buried Copernic instead of confronting and battling it.

The nationwide demonstrations after the bombing showed not only the "social usage" of the Jew, according to Trigano, but also that the Jew, "Jewish humanity, cannot, by taboo, manifest itself publicly in France *as such*," that only as an abstract and universal citizen in defense of democracy could a uniquely Jewish voice be heard. Because their particularity is prohibited by the Republic, he argued, and because both Paris and Jerusalem belong to the same culture of modernity that offers no alternative to universal citizenship, Jews have no choice but to open an internal dialogue about the meaning of Jewish existence, the arrival of "messianic Zionism" in Israel, and "the resurgence of 'the Jewish nation' in France."[44]

Both Finkielkraut and Trigano argued that contemporary Jewish life was devoid of authentically Jewish content. For Finkielkraut, the Holocaust had severed the connection between contemporary Jewry and pre-World War II Jewish culture, leaving a chasm so vast that the very idea of Jewish identity had become obsolete. Trigano believed that the Holocaust had provided definitive proof that Jews could not be truly Jewish in the diaspora. But unlike Finkielkraut, for whom the specificity of Jews was itself anachronistic, Trigano argued that until Israel shed its quest to be a state like all others, diaspora Jews should reject the otherness imposed on them by the West and embrace the particularity that was genuinely theirs. Raised in France in the aftermath of the Holocaust, of Polish parents, the non-religious and Ashkenazi Finkielkraut's understanding of Jewish identity was a cultural one, based on centuries of Jewish living in eastern Europe. After the Holocaust, that world disappeared, as did the cultural practices that had constituted Jewishness. For Finkielkraut, there was no longer any substance to Jewish

identity, only a life indistinguishable from that of his non-Jewish compatriots. Of Sephardi heritage, on the other hand, Trigano had lived a life far
more autonomous from the gentile world, one infused with Jewish learning, adherence to the laws of the religion, and a determination not to assimilate. Whereas for Finkielkraut, Jewishness was a culture from which he felt
far removed, a "memory" that enriched a consciousness rooted predominantly in secular France, for Trigano, it was a conspicuous and central part
of his being. What they agreed on was the bankruptcy of contemporary
Jewish identity, not its ideal fulfillment.

But what was the potential for either of these visions of Jewish identity
in France? The vast majority of Jews at the time were interested in sustain-
ing neither a wholly French identity, with their Jewishness relegated to the
domain of memory, nor a completely Jewish identity, characterized by an
abandonment of assimilation and a dramatic reorientation of the state of Israel such that it would fulfill its putatively messianic mission. French Jews
with Ashkenazi roots knew France as their only home and had little history
of religious commitment. They were far more inclined to understand Jewishness as compatible with French ideals and to press for their particular
rights within the institutions of French society. At the same time, many
Sephardi Jews looked to a strong Israel as their last connection to the Middle East, to a primordial culture from which they had been involuntarily es-
tranged, and they drew strength from Israel's power as a sovereign nation-
state. After the Copernic attack, moreover, both Ashkenazis and Sephardis
were unlikely to find remote either the Holocaust or the notion of Jews as
victims and were even less likely to disassociate from the seemingly inescapable Jewish component of their identity. The support of virtually the
entire French nation and the widespread celebration of difference, however
diffuse, in fact seemed to encourage the opposite: an even deeper attachment to maintaining a sense of particularity, to celebrating Jewish roots
within France. The claim to a particularly Jewish identity located French
Jews within a national culture that was now beginning to honor precisely
this kind of assertion of difference. Many Jews' unflagging commitment to
the singularity of the Holocaust trauma, the bombing of the Copernic synagogue, and the cultural shift toward extolling difference enhanced the
project of articulating a specifically Jewish identity consistent with French
citizenship.

## Israeli Nazis

In January 1981, just three months after the mass demonstrations, writer
Jean-Marie Paupert criticized French Jewry for adopting "the imbecilic pos-

ture that you bear 'no' responsibility for your misfortunes." On the front page of *Le Monde*, he chastised Jewish youth for having behaved "like Nazi hoodlums" in the days following the Copernic attack. Several well-known figures, including Simone de Beauvoir, condemned *Le Monde* for giving such "exceptional place" to a piece that recalled the anti-Semitic rhetoric of the 1930s.[45] But by the summer of 1982, the association of Jews with Nazis was less outlandish. The Israeli invasion of Lebanon in June, an August terrorist attack on Goldenberg's, a popular Jewish delicatessen located in the heart of the Marais, followed in September by massacres at the Sabra and Shatilla refugee camps in Lebanon, turned Holocaust discourse on its head.

Divided over the policies of Israeli Prime Minister Menachem Begin, with most on the Left vehemently opposed, French Jews were virtually unanimous in their denunciation of the press's widespread deployment of Holocaust imagery to characterize the war. The perpetrators of the Goldenberg's attack, they contended, could only have felt encouraged by such reckless analogies to the Holocaust. "I have the impression," complained Marek Halter, "that, consciously or not, the feelings toward Jews that many people kept inside and were impossible to express . . . found in the siege of Beirut an excuse, an outlet. They [on] could finally treat the Jews as assassins and even Nazis." From now on, contended novelist and literary critic Philippe Sollers,

the Jew is the executioner. And even the Nazi . . . Hence the anti-Semites will be able to say "we were not really guilty because ultimately it is quite clear that they are the murderers in Lebanon" . . . They relieve themselves of guilt by making the Jews feel guilty. These new anti-Semites are trying to secure for themselves a retroactive innocence.

The irony, added Finkielkraut, is that one can now hate Jews by recourse to anti-Nazism. "[T]he majority of journalists side with victims, whatever their camp . . . It was enough for the Palestinians to appear as victims for their cause to be sanctified. . . . " The "whatever" attitude about which *Le Monde* critic Enard had complained after the Copernic bombing crystallized in the wake of the war in Lebanon as a reflexive empathy for anyone portrayed as a victim.[46]

Asked to comment on "the Oradour perpetrated by Israel in Lebanon" during a July trip to Budapest, President Mitterrand responded that "when military interventions encounter resistance, they provoke Oradours. I did not accept it in France, and I will not accept it in Lebanon." Mitterrand's remarks elicited broad condemnation from Jews, especially Jewish youth, who continued to threaten reprisals. Begin attributed the Goldenberg's attack to "shocking declarations about 'Oradours' and the ill-considered remarks of the French press regarding the war in Lebanon." If the French government did not put an end to neo-Nazi attacks against Jews in France, warned the Israeli prime minister, he would appeal to young French Jews to ensure the defense and dignity of the Jewish people. Although most public Jewish personalities, including Jewish Renewal leader Hajdenberg, discounted the notion that French Jewry was answerable to Begin, they continued to press for the rights of French Jews as Jews.[47]

In a long interview with *Le Matin*, Grand Rabbi René Sirat chastised Jewish youth for recent threats and hostility. "It is inexcusable," he said. "The Jewish community demonstrated a great maturity after the attack on rue Copernic. I expect of it today the same maturity, the same calm." When asked if he was concerned that the Goldenberg's attack had failed to produce national solidarity with French Jews, Sirat was unequivocal. "Not at all. I received some 100 messages of sympathy from prominent figures as well as French citizens. . . ."[48] Sirat, however, clearly sensed a shift in national sentiment. His desire to see again the "maturity" that the Jewish community had exhibited after Copernic, a response that had included random acts of violence against alleged anti-Semites and a discourse that swore to protect Jews at all costs, was motivated at least in part by an awareness that the Goldenberg's attack had not provoked a gesture of solidarity even remotely resembling the conspicuous alliance of October 1980. A demonstration such as the one after the Copernic attack, wrote *Le Matin*, was "unimaginable."[49]

But what explains the absence of a mass identification with Jews, especially in the face of a terrorist attack even bloodier than the synagogue bombing? The violence in the Middle East, the Communist Party's outspoken opposition to Israel, and the Socialist occupation of the Elysée no doubt militated against mass left-wing participation in a Copernic-like protest. But a letter in *Le Monde* from Vitry-sur-Seine Socialist Marc Ludger captured best the apparent contradiction.

The blood of innocent victims has flowed in Paris. It has flowed in Lebanon for two months without moving leaders of the Jewish community.

Must the State of Israel's politics of terror be absolved by the sole fact that it is covered by the word "war," or is the terror only terrorist because Jews died in Paris?

France's politics in Lebanon are just because they are on the side of right, of suffering . . .

Remember, Jewish friends, the attack on rue Copernic: we were at your sides in Paris during the enormous people's parade.

Today, again, we suffer with you.[50]

"We suffer with you," the letter said, but "we will not be at your side" was what it implied.

If the "side of right" was the side of suffering, Israelis in Lebanon were clearly the enemy, and this made it difficult to separate the violence committed against Jews in the Marais from the violence committed by Jews (Is-raelis) in Lebanon. For Jews had not conveyed effectively their simultane-ous commitment to and independence from Israel. They had failed to make clear the distinction between their unconditional support for Israeli state-hood and their conditional approval of particular Israeli governments, and this made it difficult for others to distinguish French from Israeli Jews. De-spite widespread recourse to Holocaust imagery, moreover, non-Jews did not subscribe to the notion of Holocaust trauma that stipulated *a priori* the impossibility of Jews or Israelis being Nazis. A nation highly identified with victims, especially victims of fascist and right-wing oppression, was unlikely amidst mass violence in the Middle East to respond to anti-Jewish violence in a way that might have resulted in demonstrations similar to those of 1980. Because it was unclear to many where Jews/Israelis fell on the fascist/anti-fascist divide, public solidarity was as restrained after the Goldenberg's attack as it had been virtually absolute after the synagogue bombing.

Holocaust rhetoric had been so pervasive in the aftermath of the Coper-nic violence that its connection to the Nazi genocide of the Jews or the anti-Jewish violence of the synagogue bombing was incidental. This had en-abled the assignation of the Nazi epithet to any entity perceived to exercise "fascist" terror. Following the September 1982 debacle in Sabra and Shatilla, when Israeli soldiers guarding the two Lebanese refugee camps were ac-cused of enabling Syrian Phalangist commandos to massacre the settle-ments' inhabitants, the "Nazification" of Israel reached its apogee. The Holocaust is no longer more than a screen for the delirium of Israeli lead-ers caught up in a spiral of violence, wrote Gerard Dupuy in *Libération*. "The Israelis will say: 'We didn't want this, we didn't know.' But do they [*on*] think that the German population . . . would have acknowledged the existence of Dachau or Auschwitz?" Serge July painted a searing portrait:

Women, children, old people, men: tortured, assassinated en masse simply because they belonged to a people, in this case the Palestinian people. This is quite simply a crime against humanity. The end of the Second World War did not put an end to such crimes . . . It is a Copernican revolution: indirectly, at least, if not directly, Jew-ish leaders, survivors of the Nazi extermination, have covered up a crime against hu-manity. The unthinkable thus has been produced. . . . [51]

Faced with the characterization of Israelis as Nazis and anti-Israel head-lines reading "Never Again!" and "Our New Yellow Star," Jews outraged by the recent events in Lebanon were adamant that the killings had not been perpetrated by Israeli soldiers, that analogies with the Holocaust were en-tirely inappropriate, and that Israeli politics, however atrocious, could not justify attacks such as the one on Goldenberg's. Finkielkraut, for example, called for Begin's resignation but argued that after the carnage at Sabra and Shatilla, "the comparison between Israel and Nazism is still stupid and scandalous."[52] The following year, in *La Réprobation d'Israël*, Finkielkraut offered a scathing critique of Holocaust rhetoric. On what he perceived to be the tendency of some Jews to use the Holocaust to justify the invasion of Lebanon, he wrote: "This jubilation in telling oneself 'nobody loves us' must be combated on two grounds: because it criminalizes all grief toward Israel, and because in enlisting Jewish history, it banalizes it and catapults it into oblivion." But he also argued that the "analogy" between Jews and Nazis was giving way to a "filiation" between Judaism and Nazism. He criticized the press for assimilating Palestinians in West Beirut with the combatants of the Warsaw Ghetto, the annexation of the Golan with the absorption of the Sudetenland by Hitler, the Six-Day War with the "fascist" Japanese aggression at Pearl Harbor, the mark of Palestinian prisoners with the yellow star, and the death of women and children under Israeli bombs with the Holocaust. A lot of Jews were appalled by the events in Lebanon, he wrote. "But this language has dissipated that trauma and, if I dare say it, has 're-Beginized' them."

In fact, the authentic popularity of the Jews in Europe in the last twenty years and their current disparagement proceed from exactly the same feeling, the same *Christian complex*: they [*on*] liked in Jews the martyr and the image of the persecuted; they reject them now for having betrayed that so-called vocation. It is *the identification of the genocide with the passion of Christ and the crucifixion* that merited Jews their recent prestige; it is their infidelity to that image today that fuels the indictments of those who make public opinion. Momentarily deified by Auschwitz, the Jews thus risk, via Israel, to return to their destiny of deicide.[53]

For Finkielkraut, as for critics after the Six-Day War, Jews won sympathy only as martyrs.

With the publication of *The Imaginary Jew*, Finkielkraut had challenged those Jews who identified with victims of the Holocaust; in *La Réprobation d'Israël*, he found the identification of Arabs in the Middle East with Holocaust victims even less persuasive and decried the abstraction that the public had made of the Nazi genocide. But the events of the early 1980s made clear that the Holocaust as a metaphor for persecution and victimization was expanding rather than contracting. Its meaning, which Jews, too, had been hard pressed to clarify, was becoming increasingly abstract: remote in its specificity, immediate in its applicability. The genocide, wrote Finkielkraut, constitutes for Jews an irreparable loss, one without restitution or compensation. "To forget, to give meaning, we are forbidden to do either. It is between these two prohibitions that memory survives."[54] And it was within the parameters of those interdictions—the taboos of trauma— that many Jews confronted the Holocaust metaphor during the Barbie controversy.

## CHAPTER FIVE

# The Holocaust as Metaphor II
## The Klaus Barbie Affair

By the early 1980s, the Holocaust had become firmly ensconced in the land-scape of French public discourse, but deep disagreement existed over the extent to which it could figuratively represent other instances of mass re-pression and suffering. Under what circumstances was it appropriate to portray those who had been perpetrators or victims before and after the Holocaust with language born of the Nazi genocide? Could one speak meaningfully of metaphoric Nazis and Jews? Strong opinions notwith-standing, this was a debate that took place largely on the margins of public discourse. Tensions about the Holocaust were real, and there were those, especially Jews in summer and fall 1982, who made clear their displeasure with one or another representation. But conflict over the singularity of the Holocaust tended to be secondary to the more immediate controversies that genocidal imagery was invoked to illustrate.

That changed in 1983, when Klaus Barbie, head of the Nazi security po-lice in Lyon from 1942–44, was extradited to France. After his arrest, the nation began a protracted debate over whether the genocide of the Jews was legally different from torture and persecution of the Resistance. If the Nazi internment and mass killing of Jewish civilians were legally distinct, then Barbie would stand trial only for his alleged contributions to the Final Solution. If, however, the Nazi murders of Jews and resisters were com-mensurate according to the law, then Barbie's crimes against the Resistance, headquartered during the war in Lyon, could be included in the indictment. Suddenly, as most Jews and former members of the Resistance lined up on opposite sides of the dispute, virtually the whole nation seemed to be preoccupied with the question of the Holocaust's uniqueness. No longer a peripheral conflict, the relative singularity of Jewish torment was now at the heart of political debate. And the rival suffering belonged to the Resistance, whose martyrdom had been the pillar of the nation's postwar reconstruction and at the center of national iconography. The 1987 trial, during which Barbie stood accused of crimes against both Jews and Resistance fighters, demonstrated the elasticity of the Holocaust metaphor as well as the perils, for many Jews, of trying to transmit trauma in a shared discursive context.

## The Barbie Affair

In 1982, French Minister of Justice Robert Badinter began a judicial inquiry against Klaus Barbie for crimes against humanity. Previous French officials had known at least since 1963 that Barbie was living in Bolivia under the assumed name Klaus Altman, but efforts to obtain his extradition from the Bolivian dictatorship had been unsuccessful. In 1974, for example, the Bolivian Supreme Court refused to deport Barbie because Bolivia and France had no extradition treaty. Neither Pompidou nor Giscard had pursued the matter. But in 1982, a democratic regime took control of Bolivia, and François Mitterrand, the first Socialist president of the Fifth Republic, was persuaded to seek Barbie's return. At the end of the year, a French court issued a warrant for Barbie's arrest, and in January 1983, the ex-Nazi was taken into custody by Bolivian authorities. On arrival in France, the so-called "butcher of Lyon" was incarcerated in Montluc prison, where so many of his victims had been tortured and imprisoned forty years earlier. Barbie was formally charged on February 5, 1983, thus opening a new chapter in the story of postwar Holocaust discourse in France.

A few days after the indictment, a poll indicated that most French people approved of the extradition and planned to follow the trial with interest.[1] But discord soon followed. During the Nuremberg trials, in 1945, the International Military Tribunal had created a classification of World War II offenses: crimes of aggression, of war, and crimes against humanity. The latter was designed to enable the autonomous prosecution of offenses committed against non-combatants, to protect populations that had not been actively at war with the occupying power but which nonetheless had been victims of systematic persecution. The identity of the victim, in other words, determined whether an action constituted a crime against humanity. It was on this definition that the French National Assembly had voted in 1964 to exempt these offenses from any statute of limitations, although the Nuremberg tribunal had made no such distinction regarding prescriptibility. Because Barbie's crimes against combatants fell under the rubric of war crimes, for which the statute of limitations in France had expired, the 1983 indictment was restricted to offenses committed against civilian populations, or more specifically, to crimes against Jews. Although they had long insisted that they were volunteer combatants and had enjoyed the benefits as such since the end of the war, many former resisters were upset by what they perceived to be the legal system's unfair hierarchy of suffering, one that recognized crimes against Jews but not against Resistance fighters. In addition to Barbie's victims and their families, several organizations, including the FNDIRP and the National Association of Former Resistance Combatants, joined the case as civil parties shortly after the indictment was announced.[2]

In June, Jacques Vergès, a former attorney for the Algerian National Liberation Front (FLN)[3] well known for supporting the Far Left, assumed sole responsibility for Barbie's defense. Though they were opponents in the Barbie case, Vergès and Resistance organizations agreed that the indictment had inappropriately excluded pursuit and murder of Resistance fighters from its definition of crimes against humanity. But whereas former combatants feared that their sacrifice and suffering would be ignored, Vergès argued that it was the dishonor of the Resistance that the justices were trying to conceal by narrowly interpreting the law. He challenged the indictment in particular for omitting Barbie's alleged torture and murder of Resistance hero Jean Moulin. Though many historians had long acknowledged Moulin's betrayal, that he had been "handed over" to the Germans by turncoats within the Resistance, Vergès claimed to have "secret documents" to prove it. Far from heroic, he suggested, the group had been populated by traitors, many of whom were now prominent politicians who feared that the "truth" would be revealed if too much attention were focused on Moulin.[4] Drawing on the nation's continued idealization of the Resistance and fears that its image might somehow be tarnished, Vergès managed to shift public discourse from Barbie's crimes against Jews to the character and probity of the Resistance. Associations of former resisters and groups such as the League of the Rights of Man then lobbied to broaden the crimes against humanity law not only to ensure that Resistance suffering was recognized but to protect the group's honor.[5]

Jews and non-Jews were largely divided over Barbie's indictment. Non-Jewish opinion was overwhelmingly in favor of a broad interpretation of the crimes against humanity law. For much of the nation, the Gaullist myth rang true: France *was* the Resistance. That was why de Gaulle, on his triumphant return to Paris in 1944, had refused to declare a new republic: the old one had never ceased to exist. Even if "The Sorrow and the Pity" had shown that more than a few outlaws at Vichy had collaborated, in other words, the bulk of the population had supported the Resistance, the legitimate steward of France. Vergès's attack on the Resistance, therefore, was also an assault on national integrity. This was not the first time that someone had challenged the notion of France as a model of democratic universalism. In *L'idéologie française* (*The French Ideology*), a 1981 book which alleged that France was fundamentally a fascist country and that celebrated thinkers on the Left in fact had been well-masked fascist ideologues, the young Jewish philosopher and activist Bernard-Henri Lévy had tried to shatter the country's universalist image. The book inspired widely varying reactions. Most scholars and intellectuals harshly criticized it for cynically misrepresenting French history, but more than a few emphasized the importance of its message. Whereas Lévy's wrath had been reserved for Pétain, the Vichy regime, and their precursors, however, Vergès was tampering with the Resistance, and most non-Jewish opinion favored expanding the law to preserve its legacy.[6]

Like their compatriots, most Jews expressed gratitude for the accomplishments of the Resistance and recognized the sacrifices of those who had fought on its behalf. But they also felt that the Holocaust was distinct, that despite the suffering of those who had represented "true France," one could not meaningfully compare the two. The dominant Jewish voices, therefore, advocated a restricted law, one that recognized the Holocaust as a trauma and that underscored its particularity in spite of its more universal implications. In public discourse surrounding the trial, many Jews continued to express both a devotion to France and a belief in the Holocaust's incomparability. This proved to be a delicate balancing act, as the singularity inherent to the trauma seemed to diminish the suffering of the Resistance and to separate Jews from one of the most revered institutions in France. Consequently, by supporting an exclusive law, Jews appeared to stand apart from the rest of the nation. Many would struggle during the trial to reconcile their attachment to the Resistance, as French citizens, and their identification with Holocaust victims, as Jews.

On December 20, 1985, the Court of Appeal handed down a new interpretation of crimes against humanity. It stipulated that such crimes consisted of "inhuman acts and persecutions committed systematically in the name of a State which practices a policy of ideological domination . . . not only against persons for their membership in a racial or religious group, but also against opponents of such a policy, whatever form their opposition might take." The court declared that "neither the motives of (certain) victims nor their possible status as combatants can preclude the existence of an intentional element on the part of the accused in the offenses being prosecuted." What was decisive in the determination of crimes against humanity was not the identity of the victim but the fact that the offenses committed "were presented as politically justified in National Socialist ideology by those in whose name they were perpetrated."[7] Having just completed their case, Lyon prosecutors were forced to reopen the Barbie file to determine if other complaints now could be heard. They again passed on Barbie's alleged torture of Moulin but added three new charges to the indictment. The ultimate trial dossier included several allegations made by individuals as well as three collective crimes: the liquidation and deportation of the Lyon UGIF, the Jewish organization created by Vichy to facilitate its dealings with the Jewish community; the deportation of forty-four Jewish children hidden at a school in Izieu; and the deportation of the last train from Lyon, carrying both resisters and Jews, on August 11, 1944.

## Revisionism, "Genocide," and the Catholic Church

Meanwhile, in April 1983, a Paris appeals court upheld a lower-court ruling ordering Robert Faurisson to pay a symbolic franc in damages to several anti-racist organizations and groups representing former concentration and death camp inmates.[8] Faurisson had created a stir in a 1978 *Le Monde* article that denied the systematic extermination of Jews during World War II and then again in a 1980 book prefaced by American linguist Noam Chomsky. Despite the fact that most respected historians had declared the Faurisson thesis an outrage, however, the so-called revisionist school continued to make inroads into major universities. In 1985, the University of Nantes granted a doctoral degree to Henri Roques for a thesis that embraced revisionism. Of the four members of the examining committee, none was a specialist in World War II—one was a professor of medieval literature—and three had strong ties to the Far Right. In the scandal that ensued, Roques conducted radio and television interviews and groups on the Far Right sold cassettes of him reading his thesis introduction. Historian Pierre Vidal-Naquet, whose essay "Un Eichmann de papier" in 1980 had been the first detailed and scholarly refutation of Faurisson, denounced the "media campaign" that he feared would legitimize revisionism as a respectable intellectual position. He warned against even debating "someone who tries to prove that the moon is made of Roquefort cheese." The degree was eventually revoked, but the Roques dispute kept the Holocaust in the news.[9] During the Barbie trial, groups on the Far Right turned to the works of Faurisson and Roques to call for the rehabilitation of Pétain. Resistance stalwarts compared Vergès to Faurisson while *L'Humanité* claimed that those who criticized Stalin were no less odious than Faurisson. At the same time, one of Barbie's attorneys complained of "a ringing Faurissonism" in France regarding Algeria. He accused a young generation of intellectuals of

"Faurissoning" with respect to French colonialism and charged Jewish lawyers with creating "Faurissonades" about Israel's crimes against humanity.[10]

Despite Socialist occupation of the Elysée, the National Front (FN) captured eleven percent of votes in the June 1984 European elections, by far its strongest showing to date, and in March 1986 it won almost ten percent of the seats in the French parliament. Following the March elections, Mitterrand was forced to take on Gaullist leader Jacques Chirac as prime minister, thus initiating the first governmental "cohabitation" between Left and Right in France. Amidst debates about Barbie, the Far Right, and Holocaust revision, past massacres that had long been recognized as violent and horrific were recast as genocides. In 1986, Reynald Sécher published *Le Génocide franco-français: le Vendée vengé*, which claimed that the killing of Vendéens during the Revolution had constituted a genocide. In the book's foreword, noted historian Pierre Chaunu embraced Sécher's thesis. The war in the Vendée, he wrote, constituted "a sixth-column genocide that sought to burn and annihilate everything . . . This war was *the most horrendous of the wars of religion and the first ideological genocide*" (italics in original).[11] Strong new interest developed in the Turkish massacre of Armenians during World War I and especially in its quality as a genocide. Books about the killings, as well as newspaper and magazine articles referring to the Armenian genocide, began to appear more frequently. And in June 1987, near the end of the Barbie trial, an advertisement in *Le Figaro* announced that the European Parliament had passed a resolution that "recognized the Armenian genocide." The half-page announcement, sponsored by the Franco-Armenian Solidarity, paid homage to the Armenians who "for seventy years had been in search of an elementary demand for equity." It did not state with whom or what equity had been desired, but the implication, especially during the eighth week of the Barbie trial, was that the slaughter of the Armenians finally had been recognized as commensurate with the Holocaust, that the tragedy had been "elevated" to the status of genocide.[12]

In addition to the expanded definition of crimes against humanity and increasingly widespread Holocaust imagery in public discourse, a series of issues having to do with the Catholic Church fueled a growing Jewish anxiety about the universalization of the Holocaust. In 1986, controversy developed over a group of nuns hoping to establish a convent at Auschwitz. The order's founder, Sister Marie-Theresa, argued that the sisters' presence was "a grace accorded by all the martyrs of Auschwitz" and that they were there also "to pray for the Jews." Many prominent Jews spoke out against what they perceived to be the "Christianization" of the Shoah. At an international meeting of Christians and Jews held in Geneva that March, Ady

Steg, a professor in France and a prominent voice in European Judaism, took great pains to articulate what he perceived to be the irreducible specificity of what Auschwitz symbolized, "that something unique, inconceivable, unthinkable and ineffable which is the Shoah." He took particular umbrage at the notion that Auschwitz symbolized Catholic martyrdom, which he argued was tantamount to erasing the Holocaust.

How could we not be outraged by this triumphant appropriation of the Shoah, this effacement and clever theft that can only lead to the negation of the Shoah?

My God, how thick must be the new Jewish ashes covering this land for the Polish to understand the Shoah! For us, it is precisely because this is a question of Poland that the stakes are so great.

We will oppose this offense against justice with our dignity, sorrow, and determination. Every day and everywhere we will proclaim that we do not accept the appropriation and Christianization of the Shoah.

Steg implored the sisters not to "distort the symbol of Auschwitz" by planting a cross on its landscape. "If you refuse to hear us, know that we, the living Jews, in the name of the dead, will challenge the good that you pretend to accomplish."[13]

Shortly after the Auschwitz convent was proposed, Pope Jean-Paul II beatified Edith Stein, a converted Jew who had become a Catholic nun and died at Auschwitz. For the Pope, Stein was the embodiment of the universal meaning of Auschwitz. "We kneel before this great daughter of Israel who, in Christ the redeemer, discovered the fullness of faith and her mission toward the people of God." Stein, said the Pope, "was an heroic example of how to follow Christ." In *La Croix*, following printed portions of the Pope's homily, Jean Potin commented that Stein was "inseparably a martyr of the Christian faith and a victim of the Shoah. She is in the image of Paul, that man so proud of his belonging to the people of Israel, who desired to be cursed, even separated from Christ for his brothers, those of his race." Her death at Auschwitz "revealed to the Church that it also was affected by the Shoah." Similar opinions appeared throughout the French press, and many Jews complained that Christians were commandeering the Holocaust. Henri Smolarski criticized the Pope's remarks in *Tribune Juive*.

If one believes that there still exists a temptation for Catholics to proselytize, one would say that the Church wanted to signify that the Jew who converts does not betray his people. He is even more loyal to his people since Jesus would be the accomplishment of the Jewish faith. Edith Stein, or the model Jew.

Stein's death was tragic, Smolarski agreed, but it was no different from the fate of six million Jews. Since her baptism did not provoke her deportation and was not the cause of her death, "why this distinction today?" The Church's strategy throughout the Holocaust was silence, he argued. Why should the Pope make the Holocaust a Christian symbol today? Both Stein's beatification and the potential convent at Auschwitz added to Jewish fears that the meaning of the Holocaust was being misconstrued.[14]

## Crimes Against Humanity and Other Barbies on Trial

Over 800 journalists had been accredited for Barbie's trial, and the courtroom was packed when the proceedings began in May 1987. But the chambers were "rather sparsely populated," according to *Le Monde*, once Barbie—after declaring that he was a Bolivian citizen who had been illegally extradited and that he considered himself a hostage in France—had been excused from the courtroom. *Lyon Libération* counted ten journalists in attendance by week seven. Although the circumstances surrounding the arrest and death of Jean Moulin were not included in the trial dossier, most observers agreed that it was to Moulin that Barbie owed his notoriety. All one has to do, wrote journalist Maurice Szafran, is walk around the courthouse and pass from one small group to another.

[T]o listen, simply listen . . . what? A few anti-Semitic remarks, of course, but quickly stifled. Everywhere, a desire that one has to admit is identical to Vergès's: to talk about Jean Moulin. To know; to stop talking "nonsense" about the Resistance . . . Of the children of Izieu the people of Lyon do not speak. Or only a little.

*Le Figaro* published remarks from people attending the trial on its first day, all of whom declared that they had come to hear what Barbie had to say about the Resistance. Speculation about the possibility of a second Barbie trial, devoted exclusively to the Moulin affair, continued throughout the proceedings.[15]

The appeals court's 1985 decision had not put an end to disagreement surrounding crimes against humanity. Pierre Truche, the prosecuting attorney, had lobbied intensely for a restricted legal definition but was forced during the trial to make a more inclusive case. Among those who had signed on as civil parties, moreover, were associations of former resisters and organizations of Holocaust survivors. United by a desire to prove Barbie's guilt, the attorneys for these groups nonetheless were also deeply divided over the parameters of the law and at times had trouble presenting a united front. It was clear by the end of the proceedings that a common goal had not erased or even attenuated their mutual suspicion. Communists, for their part, complained throughout the trial that their heroism and suffering were being ignored, and Resistance admirers continued to regret the omission of the Moulin murder from the indictment. Because most people agreed that Barbie should be tried for all of his crimes, public discourse was replete with painstaking analyses of how torture of Resistance fighters was

as horrific as the deportation and killing of Jews. But the broad interpretation of the crimes against humanity law had opened the trial door to more
than the Resistance. Discussions in and out of the courtroom stretched well
beyond the initial controversy to include all the victims of Nazi ideology,
other World War II tragedies, apartheid, racism, and "the Barbies of today."
As after the rue Copernic bombing, the Holocaust became a metaphor for
repression and oppression broadly defined.

In defense of the extended law, many argued that both Jews and resisters
had fought against a common system; that if the war had endured another
few months, the Resistance would have faced the same fate as the Jews; and
that all had been killed in the same spirit. The court, wrote *Le Monde* journalist Jean-Marc Théolleyre before the trial began, prevented an ugly divorce between "survivors of the Resistance, a race nearing extinction, and
the heirs of the victims of the Holocaust of the Jews." That Resistance "survivors" were a "race" and contemporary Jews "heirs" of Holocaust victims
indicated the moral capital associated with racial identity and the cultural
status accorded to descendants of the Nazi genocide. For former government minister Roland Dumas, a civil party lawyer, the idea of distinguishing Jews from resisters was contemptible. When we first took our shovels
to the mass graves, he asked the jury, "do you think we were trying to differentiate between the Jew and the resister who had been shot? They both
had their mouths filled with dirt."[16]

*Le Figaro*'s Pierre Bois argued that a restricted application of the law
would have been reminiscent of "that famous selection practiced by the
Third Reich at the entrance of the camps." For Bois, the law's expansion was
a symbolic rejection of Nazism, and as such, a powerful repudiation of Nazi
ideology and practice. For many of the most vocal Jews, on the other hand,
the revised law served to conceal the Nazi logic behind the Holocaust. The
court's decision, said famed Nazi hunter Serge Klarsfeld, who had pursued
Barbie since the early 1970s and had brought crimes against humanity
charges against Jean Leguay and Bousquet,

banalizes what happened to the Gypsies and the Jews, who are in my opinion the
only victims of crimes against humanity. I do not think that public opinion can confound the inhuman treatments inflicted on resisters and the fate of Jews or Gypsies
deported with women and children. To know that one dies for a cause but that your
family is safe, that is nevertheless a profound consolation.

In an interview with *Lyon Figaro*, lawyer Alain Jakubowicz vowed to "reclaim" the specificity of the Nazi genocide of the Jews. There is a difference,
he said, between a resister who assumes the risk of being shot and in so doing commits a "positive" act, and the children of Izieu, "arrested, deported,
and gassed on arrival at Auschwitz because they were Jews while the majority among them did not even know what the word 'Jew' meant."[17]

*Le Figaro* columnist André Frossard, considered by many to be a voice of conscience in France, was one of the few former resisters to argue strongly for a restrictive law.[18] "It is difficult to isolate that difference, that specificity to the Holocaust," he wrote. "It exists. It is surely real. One can feel it. Izieu is pure horror. It is shame. It is something that cannot be seen anywhere else." In his testimony, Frossard recounted what he had seen as a prisoner for several months at Montluc: generations of an entire family—grandfather, father, mother, a young pregnant woman, and several children—marching to their deaths while an SS officer laughed; a Jewish man forced to learn and repeat in German the phrase "the Jew is a parasite who lives on the skin of the Aryan people and he must be eliminated" every time the barrack door opened. "For me, it is not the same thing to torture a resister. Torture did not degrade a Jean Moulin, it does not diminish the dignity of a combatant." A crime against humanity, he contended, "is when one executes, when one kills someone for the sole and unique reason that he is born. When we seek to provide a better definition, we do worse." Ironically, it was Frossard, the former resister, who best conveyed the sense of trauma to those who argued that Barbie was essentially being tried twice for the same acts under a law that had not existed when the alleged crimes were committed.

This trial is not a question of common law. It is totally beyond standard penal scope. [Barbie's] inculpation for crimes against humanity exceeds, escapes all common law. To such a degree that we [*on*] had been unable to predict that the Nazi horror was possible. That is why it was necessary to make the law retroactive. This is the only case where the retroactivity is justified by the horror of the crime.[19]

But just as the rue Copernic bombing had stimulated a diffusion of the Holocaust as a metaphor, the widening of the crimes against humanity law encouraged a universalization of the Barbie trial, or an extension of its conceptual scope beyond Jews and the Resistance to a seemingly limitless expanse of issues having to do with persecution and victimization, including other wartime atrocities. *Rivarol*'s Charles Filippi, for example, pointed to the Dresden bombings, "a gigantic gas chamber" that killed two hundred and fifty thousand people in two days. Drawing on the language and logic of those professing the Holocaust's singularity, Filippi suggested that the bombing was worse than the Nazi genocide.

*Humanly speaking, this was the most terrible carnage in history in the sense that never had so many people been annihilated in such a small space and in so little time.*
At Dresden, like Izieu, there was no battle between combatants . . . [This] hurricane of fire with effects comparable to nuclear bombs is as unjustifiable as that, on a reduced scale, of the Gestapo in a refuge of Jewish children.

He criticized Frossard, who had challenged the notion that the Holocaust could be compared to the bombings. As much at Dresden as at Izieu, he argued, people were not killed "for what they did in the war but for what they were: Germans or Jews. . . . "[20]

The widespread affirmation of the trial's "pedagogical value" expressed both in the courtroom and in public discourse suggested that the proceedings would help to combat contemporary racism and oppression. Ugo Iannucci, a lawyer representing both Jewish and non-Jewish deportees, told the jurors that their verdict would be directed only partially at Barbie. "The decision that you render is going to remind all of the Barbies of today or tomorrow that nothing will protect them from our pursuit." In June, *L'Événement du Jeudi* published over thirty pages on neo-Nazism in the contemporary world, labeling the adherents "the twenty-year-old Barbies." This trial, Dumas told the jury, should speak to German youth and German democracy,

all that is in the heart of the Europe we hope to build . . . You must make this message ring out and resound well beyond our own borders. It must reach South Africa, where children are in prison and in danger; the Middle East, where they are frightened under bombs; Argentina, where the mothers of May Square have reclaimed their own in vain. . . . [21]

Critics, however, charged that the attention being devoted to the past, to Barbie's crimes against Jews and the Resistance, deflected much-needed energy from current problems and that the moral injunction to remember was suspect. *Libération*'s Serge July, for example, claimed that FN racism made a mockery of the trial's pedagogical purpose, "as if the two events were unfolding on planets totally foreign to one another." Writer and former resister Jean Laborde wrote in *Le Quotidien de Paris* of the terrible atrocities being carried out by various regimes around the world, including the Soviet Union, Cuba, Ethiopia, Cambodia, Poland, Chile, South Africa, and Iran. Who condemns these people? Certainly not the French government, he lamented.

In this deluge of retrospective incantations, there is something of a cheap exorcism. To appeal to pure hearts to curse the demons that skipped about forty-five years ago and at the same time to drop one's hands before what rages today, to denounce the crimes and exactions of yesterday and contemplate with a distracted eye the infamies of today, to condemn in the most severe terms a detestable doctrine that practically no longer exists and to support others which endanger the liberties of the world— this hodgepodge of indignation and complacence is a fraud.

In this world, he asked, how can we understand the Barbie trial as pedagogy? "It seems instead like a masquerade that has one name: hypocrisy."[22]

In a satirical commentary on the trial published in *L'Humanité*, Patrick Besson also emphasized the hypocrisy of the 1987 "Resistance." The courage of today's intellectuals, he wrote, will be an example for our children. When we remember that local television stations in Paris are three metro stations apart, "we understand what disinterested heroism and anti-Nazi ardor are required of the 1987 resisters to explain their combat on two stations in the same evening—and that several times a week!"

Adored by Right and Left, running absolutely no physical or intellectual risk, present all over the media, invited to three dinners every evening, the resisters of 1987 are in the end giving a good lesson to the resisters—communists or non-communists—of 1940: why resist a regime that endures when it is so simple to resist one that no longer exists?

Essayist and professor Alain Besançon agreed but argued that communists were the primary victors in this hypocrisy. What should we make of this focus on Hitlerism "as the absolute evil, in comparison to which all other evil is relative and, in a certain sense, excusable?" he asked. It means that "we [*on*] maintain indefinitely a circumstantial alliance between democracy and communism, which was justifiable as long as Hitler existed and which today no longer has any purpose." By not recognizing communism as the totalitarian abomination that it has been,

we commit a grave injustice toward those who, by the hundreds of millions, suffer now from this generic evil, those who expect, if not help, at least a modicum of attention from us. The indefinite commemoration of past crimes, which is necessary to prevent memory from disappearing, can only continue to make sense if it does not overshadow those crimes taking place before our very eyes.[23]

Meanwhile, *L'Humanité* complained throughout the trial that the courts and French television had colluded "to erase from collective memory the place occupied by the PCF [French Communist Party] in the Resistance." Apparently, the communist daily chafed, "[o]ne has to be a Jew and not have lifted a finger against the Nazis to have the right to demand explanations from Barbie." Regardless of his faults, Truche deserves praise for not allowing the trial to be "confiscated by the evocation only of the Holocaust."[24]

## The Unique and Universal Holocaust

Jews, the potential "confiscators" to which *L'Humanité* alluded, were in something of a bind: to insist that the Holocaust was an incomparable event, that it shared nothing with other horrors, was impossible for all but the most entrenched defenders of trauma and would provoke the disdain even of those sympathetic to Jewish suffering. Such a position also would seem to diminish the ordeal of the Resistance, heroes with which Jews, as citizens of France, also felt strongly identified. To emphasize only the commonalities between the Holocaust and torture of the Resistance, however, would have denied the uniqueness that so many Jews believed was at the core of the Nazi genocide. In the end, in public discourse both before and during the trial, many Jews continued along the path set out by critics such as Jean Daniel and Raymond Aron during the Darquier Affair. That is, they stressed the Holocaust's uniqueness but at the same time spoke of it as a human tragedy, one that tied Jews to people who suffered around the world. And in a discursive context where metaphors of the Holocaust abounded, the specificity that they sought to emphasize as Jews was undermined by their simultaneous sense of connection to others.

Lawyer Alain Jakubowicz, for example, argued that a "chasm" separated Barbie's Jewish and non-Jewish victims but also admonished the jury to "prevent all the Barbies, all the falsifiers, from beginning again . . . If they succeed, it will not be their fault but yours." When Richard Zelmati, who represented several Jewish organizations, was asked why he had chosen to participate in the trial, he responded without hesitation, "because I am a Jew." He wanted to portray the unique horror of the genocide, "to explain the inexplicable." Yet he also warned during the trial that Nazi barbarism, which had targeted "Man" because he was Jewish, could rage again in other guises. "Tomorrow," he said, "Man can be persecuted because he has AIDS, because he is an Arab. . . . "[25] Both Zelmati and Jakubowicz emphasized that the Holocaust had particular meaning for Jews, that it was distinct, but also indicated that the verdict would have far-reaching consequences. Rhetorically, or logically, this position made sense. But once the crimes against humanity law had been extended to the Resistance, any notion of the Holocaust's singularity or the particularity of Jewish identity was difficult to convey in a public discourse dominated by metaphors of suffering.

More than a few Jews contended that the Holocaust was so unspeakable that it could not be properly addressed in any trial, whatever the parameters of the crimes against humanity law. We cannot represent the anguish of the forty-four Jewish children of Izieu, wrote Smolarski in *Tribune Juive*, because "Auschwitz is beyond all imagination."

Between the Jewish child entering naked and trembling into the gas chamber and the great deployments of judicial procedure, between that pain and the indignant, icy, and tumultuous hearings, between the child's infinite distress and the verdict to come stretches a no-man's-land, a terrifying void. What regard, what pity can fill it?

No one championed the ineffability of the Holocaust more vociferously than survivor Elie Wiesel, who had spent his first years after liberation in France. The Holocaust, he said in written testimony read at the trial, "de-fies and surpasses all answers. If someone pretends to find one, it can only be false."

I know that we must speak, I do not know how. As it is an absolute crime, all language can only be imperfect. Herein resides the survivor's feeling of helplessness. It was easier at Auschwitz to imagine oneself free than it would be for a free person to imagine himself a prisoner at Auschwitz. Thus, the problem: whoever did not live the event will never know it. And yet, the survivor is conscious of his obligation to testify. To tell.

I do not seek to minimize or deny the suffering of others, our comrades and friends, whom our common enemy punished with an unpardonable brutality, said Wiesel. But as a Jew, he stressed, "I insist on this point: all of Hitler's victims were not Jews; but all Jews were victims."[26]

Yet even Smolarski and Wiesel could not avoid adding to the expansion of the Holocaust metaphor. Though they captured the spirit of the trauma—Auschwitz was "beyond imagination" at the same time that survivors' testimonials were "justified"; survivors "must speak" but they "do not know how"; they know that those who did not experience the Holocaust "will never know it" but feel nonetheless an "obligation to testify"—they also generalized from the Holocaust in ways that, no matter how meticulously qualified, buried the trauma. While Smolarski argued that the Holocaust was literally inconceivable, he also contended that "Auschwitz and Barbie have reappeared or are reappearing under different forms" and justice requires the accusation and punishment of Barbie "and those like him." Wiesel, who told *Le Progrès* that no one had the right to compare anything to the Holocaust, also said that the Nazi genocide was "the beginning of experimentation in the laboratory of the inferno . . . Auschwitz signifies the past and Hiroshima the future. My wife and I were at Hiroshima before coming to Lyon: it's symbolic."[27] The trial, he said, "must bring honor to memory." But to speak about "memory," "justice," and "victims"—the same vocabulary that most of the public employed to describe torture of the Resistance, apartheid, and French racism—was to make one's self simultaneously understood and misunderstood and to exacerbate the dialectic of trauma. In public discourse surrounding the Barbie trial, no amount of precision could make the specificity of the Holocaust resonate above the din of its wide-ranging significance.

Others also struggled to convey the ineffable. Klarsfeld represented the Izieu children at the trial, and in his courtroom remarks he faced the dilemma of how to communicate what he understood as the unimaginable plight of these children without resorting to the conventions of public discourse that might somehow deny the unique horror of their deaths. Perhaps in an attempt to overcome this potential impasse, to present the event in its unmediated horror, Klarsfeld devoted his civil complaint to reading the names and biographies of Izieu children as well as letters they had written.

Sami Adelsheimer was only five years old. His mother, Laura, had been deported November 20, 1943, nine convoys before his own. Sami did not return. Max Lerner was seven. Max did not return. Otto Wertheimer's parents were deported August 17, 1942. He was left alone. He was twelve. Otto did not return. Egon Gamiel was eight years old. His parents were delivered to the SS by Vichy then deported August 17, 1942. Egon did not return. . . .

Claude Lanzmann's "Shoah" presented a similar quandary. It had earned broad critical acclaim from Jews and non-Jews alike when it first appeared in 1985, but few moviegoers had been willing to commit to the nine-hour film. Its television broadcast during the Barbie trial, for which a poll estimated over five million viewers, provoked discussions of the widespread horrors of World War II and the need to combat racism in contemporary France. While Jewish suffering was hardly ignored, commentary on the film often emphasized the Holocaust's meaning for "humanity" in a continued diffuse identification with Holocaust victims. As *L'Humanité* wrote, to see the film was "a civic obligation. It is a sufferance due from us, 'survivors,' to the six million souls seized by the night and fog of history."[28] Here, according to the communist newspaper, humankind was a collective survivor of the Holocaust. Much like the Darquier, "Holocaust," and rue Copernic controversies, as well as Klarsfeld's pursuit of Barbie, the 1987 broadcast of "Shoah" promoted a broader understanding of the Holocaust and diluted the very specificity that Lanzmann and others had attempted to convey.

The tension between the general and the specific, revealed in various aspects of the Barbie trial, betrayed the long history of Jews in France since their emancipation. "A people, like an individual, must have its memory," Jakubowicz told the court. "The people of France have not given it up, nor have the Jewish people, and I am here to claim that double memory: of the Jewish people, who are my people, as of the French people, who are my people." But in the midst of the Barbie proceedings, where the two memories were often at odds—and where Jakubowicz himself had vowed to rescue Jewish memory—what did this dual belonging entail? What did it mean to be both Jewish and French? Debates surrounding the trial, which revealed that even Jews passionate about the uniqueness of the Holocaust were deeply attached to France, betrayed the continued underlying tension between French and Jewish identity. This, perhaps, was what Lanzmann was trying to express when he described, among other reasons, why he had not addressed the Vichy regime in "Shoah." "To make this film," he said, "required distance, to not be too overwhelmed. France is too close to me."[29]

The potency of this identity conflict varied even among those who had suffered directly during the Holocaust. Auschwitz survivor and former government minister Simone Veil was skeptical from Barbie's arrest that a trial was appropriate. She worried that such proceedings, in addition to banalizing the Holocaust, would unnecessarily open old wounds and plunge France back into a climate of civil war. Writer Marek Halter, on the other hand, was less concerned about awakening old demons. "I was not in France during this epoch," he said. "I lived my childhood in the Warsaw Ghetto and I do not feel implicated in this French civil war. On the other hand, I feel perfectly French and responsible for my history." Unlike Veil, Halter had not been raised in a household where, as Veil biographer Maurice Szafran wrote, "there was only one objective: to melt into the nation and proclaim the worship of the homeland." Having come to France after his experience in the Warsaw Ghetto, Halter endeavored to acculturate in a manner that accented his Jewish identity. For Veil, whose family for generations had been devoted to the Republic, internment and deportation had not obligated her to renounce the Jewish project of assimilation.[30]

As in the demonstrations following the Copernic bombing, moreover, younger generations of Jews demonstrated a markedly more radical approach both to the trial and to their Jewish identity in France. At a Côte d'Azur conference of Jewish youth entitled "To be a Jew: Heritage or Engagement?" for example, Bernard-Henri Lévy complained of "an immense taboo" on talking about France's role in the rise of fascism and the Holocaust. If the trial produced discord among the French, argued the controversial author of *L'idéologie française*, that would be positive "because a country cannot live like a sleepwalker and be absent from its own memory." A journalist in *Tribune Juive* wrote similarly:

The Jews who fear being cut off from the national community by reopening old wounds that should be cauterized; the resisters, Jewish or not, who fear that we [*on*] are deforming the image of a France resistant to oppression—they press us to drop these old memories and to let the languishing and weak old men who no longer have much to do with the bastards they were yesterday die in peace.

I think they are wrong. The honorable task of our generation is to keep memory alive, not hallowed with a fictional halo but purified, totally conformed to the reality of the fact. We owe it to the generation of our parents to transform our "imaginary Judaism," whose roots draw partially on the memory of the Shoah, into a battle for truth.[31]

For these young Jews, confrontation with the whole history of the Holocaust, including France's role, was necessary regardless of the pain such an encounter might provoke.

## The Limits of Metaphor?

Although French conduct during the Holocaust remained peripheral in public discourse surrounding the trial, for Vergès it was the republican ideal, the honor of France, and the oft-proclaimed moral superiority of the West that were in the dock. Capitalizing on the Holocaust metaphor he had helped create, Vergès argued that Barbie's crimes were no worse than those committed by colonialist powers. He cited French offenses in Algeria, including the torture of FLN members and massacres of entire villages, as evidence that the Fourth and Fifth Republics were equally guilty of crimes against humanity. He further argued that the 1964 French law eliminating the statute of limitations on such charges had been passed primarily to prevent left-wing lawyers like himself from inundating the courts with charges stemming from the Algerian War.[32] We know what racism is, he told the court. "We bow before the martyrdom of the children of Izieu because we mourn for the children of Algeria." Barbie, said Vergès on the final day of his remarks, has been promoted to the rank of "expiatory victim" or "accused emissary" of a France always vulnerable to the "mania of purification," a "complex analogous to the masochism of the repressed."[33]

Most commentators, Jews and non-Jews alike, found Vergès's "amalgam" of offenses problematic, even if they agreed that the crimes he invoked should be punished. Roland Rappaport, former FLN lawyer and one of the few Jewish civil party attorneys to endorse the expansion of the crimes against humanity law, underscored that what happened in Algeria "was not inscribed in a project" as the Holocaust had been. Historian Pierre Vidal-Naquet, an outspoken critic during the Algerian War, argued that the behavior of French soldiers did indeed constitute a crime against humanity, and that for French justice to be coherent, the perpetrators of Algerian crimes also should be judged. However, he continued, "we should admit, as horrible as it might appear, that there are degrees in the crimes."

If it is clear that France committed crimes in Algeria, it did not commit the most serious of these crimes, the crime of genocide. No one wanted to make the Algerian people disappear, as Hitler and Himmler wanted to wipe out the Jews and the Gypsies, as the young Turks had wanted to eliminate the Armenian people in 1915 . . . Indisputably, on this terrain, Barbie can be legitimately accused and judged.

Algerian-born Jean Daniel, another vocal opponent of French colonial violence, praised Vidal-Naquet for demonstrating that there was "a hierarchy in the atrocious, a degree in the crime, and that all that took place on Algerian soil twenty-five years ago could not be compared to what had happened in Germany and the territories it occupied."[34]

Recalling the Izieu deportation, Vergès argued that those responsible for the death of children in Vietnam (the United States), Algeria (France), and at Deir Yassin (Israel) were "in the same boat" as Barbie. Jean-Martin Mbemba, one of Vergès's associates during the trial, spoke about abuse during the construction of the Congo railroad. Thousands of black cadavers littered the tracks, he told the jury, before the colonizers turned to women, children, and the handicapped.

André Frossard said that there had been no battle of Izieu, no combatants of Izieu, and that these children had died because they were Jewish. There was no battle of the railway. These people died because they were Negroes, and when I hear it said that these crimes cannot be assimilated to crimes against humanity, I wonder if we [*on*] are talking about the same thing.

But it was the third member of the defense team, Algerian lawyer Nabil Bouaïta, who caused the greatest storm. "History is rich in genocides, crimes, and abominations of all orders," he told the jury. "But if Jewish sufferance must on every occasion be the greatest among all others, my compassion goes cold." I do not see the difference between a crematory oven and a phosphorous bomb, he said, "and I do not distinguish between Nazi atrocities and those committed in Vietnam by the Americans or in Lebanon by the Israelis."

   At this point, Michel Zaoui, lawyer for the Fédération des sociétés juives de France, stood up and indignantly addressed the judge. I am not accustomed to interrupting a colleague, he said, "but it is intolerable, under the pretext of talking about crimes against humanity . . . for them to say that Israel is as guilty as the Nazis. . . . " Zaoui asked that the hearing be suspended so that he and other attorneys could prepare a response. Lawyer Eric La Phuong, representing a group of resisters, then arose and spoke with equal consternation. "It seems to me totally inappropriate for the civil party to have the right to respond to every argument of the defense. It is neither for the civil party nor the defense to say what it believes to be the sole truth but for the jurors. . . . " At the end of the day, outside the courtroom, several lawyers representing Jewish claims rejected the accusation that they had violated the trial's procedural rules. "Our Jewish sensibility has been rankled by an anti-Semitism, at once simple-minded and insidious, under the guise of anti-Zionism and attacks against the State of Israel," said one counselor. Zaoui spoke of the rage that had driven him to interrupt Bouaïta. "There is a time when one must know how to say no to that which is intolerable . . . And it is intolerable to hear it said that the 'Jews' of Israel use the same arms as their executioners." The victims of Auschwitz and Izieu have been offended, said several Jewish attorneys. "When the defense invokes 'a Nazified chosen people,' there is no longer any ambiguity. And the civil parties were insulted!"[35]

   But the reality was that *some* of the civil parties were offended. When La

Phuong reprimanded Zaoui—an intervention that earned him praise from several of his colleagues and applause from the audience—he made clear that for Resistance lawyers, Bouaïta's reference to Sabra and Shatilla was no more egregious than any other component of the defense's "amalgam" strategy. The association of Israel with Nazi Germany was from this perspective unexceptional alongside similar analogies to Algeria and Africa; the identification of Israel with Nazis carried no particular meaning because the Holocaust itself was not unique among the crimes for which Barbie was on trial. Despite broad disagreement over the definition of crimes against humanity, the breadth of the Barbie dossier, and the extent to which the Holocaust could be universalized, civil party lawyers had acted largely in consort throughout the proceedings. What brought the rift to the surface was the same "intolerable" Israel-Nazi analogy that had provoked the ire of a broad spectrum of Jews since the end of the Six-Day War and that continued to unite Jews with varying political sensibilities. "What happened is upsetting, indecent. And it doesn't help the Arab cause . . . " said Halter. "I was the first to defend Palestinian children, but leave mine alone!" Alain Finkielkraut found it "sad" that only Jewish lawyers had protested. Long after the trial, he reflected on a moment earlier in the proceedings, when Henry Noguerès, president of the League of the Rights of Man, had interrupted Vergès and warned him against making unsubstantiated allegations against the Resistance. No civil party lawyer, including La Phuong, had protested this disruption. In announcing, "'I am not here to defend the state of Israel,'" wrote Finkielkraut, La Phuong

signified that Mr. Zaoui *was* Israel's defender and that his gesture was motivated not by concern for the truth but by the interests and image of the country he was representing at the hearing. Only a militant Zionist—and who would be more susceptible—could contest the defense's right to identify Sabra and Shatilla with Auschwitz, phosphorous bombs with crematory ovens, the Jewish idea of the chosen people with Hitlerian racism. Confronted with this skittish nationalism, Barbie's lawyers and those of the Resistance associations found themselves on the same side of the barricade. Each one was leading the same combat to dislodge the Jews from their position of monopoly and to take the crime against humanity away from its monopolizers.[36]

After the jury found Barbie guilty—the only verdict possible, Dominique Jamet wryly noted, in a system where the jurors could return home every night to watch "Shoah" on their televisions—this combat continued in both subtle and direct ways. Because, as Finkielkraut wrote, the trial demonstrated that Hitler had become a paradigm, "Hydra with a thousand heads . . . annihilated only to be immediately reborn in other places and with other faces."

The French at Sétif, Americans at My Lai, Jews of the UGIF or Zionists at Deir Yassin, the whole world is Nazi, said Mr. Vergès, in effect, the whole world except the Nazis themselves. Because they are the losers. Crushed by the Allies, having served as a guarantee or excuse for the creation and the expansion of the racist State of Israel, how could they be absolutely evil, that is to say Nazis?[37]

To underscore the trial's universal import and the magnitude of the social forces that had converged on the guilty verdict, *Le Patriote Résistant* published a laudatory editorial entitled "We Were All the Civil Party" on the front page of its July issue. The jury's conclusion, it emphasized, was a victory for everyone.

Victory against forgetting, victory against those who banalize, victory against those who practice the amalgam, victory for history, victory for all those who said from the beginning that it was a question of judging an ideology in judging a man, product of that ideology . . . victory also of the witnesses, these witnesses who wrested words from their memory and made the acts of the sinister "butcher of Lyon" reappear. Victory for the Resistance, that Resistance whose stature Mr. Vergès said would not emerge enhanced and against which he was incapable—and for good reason—of delivering the promised accusation. Victory equally for the civil parties who knew how to preserve their unity on the essential.

The victory, the editorial stressed, was "for all of you: deported, interned, families, survivors of a time of hate and contempt" because "you were all the civil party, and you are also the artisans of this victory of memory." Later that month, a *La Croix* contributor challenged more directly the Jewish "monopoly" on suffering. "Jewish martyrdom, as immense as it is, is not unique, just as the West is not unique."

But just as the West has and will continue to have trouble rethinking history, so do the majority of Jews accept poorly—indeed, not at all—to not be the only, or in a way, the first in the order of martyrdom. Pride? Egocentrism? Feeling of superiority? . . . Whatever it is, as our views of history expand, we see something of a rivalry of distress beginning to appear. . . . [38]

As far back as United States President Ronald Reagan's 1985 visit to the Bitburg cemetery in Germany, *Tribune Juive* cartoonist Olivier Ranson had been poking fun at this "rivalry" and its expression in Holocaust imagery. He depicted a man, standing in front of a tombstone marked "Klaus Barbie," musing "he is also a victim." In another sketch, Le Pen says he wants to wear a yellow star like the one Jews were forced to wear in the occupied zone because he feels excluded from French politics. A cartoon during the trial satirized Kurt Waldheim, the new Austrian president who recently had been accused of having collaborated in the Nazi murder of Jews. Complaining about the controversy, Waldheim whines, "I continue to suffer from the war . . . more than Elie Wiesel!" And the following month, after *Figaro Magazine* columnist Alain Griotteray had argued that it was the Pope's prerogative to pardon Waldheim, Ranson commented on Griotteray's "rather complacent" attitude toward the Austrian president's visit to the Vatican. In one frame, the Pope faces Waldheim and says "I pardon you because you are a good Christian." Slightly in the background is a priest saying "We pardon you because you are the Pope." To the side, a Jew wearing striped pajamas implores "Please, act like I'm not here."[39]

### The Barbie Trial, France, and the Holocaust

No one can deny it, *Le Nouvel Observateur* had opined at the beginning of the trial: what makes Barbie so fascinating is not the deportation of the children of Izieu. "It is the capture of Jean Moulin, the torturing-to-death of the leader of the French Resistance." In fact, Vergès never alluded to Moulin during the trial. Jacques Chaban-Delmas, president of the National Assembly and a former resister, testified that there had been no traitors among resisters, and Vergès, according to Sorj Chalandon in *Libération*, chose not to challenge this "idyllic portrait of a mythic Resistance." The testimonies have all been heard, wrote *Le Monde*'s Jean-Marc Théolleyre, and "France has not capsized, the Resistance was not shaken." While most observers recognized that not all resisters had been heroes, they also agreed, in the words of *Le Canard enchaîné*, that it had not been "*fundamentally* a movement of bastards."[40]

The strength of French identification with the Resistance and the failure of Vergès's defensive strategy left the Gaullist myth bruised but still resonant. In diatribes against colonialism and Resistance deception, however, Vergès had cast a pall over the French past similar to the shroud of Lévy's *L'idéologie française*. It was in debates surrounding the trial, in fact, that the outlines of a battle over national identity began to take shape. On the one side were proponents of the Gaullist myth, champions of a France epitomized by revolutionaries, republicans, Dreyfusards, and resisters. On the other side, promoted in rhetorically distinct ways by men like Vergès and Lévy, were those for whom true France had been embodied by monarchists, anti-Dreyfusards, and collaborators. This was the classic antinomy between "the two Frances," between France as the paragon of republicanism and the acme of fascism. The terms of this discourse allowed little room for a more nuanced notion of national identity, one which recognized that French history was complex and even contradictory, that Vichy (or, for Vergès, colonialism) was *a*, but not the only, "French ideology." Once again, wrote *Esprit* at the end of the trial, we have seen France oscillate "between a gilded and dark legend." We manage "neither to detach ourselves from nor believe in the idea of a France that the Resistance would epitomize. Its persistent influence only increases the bitterness of having fallen so short."[41]

Had the real France been incarnated by the Resistance, as de Gaulle had contended, or had it been personified by the Vichy regime, as Vergès implied? The truth was that the Resistance had helped to rescue France from Nazism, but it also had saved France from itself. Debates during the Revolution had shown that intolerance could exist alongside and even within the rhetoric of universalism, indeed that a failure to distinguish that which was universal from what was French could produce decidedly undemocratic ways of thinking. And the strength of both collaboration with and resistance to Nazism during World War II indicated that the Third Republic had not resolved these competing impulses. The assumption that grounded the Gaullist myth, that France was entirely universalist, glossed over the nation's history of anti-Semitism, colonialism, and nativism just as the premise that only the Resistance was French neglected the reality of Vichy. As had been true in the revolutionary vision, the idea of France represented by the Resistance was based on a construction of the nation that was either unconscious of or unwilling to recognize its own contradictions. The Resistance was to France as the Republic was to France. But if the Resistance was not as representative as once imagined—if Vichy was equally a French product—was France, correspondingly, not as republican? As much as the Barbie trial was oriented toward World War II, the debates about the Algerian War, colonialism, and racism that surrounded the proceedings also reflected contemporary confusion over what it meant to be French, over national identity. Barbie was a symbolic atonement for French sins, Chalandon remarked, but "the phantoms will always remain."[42]

At the beginning of the trial, André Chambraud remarked in *L'Événement du Jeudi* on the coincidental timing of the Barbie hearings and Le Pen's recently announced candidacy for president. Long identified with de Gaulle's glorified history of the Resistance, he wrote, "the French are going to meet their present as much as their past . . . With Le Pen, we are witnessing a countercheck, an actualization of the trial led by Vergès." We are not in 1942 or 1943, he said, but it is difficult not to recognize a certain correspondence between then and now. Will the French resist Le Pen, or will they listen with complacency as most did during the war? *Esprit* wondered as well about the path the nation would follow. Some people think that France is rotten at its core, an editorial argued.

Contempt and condescension only aggravate the obsessive fear and humiliation that make us [*on*] hang our heads and refuse to confront our values. The only remedy is to augment our capacity to debate the past as well as the present, to stand collectively, to locate values in the community, in its capacity to be itself thanks to the understanding of its history, to share difficulties as well as hopes, thanks to the practice of being fellow citizens. This is what we call at times . . . the passage from the Republic to democracy, from the veneration to the interiorization of public values. . . .[43]

Both Lévy and de Gaulle had had it wrong, *Esprit* implied. To be a true democracy, to combat Le Pen and the forces that had led to Vichy, France must openly confront the good and the bad, the democratic and the repressive, in French history. Not long after the Barbie verdict was announced, Le Pen weighed in on the Holocaust and provided an opportunity for just such a confrontation.

## CHAPTER SIX

# "Why the War Haunts Us"
## Vichy on Trial

The Barbie trial had united in one event Jewish concerns about the Holocaust, national fascination with World War II, and popular identification with oppression and victimization. In the aftermath, Holocaust discourse took yet another turn. Controversies surrounding Jean-Marie Le Pen, the 1990 attack on a Carpentras cemetery, and the arrest and trial of former Vichy subordinate Paul Touvier became sites where the major themes in public discourse converged on a national identification with the Holocaust, or more precisely, with the idea of Jewish victimization during the Holocaust. Whereas in earlier discussions attention to Vichy and the details of Jewish suffering within France had been peripheral, now it was France's national character and its role in the persecution and deportation of Jews that were at issue. If Barbie brought the Holocaust definitively to France, Le Pen and Touvier delivered France to the Holocaust.

Le Pen had earned his share of negative press, especially after winning eleven percent of the seats in the European Parliament in 1984. But after the Barbie trial, he made a series of irreverent statements about the Holocaust that turned him into a national enemy. By making light of the Nazi genocide, whose victims rhetorically included Jews, members of the Resistance, and a variety of persecuted groups, Le Pen became the symbol of its perpetration in France. He was perceived to be the modern embodiment of collaborationist ideology, the epitome of French degeneracy at present, and his critics spoke with apocalyptic alarm about a return to Vichy. As anxiety about the past intensified, Le Pen became something of a surrogate for the

Vichy regime in public discourse. The greater the vehemence with which the FN leader could be renounced, the more completely, it seemed, France could repudiate its Vichy past. Touvier's arrest in 1989 made possible the condemnation of an actual collaborator. Touvier had been in charge of intelligence and operations for a regional division of the Milice, an organization of paramilitary brigades created by the Vichy regime in 1943 to combat the Resistance. He was not the first Frenchman to be charged with crimes against humanity,[1] but he had the misfortune of surfacing at a time when the public was beginning to fixate on Vichy. As the investigation into Touvier's past proceeded, and especially after a controversial 1992 court ruling, his case became the focal point for public discourse on the Holocaust. The tensions between history, memory, and the law that had been troublesome during the Barbie controversy exploded, and the public's growing desire to punish Vichy criminals, to establish publicly and definitively the culpability of the Vichy regime, led to legal maneuvering and conceptual slippages that parodied both justice and historical investigation.

By the time of the Touvier trial in March 1994, a conceptual divide had begun to emerge, one that distinguished the Vichy regime, guilty of crimes against humanity, from the wartime French population, innocent of such crimes and a victim of Vichy betrayal. Such a distinction echoed the long-standing Jewish assertion that the Pétain government should not be confused with the French people, that "official France" should not be mistaken for "true France," but this consensus masked a subtle but real disagreement over the meaning of the Holocaust. While most Jewish opinion suggested that the trial was an opportunity to recognize Vichy's repression of the Jews in particular, most of the rest of the nation sought to capitalize on the crimes against humanity law to disavow the Vichy regime in general. For the former, Vichy stood for the Holocaust, while for the latter, the Holocaust became a metonym for Vichy: the persecution and deportation of Jews from France became the Vichy crime that encapsulated the evil of the regime. As in controversies surrounding Le Pen, the Holocaust came to stand for Vichy, though in neither case were the so-called "dark years" critically confronted.

## Le Pen and the Return of Vichy

The popularity of Le Pen and the FN, along with violence against immigrants, continued to rise in the late 1980s. Anti-Muslim tracts, pamphlets, graffiti, vandalism against mosques, and other incidents of racist violence were common. In May and June 1986, a group calling itself French Commandos Against the North African Invasion took credit for a series of bombings in southeastern France. In three separate incidents that year, attacks on bars frequented by North Africans killed one and injured five others. A dormitory housing foreign workers was blown up in 1988, and the following year saw more deadly attacks. In the world of electoral politics, the conservative parties won a majority in parliament in 1986, which forced Socialist president Mitterrand to take on RPR leader Jacques Chirac as prime minister. With an eye toward the presidency, Chirac tried to attract Le Pen enthusiasts by assuming a tough stand on issues like crime and terrorism, which extremists linked to excessive immigration. He tightened visa requirements and also considered revising the nationality code so that no automatic rights of citizenship would be granted to someone born in France to non-French parents. Still, Le Pen captured almost fifteen percent of the votes cast in the 1988 election, prompting Chirac to announce that he had "heard" Le Pen's supporters and Interior Minister Charles Pasqua to note that "the National Front supports the same values as the majority." Mitterrand was comfortably reelected.[2]

Meanwhile, the Jacobin republic seemed to be undergoing something of a religious revival. Ultra-orthodox Jews, for example, began to assume greater prominence, including positions of leadership in key organizations, in the Jewish community. Conspicuous in their attire and demand for religious rights, they asserted their Jewishness in ways that troubled not only old-stock community leaders but Jews both opposed to and in favor of a public Jewish presence. Moderately observant Jews, who often found themselves at odds with the rigidity of some of their coreligionists, also were beginning to claim their religious rights. In June 1991, for example, the lead editorial in *Tribune Juive* complained that the first day of school in the fall would coincide with Rosh Hashanah, the Jewish New Year. "It would not have been too much for the Republic to have taken into consideration the desire of Jewish students and teachers to follow Jewish law," wrote Jacquot Grunewald. As religious Jews began to find their voice, others objected that they were being squeezed out of the Jewish community. "Who Represents the Jews of France?" asked *Tribune Juive* in July 1990. "The Jewish community in France is plural," wrote one reader, angry at remarks made by Benny Cohen, the new president of the Paris Consistory, intimating that Jews who did not adhere meticulously to Jewish law were not really Jewish. While it might have been appropriate for the president of the Republic to visit the home of the Grand Rabbi after the Carpentras desecration, the letter continued, "it is neither just nor honest to suggest to the national community—the variety of French citizens—that *only* the Grand Rabbi represents *all* the Jews of France."[3]

While Jews argued among themselves and with others about the nature of their identity in France—a dialogue that had begun in the wake of the

Six-Day War—they and the rest of the nation struggled with the consequences of ongoing immigration and the challenge it posed to old notions
of what it meant to be French. In 1989 and 1990, several young girls were
expelled from public schools for wearing the traditional Muslim veil, which
school officials contended was a threat to France's secular educational system. In the controversy that ensued, the nation was divided between supporters of public religious expression, on the one hand, and critics who believed that religion should be restricted to the private domain, on the other.
Among those who objected to the "intolerance" of the non-religious world
were many North African Jewish immigrants and their descendants, who
were now settled and integrated and often leading the communal institutions that since Napoleon had been dominated by Ashkenazi Jews committed to assimilation. Known as ultra-orthodox, these Sephardi Jews advocated a strict adherence to Jewish law that angered many traditional leaders,
who found such rigidity excessive. They argued for the right of Jewish boys
to wear yarmulkes to school, and although not entirely opposed to secular
culture, they and other supporters of the Muslim girls called for a society
that encouraged religious pluralism.[4]

On the other side of the battle were those who feared the end of French
secularism, including assimilated and largely secular Jews who inveighed
against the rise of "Jewish fundamentalism." They opposed the veil in
school and accused activists who advocated a public role for religion of
mounting a campaign against the Revolution. Marked by heated ex-
changes, the debate demonstrated the breakdown of the post-revolutionary
consensus on Jewish identity and the demise of the revolutionary republic,
constituted by a citizenry with loyalty only to France. Divided by competing visions of what it meant to be Jewish, Jews mirrored the rest of the nation, itself struggling to articulate the contours of a modern French identity
that respected particularist loyalties. The probability of some form of a
united Europe, moreover, made even more pressing the project of determining what made France *French*. Was it the Jacobin ideal, whereby unfettered citizens participated in civil society without respect for particular alle-
giances? Or was it exclusionist nationalism, which demanded "France for
the French" and refused to extend the privileges of citizenship to others? Or
was there now a third way, a pluralism that tolerated particular affiliations
in a liberal polity?

As immigration, citizenship, and national identity became prominent issues in public discourse, it was in many ways Le Pen who served as the figurative bridge between Barbie and Touvier, between the Holocaust as a
crime perpetrated by the Nazis and the Holocaust as an atrocity for which
France shared responsibility. Not long after the Barbie trial had ended, in
September 1987, Le Pen provoked an uproar by announcing on a popular

radio program that the gas chambers were merely "a detail in the history of World War II" and implying that their existence was in doubt.[5] In September 1988, he again caused a stir by using the name of government minister Michel Durafour in the pun *Durafour-crématoire*. *Four-crématoire* translates as "crematory oven." And the following year, controversy developed surrounding the remarks of film-maker Claude Autant-Lara, who had been elected on Le Pen's list to the European Parliament. Autant-Lara announced himself in favor of revisionism—"Auschwitz . . . genocide . . . we really don't know"—and attacked Simone Veil. "Whether you like it or not, that woman belongs to a political ethnic group that tries to set roots and dominate." And regarding her internment at Auschwitz: "She plays that for all it's worth. But she came back, eh? And she's doing well . . . So when someone [*on*] talks to me about genocide, I say that in any case they missed old mother Veil!" Veil chose not to respond publicly, but the headline in *Libération* was clear: "Autant-Lara declares out loud the anti-Semitism of the National Front."[6]

Though Darquier de Pellepoix's 1978 interview with *L'Express* had demonstrated the presence of an autonomous French anti-Semitism within the Vichy regime, its publication had come at a time when the French were only beginning to think critically in public discourse about Vichy and collaboration in general. The Holocaust, too, was at the time a fairly undeveloped theme, and insofar as it was discussed, it remained largely a German affair. But Le Pen espoused racism, anti-Semitism, revisionism, and a general impertinence toward the Holocaust that ran directly counter to the current of public debate. That over four million people voted for the FN in the 1988 elections made him seem even more dangerous, because he represented what was wrong with France at present. In provoking questions about national character and France's commitment to universal, liberal principles, Le Pen actualized the issues surrounding French complicity in the Holocaust. Critics focused on the reappearance of an "atavistic" anti-Semitic discourse. What is worrisome in all this, wrote Laurent Joffrin in *Le Nouvel Observateur*, is that Autant-Lara sounds so much "like the old codgers of the  collaboration who continue to tumble from the closets of French society." For the first time since the war, "a political movement has voluntarily, publicly, and repeatedly adopted an anti-Semitic discourse. In a France that until today had triumphantly prevented a renaissance of the nauseating rhetoric from the 1930s, this is an event." An analysis of a national poll about attitudes toward Jews, published in *Tribune Juive*, contended that Jews were increasingly being feared because of their "foreignness." *Le Monde* characterized the survey's results as "ambiguous," but many in both the Jewish and national press argued that a recent rise in anti-Jewish acts constituted a "third wave" of anti-Semitism and was cause for serious concern. Given the fractures in French society, the weakening of ideologies that have served as moral guides, and the ease with which everyone looks for a scapegoat, Joffrin concluded, "it is impossible not to be concerned."[7]

Shortly after the Autant-Lara dispute, a group calling itself the Sons of Jewish Memory claimed responsibility for a physical assault on Robert Faurisson, whose writings denying the existence of Nazi gas chambers had caused an uproar just after the Copernic bombing. Faurisson, according to a group statement, was the "negator of the Shoah" and "the source of the Carmelite Affair at Auschwitz."[8] The group was quickly disavowed by CRIF president Jean Kahn and former president Théo Klein, the latter of whom was directly involved in the Auschwitz negotiations, and both agreed that it was unwise to link the convent in Poland with the revisionist theses of Faurisson.[9] Yet there was a strong tendency in public discourse to turn controversies having to do with the Far Right into discussions about the dangers of Holocaust denial. No less a commentator than the respected Joffrin remarked that equalizing Catholic and Jewish victims at Auschwitz denied the historical particularity of the Holocaust and was in the "Faurissonian spirit."[10] After Le Pen's infamous "detail" comment, the *Durafour-crématoire* pun, and the Autant-Lara controversy, debates intensified over whether legislation should be adopted making illegal the denial of the Holocaust. In widely expressed consternation about a renewal of anti-Semitism, there seemed to be something particularly dangerous about revisionism. If the bombing on rue Copernic had signaled the lifting of a taboo against anti-Jewish violence, the popularity of Le Pen and the FN seemed to mark the end of the prohibition against political anti-Semitism, and denial of the Holocaust was widely perceived to be its most dangerous expression.

On the one hand, the Holocaust had been a fixture in French public discourse since the Barbie trial, when the nation had identified with the Resistance as a victim of Nazism. During the proceedings, Nazism had become synonymous with the Holocaust, which itself remained largely an event in which France itself was not implicated. Given the status accorded to victims in popular discourse and the extent to which the reputation of the Resistance had been linked to its persecution by the Nazis, it is not surprising to find a wide array of opinion sensitive to any sentiment that denied the reality of that suffering. On the other hand, although Autant-Lara appeared to be a partisan of Holocaust revisionism, Le Pen's remarks seemed to reflect more the kind of "banalization" of the Holocaust that many Jews had worried about since the Darquier interview than any concerted effort to deny the existence of gas chambers. His anti-Semitism, moreover, was largely unmarked in rhetoric and fact by the kind of deadly violence associated with Nazism and the Holocaust (and with FN racism). As historian Pierre Birnbaum has written, the inhibitions against acting on racist prejudices were far less powerful than those that discouraged anti-Semitic activity.[11] Why, then, was there such concern about revisionism? Why did commentary hostile to the Far Right (and mainstream public discourse was overwhelmingly anti-Le Pen) almost invariably weigh in against Holocaust denial as though it were a, if not the, central concern?

The key was an unexpressed consensus about the role that the Holocaust played in discrediting the Far Right and the Vichy regime. Jean Daniel had some sense of this when he argued that "Faurissonism" was a phenomenon only partially about Faurisson himself, that it alimented all kinds of thinking on the Far Right. The reasoning, he argued, was as follows: "if the genocide did not exist, then French anti-Semitism can gain respectability. . . . " If Pétain was only Hitler minus the genocide, he explained, by suppressing the genocide, the Far Right could reclaim both Pétain and Hitler and in the process rehabilitate an ideology that had been disparaged since the end of the war. What was important for right-wing extremists, in other words, was that the Holocaust had not taken place. "Since in sum it was the genocide that discredited the National Revolution," wrote Daniel, "it is necessary to challenge the very reality of that genocide."[12] Because, in other words, it was the Holocaust and not simply anti-Semitism that ultimately compromised Vichy in the eyes of contemporary France, Le Pen's revisionism, however peripheral to his larger political agenda, was an especially potent weapon for those who sought to repudiate both the FN and the Vichy regime. During periodic developments in the prosecution of alleged French war criminals, and especially since the Barbie trial, the reality that France would be called upon to account for its role in the persecution and deportation of Jews had become clear. As the Holocaust increased in salience in public discourse, a certain anxiety about Vichy, a desire to draw a distinct line between the past and present, became apparent. With popular identification with the Holocaust high, accusations of Holocaust denial were a powerful way to discredit the FN and disinherit the Pétain regime. By focusing on his remarks about the Holocaust, the public could disown both Le Pen and the (Vichy) ideology that animated him.

If the FN was the contemporary embodiment of Vichy, however, popular opposition to Le Pen undermined both the current Far Right and Vichy ideology without paying any real attention to the past. Instead of opening a national dialogue about collaboration, and in particular, about French persecution of Jews, denunciation of Le Pen via a critique of Holocaust denial actually created a certain distance between contemporary France and the Holocaust. By condemning Le Pen, one could dissociate from French contributions to the Final Solution without examining them. Once Holocaust denial was attributed to Le Pen and the FN leader effectively isolated from the respectable French community, further distance was created between the French nation to which most people felt they belonged and the France involved in the deportation of Jews. To blame Le Pen was a clear acknowledgment that something was and had been rotten in the hexagon, but it was also a relatively painless projection of guilt that required no assumption of responsibility for or examination of the ideologies and events in question. In discussions about the danger of extremist politics, "opposition" to the Holocaust and disavowal of Le Pen made possible a decidedly a-historical non-confrontation with history. Language that suggested a critique of the past in fact masked a certain orientation away from the past. Anti–Le Penism served in this way as a surrogate for a critical investigation into Vichy politics and French collaboration, and preoccupation with revisionism in the rhetoric of Le Pen displaced critical examination of Vichy's role in the Holocaust. In this way, the ostracization of Le Pen in the late 1980s marked the first step in the distancing of the nation from the Vichy regime.

## Touvier's Arrest

A former member of the Milice twice condemned to death in absentia, Paul Touvier had lived on the run, assisted by friends in the Church hierarchy, since 1946. Once the statute of limitations on his crimes had expired in 1967, the death penalty was lifted, and in 1971, against the counsel of his advisers, President Pompidou granted Touvier a pardon. "Are we forever going to keep bleeding the wounds of our national disagreements?" Pompidou asked. "Has the moment not come to draw a veil, to forget these times when the French did not like each other, were tearing each other to pieces and even killing each other?" When the press publicized the pardon, which had been kept relatively quiet by the Elysée, the public was outraged, but it was not until ten years later, after protracted legal wrangling, that a Paris court issued an international warrant for Touvier's arrest. In the meantime, the former *milicien* remained in hiding. In 1979, he defended himself in a pamphlet entitled *My Crimes Against Humanity*, and in 1984, a regional newspaper announced his death. Few were fooled, and rumors circulated that French authorities were aware of his whereabouts and could take him into custody if they so desired. On May 25, 1989, newspapers around France heralded his capture.

The arrest renewed debates about imprescriptibility and retroactive crimes first heard during the Barbie controversy, but even some of the most outspoken skeptics of crimes against humanity trials indicated that once Barbie had been tried, France could not "wriggle out of responsibility" when it came to Touvier. As Veil told *Le Figaro*, people in France would not be able to understand why the government had pursued and tried Barbie, a German who could have put forward as his defense that he was fighting for his country, and had chosen not to judge Touvier, a Frenchman who tortured and assassinated other French people. For many commentators, a trial would be an opportunity for the French to shed light on the nation's past, confront their conscience, enhance collective memory, and judge the collaboration. "A people cannot live its present if it does not assume the reality of its past, if it does not demand of itself the most accurate writing of its history," wrote Bruno Chenu in *La Croix*. "Willful amnesia does not ennoble humanity."[13]

Yet the anxiety was palpable. As Philippe Boucher wrote in *Le Monde*, Barbie was taken with nothing but the shirt on his back and his memory, but Touvier was captured with "poisonous sweets," suitcases of notes that could implicate a range of officials and institutions in France. While former Barbie attorney Jacques Vergès gleefully announced the "trial of the entire French society and not of an isolated man," newspaper headlines following Touvier's arrest—"The Ghost of Vichy," "Touvier: Vichy before the Court?" and "The Trial of France"—contained an ominous sense of foreboding. Leave the collaboration and Vichy to the historians and judge Touvier as an individual, warned André Frossard, then a member of the Académie Française. If not, "old national demons will resurface." These demons, it was well understood, had to do with the Vichy regime and the extent of both governmental and popular collaboration with the Nazis. More or less contained since 1945, these demons had come dangerously close to provoking fractious and protracted national debate during the Darquier de Pellepoix and Barbie controversies. What a trial threatened to expose, wrote Alain Guérin in *L'Humanité*, was the fact that from one end to the other in the chain of complicity, and even in the shadow of the Vatican, the clergy, businessmen, politicians, and civil servants who protected the French citizen Touvier "were all French, terribly French."[14]

In the meantime, just before Touvier's arrest, controversy had broken out over the impending visit of Palestinian Liberation Organization leader Yassir Arafat to the Elysée. Much of the Jewish community was furious with Mitterrand for having extended himself to a man they believed was a terrorist, and leaders of several Jewish organizations wrote an open letter, published in *Le Monde*, expressing their indignation. Responding to criticism of the Church and to Le Pen's suggestion that the Mitterrand government had "served up Touvier to the Jews" to offset the unpopular Arafat visit, *Aspects de la France* warned: "Campaign against France, campaign against the Church: those who lead them do no favor to the Jewish community, of which certain representatives go too far. The French could begin to notice."[15] Suspicious, too, that the government had considered it necessary to "toss Touvier's head to the Jews in compensation," Annie Kriegel wrote in *Le Figaro*: "We are finally going to be able to conduct, in opinion and in the courtroom, quite the trial of the Catholic Church, as well as the trial of France, Vichy, and de Gaulle, all mixed together in the same execration. . . . "[16]

Though she rejected the notion of a singular, unified Jewish community and on numerous occasions had criticized Jewish organizations,[17] Kriegel, herself a Jew, would have endorsed neither the anti-Semitic implications of the monarchist newspaper's statements, which deliberately separated Jews from "the French," nor the anti-republican ideology that the paper unapologetically propagated. But both Kriegel and *Aspects de la France* concurred that an otherwise disparate collection of ideas and institutions might find themselves incriminated in any Touvier proceedings. The Church, as *Aspects de la France* implied, was in the minds of many French people, and not simply monarchists or devout Catholics, inextricably linked to any idea of "France," and this had been especially true under Vichy. A campaign against the Church could appear as an assault on France. Moreover, if a member of the Milice, a creation of the Vichy regime, were to face charges for crimes against humanity, Vichy would also be implicated in crimes against Jews. And if the regime were on trial, so, too, would de Gaulle and his version of history be judged. How would "the French," Jews included, respond? The nation and the state, French heroes and French myths—all would be before the jury in a Touvier trial. This explains "why the war haunts us," as a *La Croix* interview with historian Jean-Pierre Azéma was billed.[18] Touvier was perhaps not the best representative of collaboration, but the affair had the potential to re-divide the nation.

## Carpentras

By 1990, Le Pen had become a symbol of all that was wrong with France, both historically and in the present, and repudiation of the FN leader became something of a mantra in all but the most extreme right-wing public discourse. This anti–Le Penism reached its apex following the desecration of a Jewish cemetery at Carpentras in May 1990, when over thirty gravestones were pillaged, and the body of a recently buried man exhumed and mutilated. President Mitterrand immediately called on the French to "get a hold of themselves" while RPR president Jacques Chirac spoke of a crisis "for which we are all responsible." The Left accused conservatives of going too far in publicly sympathizing with FN concerns, while parties on the Right accused the Socialists and Communists of having provoked the Carpentras desecration with radical immigration and citizenship policies. Critics compared the defilement to Auschwitz; Jean Kahn remarked that even the Nazis had left Jewish bodies in their graves. Demonstrations were held throughout France, and over 200,000 people marched in Paris. In an event that recalled the protests following the 1980 rue Copernic bombing, expressions of solidarity against racism and anti-Semitism bordered on the maudlin. The riot police (CRS) smiled at photographers, and members of several police unions, which had been accused in 1980 of sheltering known fascist supporters, conspicuously joined the march. *Le Monde* described the scene:

"You're a cop?" said a macho member of the Communist Party to a blond police officer. "Cop and Jewish, like all cops. Is that a problem for you?" responded the officer. He hugged her. The walkie-talkies of the police commissioners indicated that there, unreachable by the boulevard, the president of the Republic was suffering the warm assault of hundreds of young Jews and that the Elysée police had a lot to do just to maintain a path for survival. Mitterrand was to shake the hand of the Grand Rabbi, but having himself been mauled by the outpouring of the crowd, he had been shunted into a CRS car. Suave. A half an hour to extract the chief of state. . . .

The oldest people, under the banners of Auschwitz, recalled the past. "Do you realize that it's been barely fifty years [since the Holocaust], and they [*on*] no longer think about it?" Kids told each other they were ready to give Le Pen a piece of their mind. The police pleaded with them to come down from the roof of the minister of agriculture's car.[19]

The night of the demonstration, all French television stations simultaneously broadcast "Night and Fog," Alain Resnais' 1955 film on Nazi concentration and death camps.[20]

Although Le Pen denounced the desecration and emphatically denied that his party was responsible, public discourse immediately and almost unanimously indicted him and the FN. Bernard-Henri Lévy inveighed against the "fascism" of Le Pen, Lyon mayor and RPR deputy Michel Noir denounced the "cowardice" and "hypocrisy" of politicians who did nothing to counter the successes of Le Pen, sociologist Alain Touraine called for the dissolution of the FN, and Communist Party leader Georges Marchais issued an appeal to television and radio stations to refrain from broadcasting the "poison" of Le Pen and his sympathizers. As commentators tried to discern what accounted for Le Pen's popularity, many pointed to the population's dwindling faith in the ideas and social structures that had provided guidance in the past. Touraine suggested that French society had lost "its capacity for ideological interpretation and institutional treatment of its conflicts and fears" while *Libération*'s Serge July lamented the "evacuation of politics" that made a hero of Le Pen, "the absolute opposite of aseptic technocracy. . . . " Historian Michel Winock, essayist and Académie Française member Jean-Denis Bredin, and Veil expressed similar sentiment. The waning of ideologies, religion, unions, universities, and even grade schools has left people vulnerable to extremism, said Veil in an interview. "They need an outlet . . . and they spontaneously give themselves over to a crazy leader. In France, you see, there are no more intellectuals. The political world is too cut off from deep reflection."[21]

Le Pen countered that he was the "victim" of "professional anti-racists," and many observers who hardly could be accused of racism or sympathy for the Far Right found the nation's reflexive anti-racism somewhat disingenuous. If, as many had argued, the decline of ideology and social institutions had created space for the demagoguery of Le Pen, still others suggested that anti-racism had itself become an ideology, or an end unto itself. Finkielkraut reiterated what he had written in *La mémoire vaine*, after the Barbie trial.

What is serious today, in the collapse of communism, is that instead of being an arm of combat against racism, anti-racism tends to be substituted for communism, to play its role . . . [It] takes the place of ideology for a Left that has lost its bearings and its principles . . . It is an anti-racist *identity* that requires the existence of its adversary, Le Pen as it happens, and not a combative anti-racism that wants to eliminate its enemy.

As for the slogan and protest banner reading "We are all responsible," Pierre-André Taguieff, professor and president of a group that monitored anti-Semitism, called it a "stylistic device" and questioned the depth of public engagement. "I was struck in this affair by the discrepancy between sincere indignation and the extraordinary flood of stereotypes and cliches . . . Unanimous demonstrations like this tend to create a veil of illusions."[22]

Violent attacks against immigrants in the recent past suggested that the problem of racism and prejudice was more than discursive. Yet, although Le Pen's popularity and inflammatory remarks about North Africans, Jews, homosexuals, and anyone else he deemed not French had inspired among certain segments of the Left a vigilance against any hint of nativism, no coordinated, mass condemnation had materialized. Why had there been no outpouring of indignation after these incidents of racism? Other cemeteries had recently been ransacked. Why had there been relatively lackluster response? Why was it the defilement of the Jewish cemetery at Carpentras that provoked such intense reaction? The disentombing of and attempt to impale a recently buried body certainly inspired particular revulsion, but this fails to account for the gulf between the conspicuous post-Carpentras anti-racism and the comparatively muted character of earlier reproaches. Though the rhetoric of the Far Right was laced with both anti-Semitic and racist imagery, it was immigrants, not Jews, who were the overwhelming victims of xenophobic attacks. A variety of Jewish and non-Jewish public figures, including Lévy, Frossard, Bredin, Robert Badinter, Grand Rabbi Joseph Sitruk, former *Esprit* editor Jean-Marie Domenach, and former government minister Léo Hamon, speaking at various moments in the Carpentras aftermath, stated their firm belief that France was not at present anti-Semitic.[23] Why, then, was it a seemingly anti-Jewish act that stimulated such formidable resolve?

The French, wrote Bredin, suffered the illusion that they would immunize themselves against anti-Semitism only by memory of the Holocaust. But the illusion was really a slight modification of the inverse: that the nation would protect itself from Vichy only by sensational demonstrations against anti-Semitism. Carpentras became a spectacle because it piqued a deep-seated angst about the Vichy past. Unlike in Germany, Winock told *Le Quotidien de Paris*, many in France had a "bad conscience" because there had been "no real debate about our moral responsibility" during that epoch. Psychoanalyst Daniel Sibony detected at the Carpentras protest "an indecipherable symptom visible only in the malaise . . . a memory lapse, something simply and implacably unsaid: the France of the young and the not so young does not know that it was officially Nazi for almost four years." The situation is aggravated, he added, when instead of "nourishing" this hunger for memory society tries to fill it with "moralistic mawkishness." Marek Halter agreed. "Le Pen is not responsible for everything," he said. There is a lacuna in French memory "because we [*on*] have never really spoken about Vichy." The purpose of such a discussion is not to make accusations "but to understand [ . . . ] If not, we will have other Carpentrases, Copernics, and rues des Rosiers."[24]

Le Pen, according to July, evoked "all that is repressed in the history of France" and therefore had been "unanimously designated as the number one ideological polluter."[25] But widespread contempt for Le Pen and ostentatious repugnance at anti-Semitism were no more a confrontation with the French past than the proliferation of the "Never Again!" slogan following the rue Copernic bombing in 1980 had been an encounter with the Holocaust. Anti-Le Pen sentiment was no more a successful attempt to assign responsibility for a violent anti-Semitic attack than had been the anti-fascism of post-Copernic discourse. Some people were indeed concerned about anti-Semitism and racism, and the mass protest served to underscore a widespread contempt for intolerance. But despite the pervasiveness of Holocaust rhetoric, including a demonstration in front of former Vichy police chief Bousquet's Paris home the day before the march, Vichy's role in the persecution and deportation of Jews was not critically confronted. To the extent that Le Pen attracted public wrath, fears about Vichy were displaced and the collaboration itself remained unexamined.

If the anti-racist front revealed a preoccupation with Vichy, it also betrayed a certain detachment from the social problems of contemporary France. The pervasive rhetoric of anti-racism in response to an act of anti-Semitism conflated racism and anti-Semitism, which, as Olivier Roy, an *Esprit* editor, wrote in a *Le Monde* opinion, were not the same thing. "The battle against anti-immigrant racism will not be carried out symbolically," he wrote, "but in socially treating the problems of cohabitation among people of ethnically diverse origins."[26] Hamadi Essid, the Arab League ambassador to Paris, explained in a *Le Monde* opinion that many French Muslims, "the preferred target of racism," wondered why no one paid attention to the profanation of their mosques and cemeteries. Those who attended the march, he argued, contributed to

the clear conscience of all those who the next day would not fail to claim their satisfaction in a country where hundreds of individuals, recognized authors of racist crimes, walked freely about with Arab blood on their hands, which obviously is an attenuating circumstance.[27]

That the mass public response was not to one of the many incidents of anti-immigrant violence but to an act of anti-Semitism, however deplorable, averted attention from the arguably more pressing issue of anti-Arab racism and violence. Thus both the history of Jews in France during World War II and the contemporary problems of racism and immigrant integration remained unaddressed in the "outbreak" of anti-racism following the pillage at Carpentras. As had been the case in earlier denunciations of Le Pen, the demons of both past and present were exorcised before having been internalized.

Nonetheless, certain Jewish activists, among whom Serge Klarsfeld was the most prominent, were determined that the Vichy regime's persecution and deportation of Jews be publicly discussed and that the perpetrators receive official sanction. The media, moreover, publicized with zeal any issues having to do with Vichy, the Holocaust, or World War II. Less than a week after the Carpentras violence, new crimes against humanity charges were filed against Maurice Papon; and in June, *Le Nouvel Observateur* published a cover story titled "The French People Who Were Accomplices to the Genocide," in response to which Papon sued for defamation. Later that summer the National Assembly passed the Gayssot law, which made it illegal to contest the existence of crimes against humanity, and in October, to mark the fiftieth anniversary of the Jewish Statute, Klarsfeld and the Contemporary Jewish Documentation Center (CDJC) organized a Senate colloquium about Vichy's anti-Jewish legislation. Bousquet was officially indicted in March 1991, after his appeals were rejected, while Robert Faurisson was convicted and ordered to pay a heavy fine that April for violation of the Gayssot law. And in November, Klarsfeld announced that he had discovered a card file containing the 1940 census of Jews from the Paris region, the so-called *fichier juif,* in the archives of the War Veterans Ministry.[28] In the aftermath of Carpentras, public discourse surrounding these and other events made it clear that Le Pen was a poor substitute for Vichy and that anti-racism would not take the place of a direct confrontation with the architects of French collaboration. The constant pressure of people like Klarsfeld and the media appetite for anything having to do with Vichy fueled national anxiety about the war years and ensured that popular desire to repudiate French betrayal during World War II could be satisfied only in the incrimination of those who had been directly responsible.

## No Grounds For Prosecution

In April 1992, the Court of Criminal Appeals in Paris issued a *non-lieu,* a ruling that there were "no grounds" for prosecution, in the case against Touvier. A panel of three judges dismissed outright ten of the eleven charges, challenging the credibility of witnesses and their ability to recall details of events that had occurred nearly fifty years earlier. The eleventh charge, that Touvier had ordered the massacre of seven Jews at Rillieux-la-Pape as a reprisal for the assassination of a Vichy minister in June 1944, was dismissed for lack of evidence that it constituted a crime against humanity. According to the 1985 court ruling, which had made possible the prosecution of Barbie for crimes against the Resistance, only offenses committed in the service of a government practicing a policy of "ideological hegemony" could be tried under the 1964 law declaring such crimes imprescriptible. Vichy, according to the judges, was not such a regime, and as a functionary of the Milice, a creation of Vichy, Touvier could not stand trial for crimes against humanity. It would be up to the Final Court of Criminal Appeals to evaluate this court's decision.

The *non-lieu* came on the heels of a report issued by a commission of historians that had been convoked by the Lyon archbishop shortly after Touvier's arrest. The commission's findings, based on unprecedented access to the Lyon diocese and made public in January 1992, indicated that numerous clergymen, some occupying relatively high positions in the Church hierarchy, had hidden Touvier and his family or otherwise associated themselves with his cause at virtually every stage in his flight from justice. Announced just over three months after the report had been issued, the court's dismissal of the Touvier case rocked the country. In a national survey, seventy-three percent of the respondents declared themselves "shocked" by the decision while only two percent said they were "satisfied." A later poll indicated that seventy-four percent of the population believed that those who had committed crimes during the occupation should still be punished, while seventy-one percent affirmed that it was necessary "to talk a lot about Vichy and the occupation." A group of widely respected historians launched a petition, published in *Le Monde*, stating that the ruling had "travestied" the history of Vichy "by specious logic, tricks of language, and genuine ignorance" and calling on others to add their signatures.[29] At the request of the Socialist, Communist, and Gaullist parties, the National Assembly ended its April 14 session early so that members could join the CRIF in a ceremony at the Paris Memorial to the Deportation. Channel 3 broadcast "Night and Fog," and Minister of Culture Jack Lang sent a copy of the film to all public and private schools, asking that it be shown.[30] *L'Humanité* claimed that the judges' reasoning followed the "Faurisson model" and was a *megafaurissonerie* (mega-Faurissonism). If there are people who deny the genocide of the Jews, wrote Bruno Frappat in *Le Monde*, why should we be surprised that three judges exonerated Touvier and Vichy?[31] Public discourse focused on the persecution and deportation of Jews as Vichy's principal offense, and Touvier's alleged murder of Jews became the paradigmatic crime of collaboration that had to be punished if France were to "come to terms with" the past.

Many of the concerns first raised during the Barbie trial took on new significance in light of the court's ruling. To what extent, observers asked, was France willing to face its history, and to what lengths would it go to avoid such a confrontation? How would the courts, historians, and various segments of the public manage the tenuous interplay between the law, history, and memory? As had been true after the appeals court's 1985 ruling, many Jews wrestled with the relationship between Jewish and national suffering and continued to ruminate on their particularity as Jews in France. At the same time, Jewish and non-Jewish opinion began to converge on an interpretation of collaboration that distinguished the Vichy state from the French population: the regime had been corrupt and betrayed the ideals of France, which the people had steadfastly upheld. At times it seemed as though the French people, like the Jews, had been victims of Vichy. Critics debated the urgency of national unity and the threat posed to the "civil peace" by those who insisted on "rehashing" the divisions of World War II. National identity was viewed through the alternating lenses of Vichy, the Holocaust, contemporary European integration, and the Mitterrand presidency. The *non-lieu* sparked profound debates about what kind of country France had been and should be. In a new Europe that would require the reconciliation of past antagonisms, most agreed that French reckoning with Vichy crimes was essential and that the *non-lieu* was a determined step in the wrong direction.

Public discourse reflected incredulity over aspects of the ruling, including the contention that Vichy had not been an ideologically hegemonic state. Henry Rousso, director of the Institut d'Histoire du Temps Présent and historian of the Vichy period, delivered a scathing attack in *Le Nouvel Observateur*. The judges, he wrote, "indulged in a demonstration whose sophistry is equaled only by a total ignorance of the Pétain regime. . . . " With the same arguments, "they could have arrived easily at the idea that Nazism had no ideology either." By ruling that Vichy was not an ideologically hegemonic state, many noted, the judges guaranteed that no French person could be accused of crimes against humanity. "Beyond judicial considerations, and beyond the Touvier case itself," wrote the renowned critic Tzvetan Todorov, author of a book on moral life in Nazi concentration camps,

the court sought to absolve and even to exonerate Vichy. This is why the judges took advantage of the occasion to issue with their ruling a lengthy analysis of French politics during the war, in the face of which the reader must wonder whether bad faith has triumphed over ignorance, or the reverse.

*Le Monde*'s Frappat concurred. "Touvier would have had to answer for his crimes if he had been German, but being French, and a murderer of French Jews, he is liable today only for a peaceful old age. One can easily imagine how this distinction will be received in Germany." His outrage extended to the court's assessment that Vichy had not been officially anti-Semitic. "So much for the Jewish Statute!" he wrote. For Bredin, the ruling "abused" history, the law, and justice.

Neither the Jewish Statute, promulgated in October 1940, nor the yellow star, nor the totality of Vichy texts excluding the Jews, nor the organized mass arrests, nor the massacres—such as the one the court acknowledged was ordered by Touvier— were judged to be adequate to assume the status of "an official proclamation" of anti-Semitism.

No anti-Semitic ideology in Vichy France? At this point, even the most impartial reader is left wondering.[32]

The decision manifested the problematic relationship between history, the law, and memory, and critics inveighed against the judges' "revision" of the Vichy epoch, their "rehabilitation" of the Vichy regime and foray into the domain of historians. "What is especially worth criticizing in the judges is not that they wrote bad history," said Todorov, "it's that they wrote history at all, instead of being content to apply the law equitably and universally." This was not the first time either that the law had been called upon to adjudicate history or that reservations had been raised about the competence of judges to evaluate the past. Concern about the blurred boundaries between the two had been raised in debates surrounding the Barbie trial, the indictments of Leguay, Papon, and Bousquet, and in disputes over how to respond to the revisionist theses of people like Faurisson. After the passage of the Gayssot law in July 1990, the courts were legally obligated to intervene in disputes about the past. The judges might have "played historians," wrote *L'Express* journalist Eric Conan, "but for years we [*on*] have been encouraging justice to pronounce history to such a degree that the law now recognizes this right."[33]

## Jewish Identity, French Identity, and Responsibility

Touvier's arrest and the *non-lieu* stimulated further debate among Jews about when and how to emphasize their Jewishness, and the vibrancy of these discussions showed that Jews continued to espouse widely varying notions of how to integrate Jewish and French identity. Some, such as professor Jean-Marc Chouraqui, praised the new Jewish assertiveness. After emancipation, he wrote, Jews seemed to accept liberty at the cost of identity. They felt like freed slaves, and in their commitment to assimilation they demonstrated a deference to their liberators that created a non-juridical but no less pernicious form of psychological alienation. "Two centuries later, for twenty years or so, French Jews appear to have been emancipated from the notion of emancipation . . . Politically, the Jews have been citizens for two centuries; mentally, one could say in the extreme, they have been citizens for a few years." Others, in the spirit of Finkielkraut, challenged the very idea of Jewish particularity in a France where Jews and non-Jews shared the same values and where the constant assertion of Jewish suffering was a weak basis for identity. "All exaltation and delight in Jewish exceptionalness and Jews' inability to be tolerated will never reap more than what has been sowed by others but what the celebration cultivates: absolute difference," wrote one critic in *Tribune Juive*. Jews and non-Jews are "French first, of the same country and the same language, the same culture and the same system of government, the same future," and differences that are enriching rather than divisive should be cultivated from this collective endowment.[34]

While student reactions revealed little anguish over how to be both Jewish and French, Théo Klein's response to the ruling demonstrated the persistence of this tension. A former president of the CRIF, Klein had been behind the 1989 letter criticizing Mitterrand for inviting Arafat to the Elysée, a letter in which the Jewish community stressed that it was indignant "because our dignity as citizens has been impugned." In a short essay, *Oublier Vichy? (Forget Vichy?)*, published in October 1992, he underscored the importance of being French to what might otherwise have appeared a Jewish response to the Touvier decision, and he emphasized that the matter interested him more as a French citizen than as a Jew. In the second chapter, titled "I Refuse to Judge This Affair as a Jew," he explained that he was concerned "as a Jew" with events in Israel, "[b]ut here I am moved as a French citizen." He quoted a letter in which a Jewish friend who had been a volunteer in the Resistance and a deportee at Buchenwald accused the panel of judges of torturing, deporting, and assassinating his fallen comrades a second time. The letter, emphasized Klein, "is not intrinsically the reaction of a Jew. It is a reaction of the wounded French citizen, gripped by his honor as a French person. I understand it and I share it. . . . "[35] That the letter had been authored by someone deported as a member of the Resistance and not as a Jew underscored Klein's belief that French, not Jewish, identity was central to his and other Jews' outrage at the court's decision, just as it had provoked their resentment over Arafat's visit to Paris.[36]

Nonetheless, Klein mused in various sections of the book about the meaning of both the Touvier decision and the Vichy era for French Jewry. In a short chapter entitled "As a Jew This Time," he argued that although there were multiple opinions in the French Jewish community, "a sort of instinct" among Jews meant that certain events, such as the recent ruling, would be experienced similarly. And "as a Jew," he criticized the court's dismissal of the case. For Klein, who characterized himself as a "French person whose parents, grandparents, and great-grandparents since the French Revolution were French" and who recalled being separated from children his age during World War II because he was Jewish, the suggestion that Vichy had not been officially anti-Semitic was insulting. But what Jews felt most, he emphasized, was their disappointment in France.

For the Jews, democracy was the true France, the very picture of the France of the Rights of Man, the France of the Revolution, the France that knew how to win not only wars but the respect of the world . . . It was this France that for them was the true France, as it is for me the true France, humiliated by the Touvier decision.

As several had made clear in the wake of the Six-Day War, de Gaulle's embargo on arms to Israel in 1969, and then again during the Barbie controversy, and as others had implied in discussions about Touvier, many Jews continued to distinguish between "official France" and "true France" and to place their faith firmly in the latter. They could criticize the ruling, along with much of the rest of the nation, and at the same time honor the France to which they had committed themselves for over two hundred years because Vichy and the *non-lieu* were false representations of "true France."[37]

The ruling also provoked discussions about national identity, especially in the wake of the Maastricht Treaty. A petition entitled "We Accuse"—an

obvious allusion to Emile Zola's essay "J'Accuse," written during the Dreyfus Affair—charged the justices with having put France, "in the era of Europe, in a scandalous situation vis-à-vis democratic Germany." Thomas Ferenczi argued in *Le Monde* that both the ruling and the treaty should open a
debate about "the idea we might construct of France and its future." Unfortunately, he lamented, the magistrates were not afraid to give to the rest of
Europe the image of a country "that does not intend to justify to anybody
what it did a long time ago and prefers to take refuge in the heavy silence of
memory." Without openly admitting it, mused Todorov, the French "are
feeling threatened in their national identity and seek to soothe themselves
by attempting to reappropriate their memory." Soon, he remarked, the state
will be only one authority among many.

But "Europe" cannot arouse the same kind of identification as "France," and so
"France" will remain. Like the other European nations of tomorrow, it will be more
a cultural and less an administrative entity . . . [T]his is a change of some magnitude, and we should not be surprised if it provokes tense identity crises. In this part
of Europe, when the rest of the continent is boiling, we will have to learn all over
again how to experience our collective belonging.[38]

At risk in a unified Europe, according to Todorov, was an idea of Frenchness based on the political autonomy normally associated with the nation-
state; indeed, part of what was at stake in the Touvier controversy was the
very meaning of "France" as a distinct entity. Those critical of the judges argued, as did Jacques Coubard in *L'Humanité*, that the decision should be
challenged "in the name of a certain idea of France, its honor, humanistic
values, respect of liberties." Others bemoaned the "uncertain idea of France"
reflected not in the judges' ruling but in the public's overwhelming reaction
against it. *Figaro Magazine* columnist Alain Griotteray, for example, fulminated against those who claimed that "the trial of Vichy" had never taken
place and decried all the talk about the Jewish Statute, "which a healthy reflex to conserve national unity had prompted everybody to relegate to the
innermost depths of collective memory."[39] As Todorov wrote, because Europe could not "arouse the same identification as France"—indeed, because
Europe had for so long served as a collective within which France sought to
forge a distinct identity—conservative segments of the French population
were seeking in a variety of ways to preserve a particular French past, one
that celebrated France, French identity, and the exclusion of all things not
French. At the same time, others closer to the Left continued to distance
themselves from social institutions and denounced the decision. More comfortable with the increasingly global character of everyday life and critical of
an exclusive sense of French identity, they were less concerned with defending cultural and political autonomy than with constructing a new Europe.

Thus the dismissal of the Touvier case served in part as a discursive site for debates about European consolidation.

"How can we demand that Germany rid itself of old demons if France is not resolved to battle its own?" asked Ferenczi in *Le Monde*. Clearly the *non-lieu* also challenged the moral authority that the nation had assumed during the Barbie trial. It threatened to dissolve the bond between France and the Resistance and at the same time to undermine the nation's identification with Jews, the *victims* of Nazism. Though popular discourse was critical of collaboration and the postwar myth that assumed a nation comprised primarily of resisters, powerful voices argued that the net of complicity should not be cast to encompass France entire. A clear distinction should be made, they contended, between *la France sous Vichy* (France *under* Vichy) and *la France de Vichy* (the France *of* Vichy, or Vichy France). *Le Nouvel Observateur*, for example, featured a set of articles on the Vél d'Hiv roundup entitled "France and the Jews Under Vichy," while Robert Toubon wrote in *Le Quotidien de Paris* of a divide "definitively drawn between [the] immense majority and the minority who, at Vichy and in the administration, dishonored themselves and France." Well-known Resistance fighter Jacques Baumel acknowledged that in 1940, "France was crushed by the mechanical superiority of the invader and the incompetence of its leaders." But "in its depths," he stressed, France "did not wallow in collaboration." There was, agreed Papon's attorney Jean-Marc Varaut, an "implicit resistance in which everyone participated."[40]

Many Jews, for whom "Vichy France" had been "official France" while "France under Vichy" had represented "true France," were among the most vociferous proponents of the distinction between the Vichy state and the French people. Klein argued that while not too many non-Jews had been courageous, life had not been easy for them, either. The vast majority "lived day to day, preoccupied with getting food and waiting for the end of this parenthesis in history. And I would not be opposed to it being said that it was France through its state that went wrong and not the French as a whole." Klarsfeld, an outspoken Jewish activist on Holocaust issues and a relentless hunter of alleged criminals against humanity, argued that "Vichy effectively contributed to the loss of 75,000 Jews and the French effectively assisted in the rescue of three-quarters of the Jews of France." He pointed out that France was the country where Jews had "the least bad" survival rate, which indicated that France "did not cooperate in its depths . . . If Vichy did not carry out collaboration with the Germans to the end, it is because the reactions of the French population checked and at times discouraged it." What Klarsfeld and others disputed was the claim that Vichy had not been a legitimate French government and therefore required no formal acknowledgment. "Certainly, Vichy was not the Republic," wrote Klein, but "we must accept Vichy as we must accept all the somber pages in the history of France. Even if I prefer Danton and see myself more in Gambetta, I can forget neither Robespierre and the Terror nor Thiers and the Commune."[41]

But precisely who was accountable for the persecution and deportation of Jews—and, by extension, for French collaboration—was nearly impossible to determine from public discourse. If France was simultaneously "on trial" and "against Vichy," if France had been "struck by amnesia" and at the same time "felt shamed" by the court's decision, who, exactly, was "France"? How could "France" be used synonymously with "Vichy" and as a bulwark against Vichy ideology? Did "Vichy" mean the epoch, as in "during Vichy," the government, as in "the Vichy regime," or France after the armistice, as in "Vichy France"? When Prime Minister Pierre Bérégovoy declared to the National Assembly that "France feels wounded" by the court's ruling, of which France was he speaking? When the esteemed writer and columnist Jean-François Revel suggested that "[w]e are dealing less with a rehabilitation of Vichy than with a fear of having known it too well," precisely whom did he mean by "we"?[42] There was broad accord that the *non-lieu* had failed to assign responsibility for collaboration but far less agreement on whether fault rested with "France," "the French," or "Vichy," all of which had become nebulous abstractions in light of the court's decision. Conventions of language meant that the boundaries between the Republic, the nation, and the state were as impossible to define as responsibility was to attribute. Remorse was conspicuously absent because the guilty party was so difficult to decipher. As had been true in the controversies surrounding Le Pen, the public condemned Vichy but did not grapple with the moral complexities of occupation and collaboration, including the relative innocence or complicity of French citizens during the war. The court and Le Pen were the outsiders, anachronistic holdouts from a France long dead, and the rejection of both the ruling and the FN substituted for critical engagement with the Vichy epoch.

Asked by *Le Nouvel Observateur* whether it was not time for "the French people" to confess the complicity of the French government in the Holocaust, André Frossard responded:

But who is going to represent the people? In any case, one is not going to demand that the president of the Republic ask for pardon. He is not guilty. Besides, to ask for pardon "in the name of the French people" would be to accept that they are all guilty, which is false . . . It seems to me that the French can feel guilty but not responsible.

My dignity as a Frenchman is offended by the Jewish Statute under Vichy. It dishonors our two heritages, the Christian and the Revolutionary. But we still cannot ask for a major ceremony of expiation. We must not confound the French people who endured Vichy and the occupation and the people who, on the other side of the Rhine, voted for Hitler . . . The Vichy regime is to be reviled, but one cannot revile the French people.[43]

Frossard insisted that it was essential to distinguish the French population from the Vichy administration. To ask for pardon "in the name of the French people" would be inappropriate, as it would falsely suggest that the French people were guilty when it was the government that had been responsible. He also argued that the distinction between "the French" and "the Germans" must be maintained, that regardless of the transgressions of certain French people, "the French" could not be likened morally to either Vichy or the German population. Germans, the perpetrators, had invited Nazism by voting for Hitler; French people, the victims, had "endured" Vichy and the occupation.[44] Frossard had argued just after the publication of the historians' commission report that to implicate the Church every time someone religious did something indefensible was "as absurd as if one accused the Republic each time that a mayor or municipal councilor was mixed up in an affair."[45] In the debate provoked by the *non-lieu*, "France" could be blamed for the crimes of collaboration no more than the Church could be deemed liable for the actions of clergymen who had assisted Touvier. The president of the Republic, as both the elected representative of the French people and the chief of the French state, could seek pardon for the actions of neither the population *under* Vichy nor the France *of* Vichy. What Frossard seemed to be arguing was that institutions or abstractions — France, the Church, the Republic — could not be held accountable for the conduct of those who acted in their name. The dilemma, then, was how to attribute historical responsibility in a meaningful way.

In November, the Final Court of Appeals partially overturned the lower court's decision. The Final Court accepted the latter's reasoning in the April ruling, including its conclusion that Vichy had not constituted a state practicing ideological hegemony, but argued that the judges had been too hasty in dismissing the Rillieux murders as a war crime. If it could be proven that Touvier had acted in collaboration not with Vichy but with Nazi Germany, an ideologically hegemonic state, he would be guilty of crimes against humanity. Touvier had acknowledged since 1959 his role in the Rillieux affair, but he claimed that he had been forced to carry out the executions by the regional head of the Lyon Milice, who himself was taking orders from the Nazis. What he had thought would exonerate him — the German order — ultimately served as the grounds on which he could be prosecuted for crimes against humanity. The problem was that the original case against him contended in clear terms that he had acted not at the behest of the Nazis but on his own initiative. As of the Final Court's ruling in November 1992, however, the German order of which there existed "no trace" needed to materialize in order for Touvier to be convicted. The prosecution team then set itself to proving exactly the opposite of what the examining judge had maintained, namely that Touvier had acted on behalf of the Nazi regime. In March 1994, Touvier would stand trial in Versailles for the 1944 murder of seven Jews. In the courtroom, the divide between the nation and the state would widen and the tensions between law, history, and memory become even more acute.

## The Touvier Trial

In the months preceding the trial, Holocaust imagery was pervasive. Between May 1992 and February 1994, the widely viewed television program "La Marche du Siècle" devoted six features to World War II, four of which placed strong emphasis on the Holocaust, and the respected journal *Esprit* published three special issues on Vichy and the Jews.[46] Memory associations multiplied, and the night before the trial, the group "Duty to Remember" organized a symbolic renaming of rue Alexis Carrel, a street in Paris's fifteenth district named for the 1912 Nobel prize-winning French doctor whose eugenic writings were inaccurately said to have been implemented by the Vichy regime. An exposition entitled "History and Memory: The Internment Camps of the Loiret, 1941–43," was scheduled for Paris that summer, and Klarsfeld's exhibition, "The Time of the Roundups," was displayed next to the Versailles courthouse where Touvier was tried. At the end of March, Simone Veil helped to inaugurate a monument to the victims of Bergen-Belsen at the Parisian cemetery Père Lachaise, and Steven Spielberg's "Schindler's List" played to an enthusiastic public throughout the trial. A Louis Harris/*Globe Hebdo*/Fun Radio poll indicated that nearly two-thirds of the adult population thought it necessary to try "former collaborators, Nazis, or *miliciens* of the Vichy regime." Fifty-four percent of the respondents agreed that "the Vichy regime was complicitous with the Nazis" while only nineteen percent supported the immediate postwar thesis that "the Vichy regime tried to limit the number of victims." Young people were especially inclined to indict Vichy. Only members of the FN in their majority (fifty-eight percent) said that the trial was unnecessary.[47]

The proceedings took place amidst a growing hostility among Jews that recently had become a national controversy. The first day of Passover, when Jews celebrate their freedom from slavery and exodus from Egypt, fell that March on the same day as the second round of local elections. Grand Rabbi Sitruk, an advocate of the ultra-orthodox, asked Jews to honor Jewish law (which, in his estimation, forbade driving, writing, and speaking to non-

Jews on holy days) and to abstain from voting. "Would Christians think it acceptable if the elections were held on Easter?" he asked in a rhetorical question that confirmed not only the prominence of the strictly observant in the Jewish community but the degree to which Jews with varying commitments were willing to challenge the Republic. By contrast, CRIF president Jean Kahn urged his coreligionists to fulfill their obligation as citizens by voting. A protracted debate ensued, prompting *Libération* to suggest that the French Jewish community had never been in such disorder. In the elections for Grand Rabbi that June, Sitruk defeated his more moderate challenger, Gilles Bernheim. Arguing that Jews should "integrate" but not "assimilate," nonetheless, even Bernheim distanced himself from the long-standing notion of assimilation. Critics in the national press worried about the "identity strain" and the "rise of anti-modernism" among Jews. "Can one ask a religious community, in the name of internal rules, to put itself at odds with the Republic, to be a pariah in the nation?" asked *Le Monde*. Jews have always lived between particularism and universalism, and at the moment, the former seems to be winning. The central question for Jews today, contended *Le Nouvel Observateur*, is "what does it mean to be Jewish *and* French?"[48]

More secular Jews, such as Klein, agreed that the diaspora was suffering from terrible anxiety. Anti-Semitism was not a problem, communities outside of Israel were assured of their safety by democracies, and younger generations of Jews were haunted less and less by the immense shadow of the Holocaust. Today, argued Klein, Jews in France are threatened not with physical harm but with "psychological insecurity." One woman criticized Jewish schools for no longer teaching the "double culture" of French Jews and feared allowing her daughter to play with observant children, for whom, she said, visiting a goy (non-Jew) on the Sabbath was a sin. Concerned about Jewish isolation, she and her husband sent their daughter to a public school and made arrangements for her to be excused on Jewish holidays. Several commentators, including Bernheim and *Tribune Juive* editorialist Raphael Drai, argued that the Jews should serve as a "precedent" for other religious communities, especially the growing Muslim minority. We have a "republican responsibility" that stems from the Revolution, argued Finkielkraut.

It is especially important that the Jews provide a model of integration for Muslims. But religious Jews wanted to profit from the veil affair and the burgeoning of Islam to advance their vision of a society split into separate communities, which nourishes an extremely unhealthy climate.[49]

Quick to demand their religious rights and a strict observance of Jewish law, the ultra-orthodox were far less inclined to speak out on issues that had little to do with religion. During the Touvier trial, therefore, they were content to praise France for having the courage to face a dark moment in its past. Sitruk, for example, expressed his admiration "for a France loyal to its democratic ideal." At the same time, continuing the more militant strain in Jewish politics first apparent in the debates after the rue Copernic attack, some activists did not hesitate to denounce what they saw as leaders' continued deference to France at the expense of a strong cultural or political Jewish identity. Among the criticism expressed was a letter written to *Actualité Juive* by a member of the association of Sons and Daughters of the Deported Jews of France (FFDJF), who complained of the "total defection" of Jewish leadership. "It's pitiful," he wrote. "I hope that community leaders are going to get a hold of themselves quickly and put in a token appearance at the doors of the Palais de Justice." Meanwhile, in a *Le Monde* interview during the trial, Israeli philosopher and Auschwitz survivor Yehuda Elkana blasted the "genocide cult, especially among those who did not live through it," for creating "an intolerable Jewish moral hubris" and "an arrogance that pretends to find legitimacy in eternal persecution." When asked what would tie Jews together in the absence of Holocaust memory, Elkana replied: "I don't want Jews to have only the memory of atrocities in common."[50]

When the trial began, newspapers throughout the country spoke of "history accused," the "lessons of history," and "history before its judges." *Evénement Junior* and *Infos Junior* ran special sections explaining the trial to young people. Many noted that the average age of the jurors was forty-one; while some critics questioned how individuals who had not lived through Vichy, occupation, liberation, and the postwar purge could comprehend the complexity of the epoch, others found their youth symbolic of the trial's didactic mission. Touvier's prosecution was an opportunity to "deliver to French young people a gigantic course in history and civics, as was the case in the Barbie trial," said Dimitri Nicolaidis, historian and editor of the forthcoming *Oublier nos crimes: L'Amnésie nationale, un spécificité française? (Forgetting Our Crimes: National Amnesia, a French Specificity?)* But critics continued to worry about the contradictions between law, memory, and history. As Pierre Vidal-Naquet wrote during the trial, history is usually written *after* justice is rendered, but the opposite was true in Touvier's case, and the consequences were potentially damaging to both. Sensing the degree to which Vichy's persecution and deportation of Jews had become a screen for anxieties about national identity, historian Annette Wieviorka worried that the Holocaust, perpetrated largely by Germany, was beginning to look like a consequence of French civil wars, an account to be settled internal to France. For some, including Alfred Grosser, a scholar of modern Germany, and writer and former government minister Max Gallo, Vichy had become a scapegoat that concealed "a strong French continuity," a French anti-Semitism that had been apparent long before World War II.

The trial, argued Gallo, should not conceal the fact that Vichy was "a parox-ysmal but not aberrant moment that is indicative of national history."[51]

By most accounts in public discourse, Touvier was being tried for French complicity in the Holocaust and Vichy's crime of collaboration; yet, legally speaking, he was on trial for neither. Instead, he stood accused of ordering the murder of seven Jews in retribution for the assassination of Vichy min-ister Philippe Henriot. Was "the miniature genocide" at Rillieux, as *Le Monde*'s Bertrand Poirot-Delpech posed the question, as systematic and bar-barous as the "big genocide?" Historian Rousso argued that the Jewish vic-tims surely had not been chosen arbitrarily but that their deaths "were not exactly part of the Final Solution," which implied systematic, industrial killing of humans just because they were born. "In principle *no* Jew was to escape the fanaticism of the Nazis. Rillieux was a crime committed in the *context* of a mass persecution."[52] Although the Milice had been created and administered by Vichy, moreover, it had become largely autonomous in its day-to-day functioning by the time of the Rillieux incident. An historically accurate account, then, would emphasize not Vichy's responsibility but rather Touvier's virtual detachment from the regime. Yet this would detract from popular desire to see not simply Touvier but Vichy indicted. Finally, how could the trial of France take place and French responsibility be as-sessed in proceedings where guilt depended on complicity not with Vichy but Germany?

By the time of the trial, it had become clear that both history and the law would be sacrificed for a memory in which the Holocaust and Touvier, and therefore the Vichy regime, would be repudiated. Leguay was dead, and in June 1993, Bousquet had been assassinated in his Paris home.[53] Alleged to have orchestrated the Vél d'Hiv roundup, Bousquet had been the highest-ranking official to be indicted for crimes against humanity and widely con-sidered the best representative of French responsibility for the Final Solu-tion. Papon, moreover, was eighty-three years old, and after fourteen years of investigation, his case remained buried in a judicial morass. At the mo-ment, it seemed that Touvier was the only candidate, however inadequate, to assume the mantle of French guilt. Countless juxtaposed photos of Tou-vier, Bousquet, Papon, and Leguay, as well as headlines reading—"Touvier, the Trial of Vichy," "Touvier Judged, France Accused," "The Trial of France"—suggested that the former *milicien* had come to personify French betrayal.[54] The courts had ruled explicitly and consistently that France was immune from crimes against humanity charges, that Vichy officials could be found guilty of such crimes only if it could be demonstrated that they had collaborated with Nazi Germany. Despite the headlines, therefore, nei-ther Vichy nor "France" was on trial. At one point during the proceedings, to the horror of his colleagues (and to the delight of the press), civil party attorney Arno Klarsfeld, Serge's son, dismissed the idea of a German order as ridiculous and argued that the Rillieux assassinations had been the Milice's autonomous response to the assassination of a Vichy minister. Nevertheless, he concluded, if there had been no German order in the Rillieux affair, the Milice was acting in "general complicity" with the Nazis, and Touvier was guilty of crimes against humanity. While Klarsfeld's remarks might appear contradictory on legal grounds, they nonetheless made sense in the register of historical explanation. "The divergence between historical analysis and the rhetorical necessities of a court are now obvious," wrote Rousso after Klarsfeld's presentation. The ultimate absurdity, he added, is that if Touvier acted alone, the jurors have to decide that "to kill without constraint is less serious than to have been an accomplice."[55]

The decline of political institutions and the dilution of moral authority that so many commentators had pointed out after the Carpentras attack continued to be a source of concern. The Republic is no longer the invulnerable block that it was under Gaullism, said Nicolaïdis, and France is in the middle of a real identity crisis. *L'Événement du Jeudi* featured a provocative story entitled "The France that the Young No Longer Desire," in which it decried the incongruity between the rhetoric that told young people they would be the architects of a united Europe and France's inability, manifested in the trial and the debates surrounding it, to overcome its own internal divisions. Critics on the Right vigorously denounced the "foreign influences" that encouraged the frenzy to divide and deny the honor of France. A cartoon in *Rivarol* portrayed a teacher addressing three students after showing "Night and Fog." "So, you understand, never again, right?" she asked them. "Don't worry, we'll watch him," replied two presumably African students, pointing at a white student. "So that he won't be an accomplice of the Nazis, like Touvier." Hopefully, said Jean-Marc Varaut, Papon's attorney, the Touvier proceedings will "put an end to the masochistic trial that France is conducting against itself."[56]

Touvier was found guilty and sentenced to life in prison April 20. That same day, immediately following the verdict, protests were held demanding the trial of Papon.

## The Nation, the State, and the Politics of Memory

In the late 1980s, and then following the pillage at Carpentras, denunciation of Le Pen had enabled many French people to renounce racism, anti-Semitism, and the Holocaust without contemplating a sense of accountability for or connection to racists, anti-Semites, and the Vichy officials and French people who had collaborated with the Nazis. Increasingly pervasive rhetoric during the Touvier polemics cemented another discursive divide, between the Vichy regime and the French under Vichy, which served a similar function: condemnation of an ambiguous "Vichy" and "Vichy France" and a far more precise differentiation of the French people from the Vichy regime allowed the nation to distinguish itself from perpetrators, to understand itself as having suffered under its leaders, and to be validated in a popular discourse that honored victims. It echoed many Jews' insistence that "official France" and "true France" were not the same, a distinction underscored in Claude Chabrol's 1993 release, "L'Oeil de Vichy" (The Eye of Vichy). "This film shows France not as it was between 1940 and 1944," reads an on-screen quotation in the opening moments, "but as Pétain and the collaborators wanted it to be seen." As historian Henri Amouroux told *Tribune Juive*, those who "instigated, decided, imposed, and executed" were suspect, but the conscience of the French was clear.[57]

In the period between Touvier's arrest in 1989 and the trial in 1994, a new narrative in public discourse implied that the French people had been victims of Vichy and that resistance on a small scale, even among those not officially affiliated with the Resistance, had been common. Historical texts, films, and news stories centered on how Vichy had harassed the French population and on what the French victims of Vichy had done to save the Jewish victims of Vichy. Marek Halter's film "*Tzedek*: Les Justes" (*Tzedek*: The Just Ones), which focused on the righteous in France and elsewhere who had hidden, rescued, or otherwise assisted Jews during the war, made tangible this image of suffering non-Jewish French citizens reaching out to their anguished Jewish compatriots. Human interest stories following the film's release emphasized the existence of heroes throughout France. And in an ironic twist that demonstrated the appeal of the concurrent victim/resister, Touvier's chief attorney used as his primary defense the argument that while the Gestapo had asked for 100 Jews and another Milice official had asked for thirty, Touvier had killed only seven in an effort to save twenty-three. "My client is Schindler!" he claimed, referring to the popular film "Schindler's List" in which a member of the Nazi party seemingly complied with Nazi policy while saving Jews.[58]

At the same time that they lauded the French people for their resistance to the Vichy administration, moreover, newspapers and magazines made an increasing abstraction of "the victims" of Rillieux. Though they turned repeatedly to imagery of the Holocaust, they spoke just as often without direct reference either to Jews or the Nazi genocide. Two weeks into the trial, Poirot-Delpech disparaged the popular homogenization of historical experience and disregard for differences in human suffering. The civil parties establish that Vichy made victims of the Jews while the defense expresses compassion for *all* the victims of the war, he wrote. "Media *bombardment* =

Dresden = Auschwitz."⁵⁹ This fetishization of victims was possible because much of the nation identified not with the perpetrators of Vichy, the France *of* Vichy, but with the victims of Vichy, the French *under* Vichy. It had its roots in public debates surrounding the Six-Day War, when Jewish identification with victims of the Nazi genocide led eventually to anti-Israeli sympathy for the Arab victims of Jewish Nazism. It was buttressed by events in the 1980s in which claims to past or current oppression gained political currency: in frequent debates about and demonstrations against apartheid, Israeli treatment of Palestinians, racism, and terrorism; in indictments of alleged French war criminals; and in discussions surrounding the Barbie trial. Controversy concerning Le Pen, epitomized in the aftermath of Carpentras, made present and corporeal a perpetrator with whom most people could claim no relationship, and the association of Le Pen with Vichy in the debates that followed created even further distance between most French people and any sense of connection to the actions or philosophy of the Vichy regime. The disavowal of Vichy exercised in the rejection of Le Pen made possible during the Touvier affair a more explicit condemnation of the Vichy government and identification with Jews threatened by the regime.

Yet Touvier was a weak proxy for Vichy or France because neither the regime nor the country was implicated in the trial. By insisting that France and Vichy were on trial when they had been eliminated from consideration in controversy that few could have ignored, the nation could simultaneously incriminate and absolve the France of World War II in much the same way that men like Bousquet, in the immediate postwar trials, had been found guilty of treason and immediately exculpated for acts of resistance. The indictments were ultimately meaningless. The intensity and persistence with which the trial was touted as a reckoning with the French past suggested a simultaneous desire to repudiate Vichy and to avoid wrestling with the complexity of collaboration. As the hearings were taking place, in fact, more critical voices lamented the trial's inability to address the real dilemmas stemming from World War II and the nation's "cowardly sense of relief." Nothing in this trial, wrote Sorj Chalandon in *Libération*, "touches the machinery of the Vichy state." For Guy Sorman, a writer and respected professor of politics, a better defendant would have been Bousquet or Papon, someone who represented the continuity between the Third Republic, Vichy, and the Fourth and Fifth Republics. Clearly Touvier is a crook, he wrote, but

what guarantee do we have that the prefect, the *Conseil dEtat* member, and the police captain who are now in office are not cast from the same mold as their predecessors and would not be capable of repeating the same crimes, in the name of "French state continuity," if a new debacle presented itself?

Among our elites at this very moment, he went on, "how many Bousquets are in power and how many Jean Moulins? One Jean Moulin for every 100 Bousquets, or the opposite? I would like to know." In the events leading up to the trial, the Holocaust had become symbolic of Vichy and the victimization of the national population at the hands of the Vichy government; by the end of the Papon trial fewer than four years later, the Holocaust would stand not just for the Vichy regime but for the French state throughout history.[60]

## CHAPTER SEVEN

# Mitterrand, Papon, and the Politics of Historical Responsibility

In the midst of the outrage surrounding the Touvier dismissal, *Le Monde* editor Edwy Plenel wondered what would become of President Mitterrand's Armistice Day tradition of placing flowers on Pétain's tomb, "this year, in 1992, fifty years after the major Parisian roundups, Vél d'Hiv."[1] Little could Plenel have imagined the commotion that would surround both the Vél d'Hiv commemoration in July and the president's November ritual of paying homage to the hero of Verdun. These events, yet another chapter in the Vichy-Holocaust drama, were only the beginning of Mitterrand's engagement as its tragic hero. The climax of this tragedy would come with Pierre Péan's biography of the young Mitterrand, *Une jeunesse française (A French Youth): François Mitterrand, 1934–47*, in September 1994, when the media began to judge the aging president's life and political career exclusively in their relationship to the Vichy regime. The nation's World War II drama, however, continued through the end of the decade, highlighted by the trial of Papon after more than sixteen years of judicial investigation.

Mitterrand's presidency proved to be a remarkably poignant moment in French history. His second term, which coincided with a spate of fifty-year World War II anniversaries, served as a nodal point where multiple societal narratives converged on the Holocaust, where a syllogistically arranged set of narrative equivalences were pervasive in national discourse:

Holocaust = victimization (after the rue Copernic bombing)
Holocaust = Vichy

Vichy = State (during the Touvier affair)

Holocaust = State

Mitterrand = Vichy and State (during the Mitterrand controversies)

Mitterrand = Holocaust

By the end of the Touvier trial, the Holocaust was not only a metaphor for victimization but also a metonym for Vichy. As a president of the Republic whose links to the Vichy regime became front-page news, Mitterrand came symbolically to stand for the Holocaust, thereby enabling the themes of Holocaust discourse that had been developing since the Six-Day War to converge in a critical analysis of both his politics and character. Fewer than two years after he died, Papon's trial provided the opportunity—denied by the death of Leguay, the assassination of Bousquet, and Touvier's nebulous connection to the Vichy regime—to declare definitively not only Vichy's guilt but the culpability of the French state.

## *Vél d'Hiv*

The court's dismissal of the Touvier case in April 1992 had provoked widespread public consternation because it seemed deliberately designed to exonerate France from any responsibility for Vichy or the Holocaust. With a trial apparently unlikely and other avenues of redress uncertain, there seemed to be nowhere to turn but to the chief of the French Republic for some official admission of France's role in the wartime persecution of Jews. On June 15, just two months after the Touvier ruling and one month before the fiftieth anniversary of the Vél d'Hiv roundup, over 200 well known figures from politics, culture, academe, and the media—known as the "Vél d'Hiv Committee"—issued an appeal asking Mitterrand to officially acknowledge Vichy's crimes against the Jews. Among the signatories were friends and supporters of the president and several moderate voices, including philosopher Pascal Bruckner, Jean Daniel, and Pierre Vidal-Naquet, who in the past had openly criticized many of the assumptions driving "memory discourse" in France.[2] The appeal argued that at the end of the war, "certain top officials in the French state of Vichy" were justifiably found guilty for treason, but "the highest governmental authorities of the Republic still have neither officially acknowledged nor proclaimed that this same French state of Vichy committed persecutions and crimes against Jews only because they were Jews." On its own initiative, the appeal went on, Vichy separated the Jews from the rest of the national community by passing the Jewish Statute, "signed and promulgated by Pétain, 'marshal of France, chief of the French state.'" This state then systematically discriminated against Jews, ordered their arrest by the French police, and sent them to French concentration camps. Ultimately, it contributed to the arrest and deportation of 75,000 French, foreign, and denaturalized Jews.

On the occasion of the fiftieth anniversary of the Vél d'Hiv roundup next July 16 and 17, we ask that the president of the Republic, chief of state, acknowledge and officially proclaim that the French state of Vichy is responsible for persecutions and crimes committed against the Jews of France.

This symbolic act is required for the memory of victims and their descendants. It is also required for French collective memory, sick with the unsaid.

It is, finally, the very idea of the French Republic, faithful to its founding principles, that is at stake.

What the signatories sought was official recognition of official wrongdoing, state acknowledgment of state crimes. In a television interview on Bastille Day, just two days before the scheduled Vél d'Hiv commemoration, Mitterrand rejected the appeal by distinguishing between the Republic, "which, legally speaking, did what it had to do," and the French state. "It was the Vichy regime in 1940," he said. "It was not the Republic . . . So don't ask the Republic for an explanation." The Vél d'Hiv Committee then issued a statement contending that "the French state is accountable for all that was done in the name of France" and that to solemnly acknowledge this responsibility was "to remain faithful to the republican ideal and to the memory of those who resisted the Nazis and their accomplices." The Committee's tone, represented in the shift from speaking of "the French state of Vichy" to "the French state," made clear that the Holocaust had now become a standoff between the president of the Republic and those who demanded the Republic's assumption of Vichy's crimes. Mitterrand, according to Daniel, had transformed a moderate and rather banal appeal into a controversy, and "divisions on this subject do not separate French Jews from other French people. The first are as equally divided as the second. It is truly a common national drama: the drama of our history."[3]

July 16, the fiftieth anniversary of Vél d'Hiv, was a day packed with commemorative ceremonies throughout France,[4] but the central event was the solemnization held on the former site of the Vélodrome d'Hiver, the bicycle stadium where Jews arrested in the roundup first had been sent. Among those in attendance were the presidents of the National Assembly, the Senate, and the Constitutional Council, several government ministers, and the archbishop and Muslim leader of Paris. Citing a schedule conflict, Mitterrand had declined an invitation to participate; a week before the ceremony, however, he announced that he would attend, thereby becoming the first president of the Republic to be present at the annual commemoration. He arrived late and was promptly greeted by boos and cries of "Mitterrand to

Vichy" from several people in the crowd, a notable contrast to the ordinarily respectful treatment accorded French presidents. Members of the radical Zionist group Betar and the Appeal of the 250 Against Fascism were thought to be the instigators, though the latter later denied having taken part.[5] As the jeering intensified, CRIF member Henry Bulawko, a Holocaust survivor and director of the ceremony, seized the microphone, castigated the protesters for having "dishonored the dead," and demanded that they "welcome the president of the Republic in dignity." The ceremony then resumed as a smiling Mitterrand, seated in the first row of dignitaries, fixed his eyes on the podium. When he rose to place a wreath in front of the commemorative plaque, he was heckled once again, though the jeers eventually were drowned out by applause. When it was his turn to speak, Robert Badinter, who was president of the Constitutional Council and whose father had perished at Auschwitz, was livid. "I am ashamed of you!" he cried into the microphone. "Keep quiet or leave this gathering! You dishonor the cause you think you are serving!" He paid tribute to Mitterrand and echoed the president's sentiments. "Whether it is a question of Jews or resisters, the Republic can never be held accountable for the crimes of Vichy officials, its enemies." A photo of an enraged Badinter, finger raised in fury at the protesters, standing behind a podium bearing the picture of what appeared to be a child of the Holocaust, became the most recognizable image of the event.[6]

The day after the ceremony, a *Le Monde* cartoon portrayed a group of people, including a judge and the revolutionary symbol Marianne, addressing a man wearing a Jewish star: "Because we told you we weren't on duty that day!" France, the state, or the Republic: which was responsible? Which was present at the scene of Vichy crimes? Was one accountable for the others? By whom and in whose name should the offenses of the Vichy regime be acknowledged? The Vél d'Hiv Committee appeal set off a painstakingly semantic discourse in which the media, politicians, scholars, intellectuals, and members of the clergy endeavored to assign responsibility for the suffering of Jews in France during World War II, a debate that Plenel characterized as "another dialogue among the deaf about Vichy France."[7] These discussions drew together long-running themes in Holocaust discourse—tensions between history, memory, and the law; popular assertion of victimization; the ongoing effort to articulate a modern French-Jewish identity—as well as issues that had become prominent in the Touvier controversy: the need for national unity and the validity of the Gaullist myth; the division between the population and the state and the extent to which the former felt alienated from the latter; and the relationship between Vichy and French national identity.

Both Jews and non-Jews were divided over how to establish responsibility for Vichy. In July 1940, the parliament of the Third Republic had voted to hand over full governmental powers to Pétain, thereby voting itself out of existence and putting an end to republican rule. For some, therefore, the question was at least partially a legal or constitutional one. The Nazis did not impose the Vichy regime, pointed out Marc Kravetz in *Libération*. Vichy was born from the Republic, made possible by the elected representatives of France, and sustained by "French functionaries" and "French magistrates" who followed the orders of a "French government." But others wondered whether the parliamentary vote had been legitimate. Is the Republic implicated by its representatives under the conditions of military defeat, armistice, and occupation, asked Philippe Rochette, another *Libération* contributor. For former government minister Léo Hamon, there was no continuity between the Republic and the French state of 1940, which came about by "violent usurpation." But, countered Plenel, parliamentary abdication was ultimately what legitimated Pétain and the collaboration. The point is not to condemn the Republic, he wrote in an article whose headline proclaimed the issue of state continuity to be at the heart of the debate, "but to argue for the responsibility of *its* state, functionaries, and high-ranking administration in the crimes committed between 1940 and 1944."[8]

Hamon and several other outspoken Jews were among the most dedicated Mitterrand apologists. Mitterrand "was right to recall that the Republic cannot be held accountable for Vichy crimes," contended Jean Pierre-Bloch, president of LICRA, the International League Against Racism and Antisemitism. "Abandoned by Pétain, the flame of the Republic was kept alive by de Gaulle, free French people, the Resistance, and the French who refused collaboration." Claude Lanzmann argued that the amalgam between the French state and the Republic was biased and that the demand for Mitterrand to officially acknowledge Vichy's crimes was "an insult to Mitterrand the man but also a travesty of the truth, a falsification of history." In a conscientiously precise statement, he asserted that Mitterrand was "chief of state . . . not chief of the French state. The chief of the French state was Pétain. François Mitterrand is the president of the French Republic."[9]

Others, Jews included, countered that the latter could not be exonerated so easily. As Plenel argued, "a French state, which was certainly the negation of the Republic but which was no less French because of it, participated actively in the destruction of the Jews of Europe." Grand Rabbi Sitruk deplored the public's harassment of the president at the commemoration but deemed Mitterrand's response to the appeal "insufficient." And Father Jean Dujardin, who had served as a church liaison to the Touvier historians' commission, suggested that "conscious or not . . . by the intermediary of its governing apparatus in that epoch," France was "complicit . . . in this profound evil." For critics, in other words, to conceptualize the issue of accountability only in legal terms was to deny its political and cultural significance. Mitterrand "responded as a jurist to a moral and political problem," wrote *La Croix*. His remarks were "juridically right," agreed Plenel, but politically and symbolically "inadequate" and "historically false." In protest, the acclaimed film director Marcel Ophuls gave back the prestigious "Prix de la mémoire" he had been awarded for "The Sorrow and the Pity" earlier that spring.[10]

On one point virtually all of the appeal's supporters and detractors agreed: the population could not be conflated with the state. Acts of resistance, mostly on the part of individuals who had been unaffiliated with the official Resistance, were praised throughout the debates. The purpose of an official statement recognizing Vichy crimes, wrote Bruno Frappat in an article entitled "France and France," is

to admit that France, at least in its official representation, was an agent of barbarism. It is not an accusation against the nation as a whole or against the people, among whom there were plenty of individuals to save the honor of the country. It is even less an accusation against the Republic. . . .

Father Dujardin argued that "the French people as a group obviously cannot be considered responsible. They suffered mightily under the occupation. Several men and women paid with their lives for the lucidity of their words and the courage of their acts." Indeed, American historian Robert Paxton, well known for his groundbreaking *Vichy France* in 1972 and *Vichy France and the Jews*, co-authored with Michael Marrus, in 1981, told *Libération* that he regretted not having focused more in the later text on those who rescued Jews. He recounted a conversation in which a former refugee had told him: "All the Jews who died perished because of the Vichy government, but all the Jews who survived did so thanks to the French people."[11]

Again, many prominent Jews argued passionately on behalf of the French population. Vichy was not the only France present during the war, wrote Lanzmann. There was also the France

of the dozens of thousands of women and men, dead under torture, felled by German bullets in the combats of the Resistance and the underground . . . If the French handed over the Jews, others, infinitely more numerous than we now admit, saved them, and there are many of us who can testify to it.

He went on to describe his own experience during the war, where he survived with false papers distributed by officials in small Auvergne villages. "These mayors would have died rather than give us up." Jean Kahn recalled the courage "of all those, just among the just, including certain police functionaries, who saved Jewish lives in spite of the danger." And Hamon pointed out that among the European countries defeated by the Axis, France had the smallest percentage of deported Jews. Germany bears collective responsibility, he said, but not France.[12]

Whether they endorsed or rejected the appeal, Jews were able to participate in a national dialogue in which their Jewish and French identities were not at odds. Because the integrity of the French people was not in question, they could maintain the long-standing distinction between "true France" and "official France" that many first had emphasized in the wake of the Six-Day War. Badinter told the audience at the commemoration ceremony that it was nearly impossible to appreciate what France in the past had represented for so many Jews, whose love for and faith in the country had been immeasurable. It was, he said, not only Jews but a certain idea of France that Vichy had repudiated. Lanzmann, who had claimed to be "too close" to France to address Vichy in "Shoah," underscored the same principle in repeated reference to the "two Frances" he encountered during the war. "I have always said, despite the crimes and horrors of Vichy, that the death camps like Treblinka and Belzec would not have been possible in France. I still believe it, even if I can't prove it."[13]

However, the vision of France as a beacon of universalism was less meaningful, even anachronistic, for younger Jews whose only experience was of a France that, like most other countries, had failed at times to live up to the principles on which it had been founded. Having grown up in the shadow of French colonialism, the atrocities of the Algerian War, racism and anti-immigrant violence, and an ever-more precise accounting of Vichy crimes, their regard for France was more equivocal, without illusion. After the rue Copernic bombing, moreover, it was no longer taboo to claim an identity that was distinct from and even at odds with being French. Young Jews therefore felt less compelled to justify a public Jewish presence because they felt less of an inherent conflict between being Jewish and French. What is more, prominent Jewish intellectuals, such as Finkielkraut and Bernard-Henri Lévy, were calling attention to the responsibility of Jews to speak out against current suffering, especially in the former Yugoslavia, which encouraged Jews to think outside themselves. The uniqueness of the Holocaust, finally, seemed less important in a social context where the status of the Nazi genocide in the pantheon of human horror was repeatedly affirmed. Indeed, it seemed to be everywhere in public discourse, at the center of national debate, and the Touvier affair had blurred much of the difference between Jewish and non-Jewish sentiment. Thus the convergence of social transformations that had become apparent around the rue Copernic bombing and had intensified throughout the 1980s and 1990s, on the one hand, and an evolving public consciousness of the Holocaust, on the other, made the rhetoric of trauma less cogent.

The day of the commemoration, members of the Appeal of 250 Against Fascism, among whom counted many young Jews, staged a sit-in in front of Bousquet's home in Paris. Later in the day, the Union of Jewish Students in France (UEJF) performed a mock trial of Vichy between the Palais de Justice and the police prefecture in Paris. Wearing the robes of judges and lawyers, the students hammered out the crimes of Vichy, "which was the regime of France." Four students, acting as attorneys for the victims, pleaded that "France assume its history finally and completely," while one voice invoked the reasoning of the recent Touvier *non-lieu* in mock defense of the accused. But it was ultimately to "the French people" that the Union president turned for judgment, calling on Mitterrand to declare "the French state of Vichy responsible for persecutions and crimes against Jews and Gypsies." That appeal resonated with those who distinguished the people from the state and true from official France. By including Gypsies, it also spoke to the national consensus on an expanded notion of Holocaust victims and revealed little sense of the trauma expressed by older generations of Jews. Meanwhile, some fifteen members of Betar brandished French and Israeli flags and handed out tracts juxtaposing photographs of Mitterrand and Pétain.[14]

## Pétain's Tomb

In the midst of the Vél d'Hiv dispute, Serge Klarsfeld claimed to have been told by sources close to the president that Mitterrand would end his Armistice Day custom of placing flowers on Pétain's tomb. The Elysée quickly denied any change in plans.[15] The cemetery ritual, the president claimed, had been instituted by de Gaulle and was designed to recognize the Pétain of Verdun, not the Pétain of Vichy.[16] Few observers, however, doubted the symbolic message that such an homage would convey, and even those inclined to give Mitterrand the benefit of the doubt over the summer could see no reason why he would choose in November to honor a man who so clearly had dishonored France. On November 11, both Pétain enthusiasts and Jews gathered on the Ile d'Yeu, where the tomb was located. The former, including the FN and rival factions of the National Pétain-Verdun Association (ANPV), had come to pay homage to the hero of World War I. The latter, mostly members of the UEJF and representatives of the FFDJF, including Klarsfeld, had come in anticipation of a presidential visit to the grave of the Vichy government chief. Despite palpable tensions, Jewish protesters did not interfere with the Pétain nostalgics and the day passed relatively peacefully. The only glitch was the weather: strong winds and a stormy sea forced the cancellation of the last boat from the island to the mainland, so all were forced to leave before the cemetery closed. At 4 P.M., the Ile d'Yeu was cleared of both ceremony and protest and the dispute seemed to be over.

At 5:15, a helicopter landed on the island. Yves Audouin, prefect of the Vendée, descended, laid a wreath on Pétain's tomb, stayed for about fifteen minutes, and then departed. According to a statement issued by the Elysée, the flowers had been placed "in the name of the President of the Republic on the tomb of French Marshals who had distinguished themselves in their command during the First World War." Although the Elysée portrayed the wreath-laying as a customary gesture, the manner in which the presidential flowers had arrived at the grave-site betrayed a seemingly deliberate attempt to conceal the act. The cemetery had been scheduled to close at 5 P.M.; even if the last boat had not been canceled, the wreath's 5:15 arrival guaranteed that Audouin would have encountered no resistance. The flowers had been ordered from a florist other than the one Mitterrand had used in previous years. And whereas the president in the past had honored only Pétain's tomb, this year the graves of several World War I marshals were decorated in an apparent effort to diminish the significance of the Ile de Yeu visit.

A few on the Far Right, such as the FN newspaper *Présent*, praised Mitterrand for chipping away at "the historical lie imposed on France." But if public opinion had been somewhat divided during the Vél d'Hiv controversy, it was much less equivocal on this issue. In fewer than nine months, an appeals court had dismissed the Touvier case and Mitterrand had refused both to officially recognize Vichy's crimes against the Jews and to institute a national holiday in their honor. In the tomb controversy, wrote *L'Express* journalist Eric Conan, "a threshold seems to have been crossed." Political cartoonist Plantu offered an image of Mitterrand exiting a florist with two wreaths, one "for Pétain" and the other "for the victims of Vichy." "Oh, and while I'm here," Mitterrand says, "make me a wreath for my Bosnian friends and another for my Serbian friends." Many Jews were incensed. Klarsfeld said he was "floored," and the UEJF declared itself scandalized that the president had acted "on the sly." Even the normally staid CRIF labeled the wreath-laying "an incomprehensible move" and called on parliament, to which the Vél d'Hiv Committee also had turned in July, to adopt a resolution acknowledging "the infamy committed on the soil of France by the French State." As had been true in the controversies earlier in the year, Jews continued to enjoy the comfort of expressing a popular position, one that seemed to affirm both their Jewish and French identities. "Our combat is not a battle of Jews for Jews but of French people for France," said UEJF members at a protest held on the site of the former Vélodrome d'Hiver. They demanded that "the president of the Republic" acknowledge Vichy's responsibility "in the deportation and assassination of Jews, resisters, and communists in the course of the Second World War." Unperturbed by the extent to which the Holocaust had come to stand for the whole of Vichy perfidy, these young Jews spoke of the regime's victims with an ecumenism that earlier generations of Jews had explicitly rejected.[17]

Debates continued to rage over the boundaries between the state, France, and the Republic as well as the extent to which the population could be separated from the Vichy regime. *La Croix* columnist Jacques Duquesne charged that "the notion of collective guilt is totalitarian and undemocratic" while *Figaro Magazine*'s Alain Griotteray criticized those who would forget "the active resistance of a few and the passive resistance of the majority." But the voices of those who argued that contemporary France could not be wholly distinguished from Vichy dominated the discussion. It is certainly true that Vichy abolished the Republic, wrote Thomas Ferenczi in *Le Monde*, "but if the nation is something more than a legal fiction, how can we deny that it was, in part, involved?" In the words of Daniel Bensaïd, a leftist intellectual and professor of philosophy, "Pétain is undoubtedly not *the* France any more than the Republic is *the* France. But Pétain is *also* France and France is *also* Pétain. . . . " We are certainly not guilty, he wrote. "We are, however, accountable and responsible." A few days after the wreath-laying, in an interview to be broadcast on the Jewish radio station Radio J, Mitterrand reiterated that "neither the French nation nor the Republic was involved" at Vichy. So when people demand that I ask for pardon in the name of France, he explained, "it's virtually intolerable . . . really, I don't understand the language. I don't consider the French nation to be involved in a politics of circumstance led by an enemy power." Neither the magnificence of Verdun nor the shame of 1942 should be forgotten, he went on. "Here we have a fundamental contradiction [that] I need to deal with, and undoubtedly I need to do it differently." He said he was "contemplating" an official gesture for the victims of Vél d'Hiv and other roundups, but he categorically refused to consider "a legal acknowledgment of any responsibility of the French Republic."[18]

Mitterrand claimed in the interview to be unmoved by his critics. "I have a clear conscience," he said. "I know how I have behaved, since my youth, during the war, and after. And I have always acted the same way." But by paying homage to Pétain and at the same time noting a contradiction in the marshal's behavior, Mitterrand opened himself to criticism from Pétain supporters and detractors alike. His insistence on decorating the tomb betrayed his true feelings about the "contradiction" between Verdun and Vichy, a sentiment shared by Pierre Pujo in the monarchist *Action Française*. As far as Pétain is concerned, Pujo wrote, "there is no contradiction in his life, which, from one end to the other, was in the service of France and the French. . . . "[19] Of course Pujo could have said the same about Mitterrand:

that his life had been devoted to France, democratic or otherwise, and that in uninterrupted service to the French state there is no conflict. *Action Française* actually proved to be one of Mitterrand's few allies in the Armistice Day controversy. Like the presidential wreath, nestled among flowers from the ANPV and the FN, Mitterrand found himself in strange company in the days that followed.

In February 1993, in an effort to head off action by the parliament, Mitterrand declared July 16 to be a "national day commemorating the racist and anti-Semitic persecution committed under the de facto authority of the so-called 'government of the French State,'" thereby simultaneously acquiescing to his critics and maintaining the distinction between the "de facto" government of the French state and the Republic. Shortly after the announcement, members of the UEJF put up a plaque at Drancy naming "the French of Vichy" responsible for having interned "Jews, Gypsies, and foreigners," affirming again and at once popular opposition to the Vichy state, many older Jews' distinction between "true France" and "official France," and a broad definition of Holocaust victims. French police, who had orchestrated the Vél d'Hiv roundup, stood imposingly throughout the inaugural commemoration, holding the French flag aloft, and the French army choir sang "La Marseillaise" at the end. Some Jews in attendance expressed dismay that a formerly private and solemn occasion had become something of a national spectacle.[20] Mitterrand did not attend the ceremony, but neither did he return to Pétain's tomb in November. By the end of 1993, the Mitterrand controversy seemed to have run its course.[21]

The Touvier trial returned Vichy and the Holocaust to the daily front pages; and as the trial neared its end, Mitterrand once again found himself embroiled in controversy. In April 1994, *We Will Enter into the Career*, a collection of interviews with former resisters conducted by Olivier Wieviorka, was published. It included a chapter on Mitterrand, excerpts of which fueled perception that the president was out of touch with public sentiment on Vichy and the Holocaust. Asked if Vichy functionaries should still be tried, for example, Mitterrand answered no. "Forty-five years later these are old men . . . it hardly makes sense anymore . . . We [*on*] cannot live forever on memories or resentment." The interviews had taken place between 1990 and 1993, but the publication of his remarks in the midst of the Touvier trial created a scandal.[22] A few weeks later, Mitterrand attended the inauguration of a museum at Izieu dedicated to the children deported by Barbie. Critics could not help but note a discrepancy between the Mitterrand Wieviorka presented, the one who repeatedly stressed his desire to see the Vichy era relegated definitively to the past, and the president at Izieu, who spoke with eloquence of the young Jewish victims. Which was the real Mitterrand?

## A French Youth

In September, Pierre Péan published *A French Youth: François Mitterrand, 1934–1947*, a biography of the president that focused on his political engagements through the initial postwar years. Widely praised for its insight and balanced judgment, the book was the source of renewed controversy. Its publication, and the bitter debates that followed, signaled the end of Mitterrand's political influence and the finale of a painful polemic surrounding the president, Vichy, and the Holocaust. Péan pointed to Mitterrand's political activism in the 1930s, noting that the future Socialist president had belonged to the nationalist, anti-parliament, and anti-communist Croix-de-Feu and had participated in at least two right-wing student demonstrations. As a soldier in the French army, he escaped from a prisoner of war camp and joined the Vichy regime in 1942. There he became a government functionary, eventually landing at the Bureau for the Reclassification of Prisoners. In December, he contributed an article for the Vichy journal *France: revue de l'Etat nouveau*. He made preliminary contacts with the Resistance in late 1942 and seems to have become active at some point in 1943. Péan uncovered letters Mitterrand had written while working for Vichy as well as a photograph of an October 1942 meeting between the future president and Pétain. He also noted that Mitterrand had been decorated with the *francisque*, the highest distinction of the Vichy regime. This and other evidence suggested that Mitterrand not only had served the collaborationist government but that he had been sympathetic to the National Revolution.

Most of the information in *A French Youth* was not new: though the details had not been emphasized, historians had long known of the president's early sympathy for the nationalist Right and his service to the Vichy government. The public, however, had not known, or had chosen not to know, and critics chastised both journalists and historians for not publicizing Mitterrand's history more insistently.[23] But there were revelations in the Péan text as well, especially news of his long friendship with René Bousquet, accused in 1978 of having orchestrated the Vél d'Hiv roundup, charged with crimes against humanity in 1991, and assassinated in summer 1993. And the fact that Mitterrand had granted several interviews to Péan while the book was being written, interviews in which he spoke without remorse of his earlier political involvement and later friendship with Bousquet, suggested that the book carried the president's blessing, indeed that Mitterrand wanted his story to be told as Péan had written it.

In response to the polemic unleashed by the biography, Mitterrand elected to participate in a nationally televised interview with Jean-Pierre Elkabbach, president of France-Television.[24] Physically diminished by prostate cancer, the president spent the first part of the interview stressing that he had no intention of leaving office before the end of his mandate and even joked about running again. But most of the discussion centered on *A French Youth*, and Mitterrand said little to alter the portrait painted therein. Péan had found no evidence that Mitterrand had been an anti-Semite, and the president swore vehemently during the interview that he had never been sympathetic to racism or anti-Semitism. As for Vichy's anti-Jewish legislation, Mitterrand claimed that it had been targeted only at "foreign Jews" and that he had known nothing about it. Vichy, he said, had been administered by both anti-Semites and "impeccably patriotic people . . . men in the upper echelons of the Vichy administration who were resisters in their souls and preparing for what would happen next. There were real resisters at Vichy." The regime, he said, was "largely condemnable"; it deserved "a certain form of condemnation." But, he added,

the Republic has nothing to do with that, and I believe in my soul and conscience that France is also not responsible; that it was the activist minorities who seized the occasion of defeat to take power who are responsible for these crimes. Not the Republic, and not France! So I will not make any excuses in the name of France. I've already said that.

Mitterrand's most controversial remarks concerned his friendship with Bousquet. He reminded Elkabbach several times that the High Court of Justice had acquitted the former chief of Vichy police in 1949. By the 1950s, Mitterrand argued, Bousquet was living a normal life and welcomed everywhere. Between 1978, when Darquier de Pellepoix accused Bousquet of organizing the Vél d'Hiv roundup, and 1986, their friendship continued. At the time, according to the president, Bousquet served on at least a dozen major advisory boards, "was a man of exceptional stature," and was "rather likeable." Once he had been indicted in March 1991, Mitterrand said, it was the responsibility of prosecutor-general Pierre Truche, not the president, to determine whether to pursue the case. "I never intervened in the slightest way to prevent him from acting according to his conscience," Mitterrand underscored. "But it has been my opinion for years that we must try to put an end to the permanent civil war among the French." Is defending "the civil peace" one of your guiding principles as president of the Republic, asked Elkabbach. "I have always said as much to government ministers," said Mitterrand. Had he advised them to impede certain judicial proceedings? "Absolutely," the president replied, especially cases that threatened to reopen old wounds. "My obligation is to see to it that after a while the French reconcile with each other." I am not against punishment, he added, but pardon is also an option, and one that serves the noble cause of French unity. He remained unmoved by his critics: "There is a formidable campaign being waged against me whose echoes you [*on*] hear almost every hour. It does not affect me because I believe it to be profoundly unjust. My conscience is absolutely clear."[25]

The president revealed an almost complete failure to grasp what Vichy represented in national consciousness. A Plantu cartoon portrayed Mitterrand during the interview. "And then," says the president, "Adolph invited me to spend the weekend at Berchtesgaden." As Elkabbach falls from his chair, Mitterrand responds, "No, hey, I'm kidding!" And to himself: "He's tense, this Elkabbach!"[26] Ravaged by cancer, betraying an air of bemused innocence, Mitterrand was portrayed in the press as the next in a string of mediocre characters who had come to represent Vichy and the Holocaust. Touvier could not acknowledge that he had done anything wrong because he seemed unable to extricate himself from the epoch he had been called upon to justify. Mitterrand, too, appeared incapable of discussing Vichy with the moral judgment that hindsight demanded. He was an anachronism, wrote *Esprit* editor Olivier Mongin, not because he was old but because he had no sense of historical time.[27] Earlier in the year, an aged and ailing Touvier had been characterized as a pitiful old man who seemed not to understand why he stood accused; an 89-year-old Pétain had struck a not dissimilar pose during his 1945 trial. And a dying Mitterrand evoked a comparable impression. Like Barbie, Bousquet, Touvier, and Papon, he refused to admit any wrongdoing.

Many Jews received the Péan biography with mixed emotions. On the one hand, in the words of Pierre Moscovici, Socialist deputy to the European Parliament, Mitterrand had demonstrated "a stronger interest in the Jewish community than any other president under the Fifth Republic." In addition to being the first to visit Israel in his official capacity, Mitterrand had been among the most outspoken allies of the Jews after the rue Copernic bombing and had made a very public point of eating at Goldenberg's restaurant shortly after the 1982 attack. Strongly criticized for inviting Arafat to Paris in 1989, he nonetheless showed firm support for the Jewish community in the wake of the Carpentras desecration. Commentators after the 1990 demonstration noted that it was the first time a French president had marched in the streets since de Gaulle's historic walk down the Champs-Elysées after the liberation of Paris. Indeed, one irate letter in *Tribune Juive* denounced the magazine's critical response to both Péan and Mitterrand for these very reasons. On the other hand, Mitterrand refused to acknowledge French responsibility for Vichy. To widespread opprobrium, he had continued to honor Pétain on Armistice Day, and only belatedly, in apparent fear of being trumped by the National Assembly, did he institute a national holiday in remembrance of Vichy's Jewish victims. Not only did he admit to having maintained a friendship with Bousquet, he seemed to believe that the relationship had been morally justifiable. This was, in the words of Moscovici, "the Mitterrand paradox." For those who believed in 1981 that the French Republic finally had elected a true friend of the Jews, wrote Yves Derai in a *Tribune Juive* editorial, "[Mitterrand's] latest 'clarifications' are hard to swallow." "The greater the affection," said Jean Kahn, "the greater the disappointment."[28]

In an official statement, the CRIF limited its criticism to Mitterrand's relationship with Bousquet and his professed interventions on the latter's behalf. While many Jews and others might have been inclined to dismiss the poor judgment of an ambitious young man, what they could not forgive was his postwar friendship with the chief of Vichy police who allegedly was responsible for the deportation of thousands of Jews. But the Bousquet connection was about more than friendship. In 1990, Mitterrand replaced the justice minister, who recently had ordered the Paris Court of Appeals to begin an investigation of Bousquet, and named close friend Georges Kiejman to the newly created post of minister-delegate. Two weeks later, in a direct reversal, the prosecutor-general asked the Paris court to declare itself incompetent to hear the case, and Kiejman suggested that "[b]eyond the necessary battle against forgetting, it is important to preserve the civil peace." This prompted widespread accusations in the press that Mitterrand was intervening on behalf of a Vichy official. Bousquet was eventually indicted in March 1991, but the scandal at the Justice Ministry became part of the Péan controversy. Klarsfeld excoriated Kiejman for favoring Vichy's absolution while Kiejman called the insinuation "an insult to the respect I have for my father, murdered at Auschwitz in 1943." In the meantime, Klarsfeld published a scathing letter to Mitterrand in *Libération*. He admitted having concocted the summer 1992 leak suggesting that the president no longer would decorate Pétain's tomb, but he criticized Mitterrand for failing to take that opportunity to be "less loyal to yourself than to those who suffered so much from the anti-Semitic and collaborationist politics of Vichy . . . Your adherence to Vichy in 1942 without taking account of the regime's state-sponsored anti-Semitism did not authorize you to try to prevent the judgment of Bousquet."[29]

If God reveals himself in the details, wrote Bensaïd, "the telltale detail of the Mitterrand fraud is René Bousquet." Indeed, the Bousquet affair was at the root of public consternation, which indicated the extent to which the Holocaust had become the most recognizable symbol of Vichy. Even segments of the Socialist Party would not countenance Mitterrand's relationship with the former Vichy police chief. Stressing that Bousquet had been responsible for the Vél d'Hiv roundup, the Movement of Young Socialists released a statement declaring its shock over the friendship and renewing the call for the president to issue a formal condemnation of the Vichy regime. Gilles Martinet argued that it would have been impossible to work at Vichy and be unaware of the Jewish Statute, and commentators both within and outside of the party were stunned to hear Mitterrand say that the Statute had concerned only foreign Jews. In fact, it had targeted all Jews, and this had been pointed out on numerous occasions in previous debates. After intense public scrutiny of all aspects of Vichy policy toward Jews, much of it in polemics surrounding Mitterrand himself, how could a citizen, much less the president, not know what every high school student today knows, asked Henry Rousso in *Tribune Juive*. There is in Mitterrand's remarks "a kind of provocation, conscious or not." In an article entitled "I am Sorry I Voted for Him," Maurice Szafran, *L'Événement du Jeudi* journalist and author of a new biography of Simone Veil, berated himself for having believed blindly in "the champion of the Left." Never would I have voted for him, he wrote,

if I had known that in July 1942, at the time of the ignominious anti-Jewish roundups, this fanatical writer who produces pages and pages had not a word, not a line of compassion for the wretched who wore the yellow star. Fifty-two years later, he has the nerve to excuse his insensitivity by drawing a distinction between "French Jews" and "foreign Jews." Disgust.[30]

## Mitterrand, the State, and National Identity

"Like a number of democracies in western Europe," wrote *Esprit*'s Jean-François Bouthors, "France is now experiencing serious problems with identity and self-confidence."[31] This identity crisis had much to do with an ambiguous national past, an uncertain future, and the decline of the French state. Clearly the barrage of controversy relating to World War II had muddied the nation's history and called to question its claim to have been a luminary of universalism. The impending unification of Europe, with the associated disappearance of the franc and French borders, made the future equally murky. And while what had been and what was to come both seemed elusive, the all-powerful French state—sullied by revelations about Vichy and on the verge of relinquishing important powers to a European Union—was unable to be a stabilizing force. A certain public disaffection from the state had been growing since the events of May 1968, and its power and influence had been diminished in recent years by regionalist movements, decentralization, decreased government intervention in the market, and the rise of more particularist identities. Although the state had long been one of France's defining institutions, Mitterrand seemed indifferent to its credibility and future. In fact, as power shifted to the *départements*, to Brussels and the European Union, he seemed content to preside over the state's dismantling. To be sure, Mitterrand was not the first president to envision a more unified Europe. De Gaulle, for example, had imagined an integrated continent as a bulwark against the encroachment of American power. But in that Europe, France was to be a central authority. Mitterrand appeared willing to cede not only formal aspects of French sovereignty but any claim to be a dominant power. It was as though he was determined to be the last chief of the glorious French state, or as one historian suggested, "the last French president."[32]

The reduced stature of the state was inseparable from the declining popularity of the presidency, and here a comparison of Mitterrand and de Gaulle is revealing. Each acted in the Elysée as though the nation were the embodiment of the presidential ego, as if what was good for Mitterrand or de Gaulle were by definition good for the nation. For most of his tenure, indeed until his final days in office, de Gaulle had successfully sculpted the presidency in his own image, never publicly doubting himself or the power he seemed convinced had been bestowed almost divinely upon him. Mitterrand, too, appeared to believe in the mysterious extenuation of presidential power and the impossibility of retraction without debasement.[33] Nowhere was this more clear than in his almost smug refusal to renounce the Vichy regime. But Mitterrand's stylistically Gaullist behavior, which had served the general so well, was anachronistic in a period where a certain deference to the authority of state was no longer in fashion. The Gaullist Republic, as *Libération*'s Oliver Duhamel had written in late 1993, was presidential, hierarchical, authoritarian, and Jacobin, dominated and even demolished by the personality of its leader. De Gaulle wanted to be head of both state and government, the unique symbol of national unity. "It was the epoch of the absolute presidency." Today, however,

we are living a period of the relative presidency. Because of the cohabitation, that goes without saying, but also because France has become a pluralist society, Girondin, dispersed, contentious—in short, emancipated. The counterbalances and challenges to established authority multiply. In the general's epoch, the Republic domesticated democracy. Today, democracy tames the Republic . . . Twenty-three years ago, France was de Gaulle's widow. Today, it has divorced the Gaullist Republic.[34]

Perhaps the greatest paradox of the Mitterrand affair was the public's simultaneous rejection and validation of the French state, its seeming disenchantment with and continued empowerment of the state. From the initial stages of the Mitterrand controversy, when the Vél d'Hiv Committee demanded that the president acknowledge Vichy's crimes, to the most recent debates following *A French Youth*, many in the nation sought an expression of remorse, some acknowledgment of failure, from the very body they criticized and whose moral command they challenged. Only the state had the social authority to speak on behalf of France and to declare its own illegitimacy. At the same time that most opinion embraced some form of decentralized administration, pluralism, and European integration—all decreases in the relative power and influence of the state—the public continued to grant the state far-reaching moral jurisdiction. The Mitterrand controversy, wrote *Esprit*'s Mongin, shows the undiminished preeminence of the state in a country whose turn to liberalism one might have thought meant a decline of the state. Indeed, in a spring 1995 poll asking people across the country what they most desired, the number one response was "a strong state." The "dominant political culture" in France, said Gaullist deputy Patrick Devedjian, "is to worship the cult of the state," and that seemed to be true even when the institution was under attack.[35]

The press made much of the differences between Mitterrand and de Gaulle, and the current president did not fare well in comparison. But what was remarkable, in light of the current controversies about Vichy and the Holocaust, was the two presidents' shared understanding of how World War II fit into the history of France. Like the general, Mitterrand refused to acknowledge any continuity between France and the Republic, on the one hand, and Vichy, on the other. From his triumphant march down the Champs-Elysées in August 1944, commemorated only a month earlier, through the end of his presidency in 1969, de Gaulle had maintained the fiction that wartime France had been a nation of resisters, that Vichy had illegally usurped the power of the Republic (which, nonetheless, continued to exist in London), and that the illegitimate regime warranted no recognition from republican France. The Resistance myth and the notion that the Republic was not accountable for Vichy had a certain credibility coming from de Gaulle because he had embodied, in the most literal sense of the term, the Republic's continuity. Mitterrand, however, had not earned the right to perpetuate this illusion. As a former Vichy functionary and president of the Republic, he could not convincingly draw such a distinct boundary between the two Frances. He could not reconstruct history "in order to make it compatible with his own hesitations."[36] Though his position was very much the same as de Gaulle's, he could not sustain it. It was the messenger, not the message, that destroyed the myth.

If de Gaulle represented the persistence of the Republic, Mitterrand personified the continuity of France. For Vichy was very much a part of the post-revolutionary French political tradition. That empires and restorations had alternated continuously with republics suggested that a deep-seated anti-democratic spirit was in continual competition with a profound commitment to republicanism. The Vichy regime, voted into power by the democratically elected parliament of the Third Republic, encapsulated this conflict. And Mitterrand, who had begun his political activity in the Croix-de-Feu, served both Vichy and the Resistance, and led the Socialist Party in opposition before becoming the fourth president of the Fifth Republic—a president who refused to renounce his allegiance to the anti-republican Vichy regime—was one of its archetypes. Those who moved from Vichy to the Resistance had successively represented "the two Frances," but Mitterrand seemed to live them simultaneously. His presidency, in the words of professor Stéphane Baumont, was a "republican, hierarchical, and sovereign monarchy."[37] The irony is that Mitterrand incarnated the association between the state, France, and the Republic that he so emphatically disavowed. By simultaneously honoring Pétain and acknowledging the "contradiction" between Verdun and Vichy, by representing the Republic and showing a certain indulgence toward the French state of Vichy, Mitterrand illustrated the very tension between "the two Frances" that he desperately tried to deny. At a time when the country sought clarity about the meaning of French identity, Mitterrand could offer only paradox. What France needs, surmised Mongin, is a president who "can invent a language that evokes the crisis of the nation at the hour of Europe," but one who is not content simply "to mimic de Gaulle."[38]

In January 1996, less than a year after leaving office, Mitterrand deliberately stopped taking his cancer medication and died. In orchestrating his own death, as several noted, he continued to be in control until the very end. "With Mitterrand," wrote longtime friend Jacques Attali, "disappears the last republican monarch, the last truly French statesman."[39]

## *The State and Responsibility*

As expected, the Socialist Party lost the Elysée in May 1995. On July 16, the fifty-third anniversary of the Vél d'Hiv roundup, new president Jacques Chirac issued the long sought-after presidential acknowledgment of Vichy's crimes. Yes, he told a crowd of several hundred gathered at the site of the former Vélodrome d'Hiver, "it is true that the criminal insanity of the occupying forces was backed up by French people and by the French State . . . France, land of the Enlightenment and of Human Rights, land of hospitality and asylum . . . committed an irreparable act. It failed to keep its word and delivered those it was protecting to their executioners. . . . " We owe the victims, he added solemnly, "a debt without a statute of limitations."

Certainly, there are the mistakes that were made, there are the offenses, there is a collective sin. But there is also France, a certain idea of France, upright, generous, and faithful to its traditions and its spirit. That France had never been at Vichy. It had long since been absent from Paris. It was in the sands of Libya and everywhere the Free French were fighting. It was in London, exemplified by General de Gaulle. It was present, one and indivisible, in the heart of those French people, those "righteous among the nations" who, at the risk of their lives and in the darkest hour of the storm, as Serge Klarsfeld has written, saved three-fourths of the Jewish community living in France and gave life to the best in this country: the values of humanity, of liberty, of justice, and of tolerance. They are the foundation of French identity and our obligation for the future.[40]

Thus the Gaullist Chirac, without directly implicating the Republic, recognized French responsibility for the deportation of Jews from France. He acknowledged that Vichy had been a French regime supported by French people and that France in that moment had faltered. He repeatedly stressed, as many commentators noted, the responsibility of the "French State." At the same time, he affirmed that "a certain idea of France," what many Jews referred to as "true France," had been absent from Vichy, thereby saving the honor of both de Gaulle and the nation. While the irony of a Gaullist leader breaking with the Gaullist myth of a France united in resistance was not lost, reaction was largely favorable—seventy-two percent in one poll supported Chirac—predictable dissent notwithstanding.[41] Chirac's expression of remorse, more damning and inclusive in its reference to "a collective sin" than anything either Jews or others had demanded in the past, seemed designed both to clearly distinguish the president from Mitterrand and to put an end to the controversy. "On this day, July 16, 1995," wrote Annette Lévy-Willard in *Libération*, "France is officially condemned."[42]

Meanwhile, the Holocaust continued to serve a variety of symbolic purposes. In September, for example, a full-page advertisement for SOS-Racisme in *Libération* featured survivor Primo Levi's poem "If This is a Man." The words "Never forget, fight always" appeared in large bold type. The following summer, the French Olympic synchronized swim team planned a routine set to the music of "Schindler's List." Swimmers were to goose-step to the pool and reenact the arrival of Jewish women in the death camps, the selection by Nazi doctors, and the procession to the gas chambers. Told by the sports minister to remove any allusion to the Shoah from the performance, the president of the French Swimming Federation said he had chosen the theme because of its "tremendous emotional value." We took a chance, he said. "If we don't do it, the team will stay in fifth place."[43]

Soon after, it became clear that Chirac's apology had marked only a temporary cessation of hostilities, which erupted once again during the trial of Maurice Papon. The last remaining Frenchman indicted for crimes against humanity, Papon had been under fire since 1981, when *Le Canard enchaîné* accused him of orchestrating the deportation of Jews from Bordeaux during his tenure as general secretary of the Gironde prefecture in the Vichy government. Papon had been responsible for Jewish affairs, and under his signature, several convoys of Jews had been sent to Merignac and Drancy, both French concentration camps, before being deported to the east. He was indicted in January 1983, only to be suspiciously relieved of all charges, following an error in judicial procedure, almost four years later. New charges were filed, and further controversy over procedure ensued. Papon maintained his innocence from the beginning and in 1990 brought a libel suit against *Le Nouvel Observateur*, claiming, "I am Captain Dreyfus." In the meantime, Jean Leguay, Bousquet's delegate to the occupied zone, had died in 1989, as had Maurice Sabatier, the prefect under whom Papon had worked and who in 1981 had publicly assumed "full responsibility for Jewish repression throughout his prefecture." Bousquet was then assassinated in June 1993. But for Papon, all Vichy functionaries indicted for crimes against humanity were dead, and the very day the Touvier verdict was announced there were calls for Papon's head. In light of the Mitterrand scandal and the public's deep antipathy for Vichy, it seemed unimaginable that Papon would escape trial. In the end, after four magistrates, four indictments, and over sixteen years of controversy, an eighty-seven year-old Papon was brought to trial in October 1997.

As the nation prepared for the third, and in all likelihood last, crimes against humanity trial to be held in France, many of the concerns first raised in the Barbie and Touvier controversies resurfaced: it was impossible to try a man more than fifty years after the alleged crimes had been committed; it was anachronistic for a jury comprised mostly of people who had not been alive during the war to judge an epoch whose challenges they could not appreciate; judicial proceedings were necessary for pedagogical reasons, to teach younger generations "what it was really like" during the war; and the trial was essential in order for France finally to confront its past. There was the by-then ritual chronicling of Vichy anti-Semitism and the regime's role in the deportation of Jews from France. Historians continued to worry about the law's ability to negotiate the nuances of history, and conservatives wondered when France would cease to flagellate itself about the past. In one poll, forty-two percent of the population, and nearly sixty percent of those under twenty-five, agreed that the nation did not talk enough about the Vichy regime. Names and details notwithstanding, public debate sounded very much as it had three and one-half years earlier, during the Touvier trial.[44]

What was different was the extent to which accountability for the Final Solution had been institutionalized. Just before the trial began, the French Catholic Church acknowledged the role played by "incessantly repeated anti-Jewish stereotypes wrongly perpetuated by Christians in the history leading to the Holocaust." In a public statement, Archbishop Olivier de Berranger lamented that in response to Vichy's anti-Semitism, "silence was the rule and words on behalf of the victims the exception." Today, he concluded, "we confess that silence was a mistake. We beg for God's pardon, and we ask the Jewish people to hear our words of repentance." As had been true after the publication of the historians' commission report in 1992, some rank-and-file Catholics opposed passing judgment on the Church and questioned the hierarchy's new transparency. Jews interviewed in the Marais the next day criticized the Church's "hypocrisy" and noted that its confession came only now that it was "fashionable to apologize." CRIF president Henri Hajdenberg, however, hailed the "historic moment" ushered in by the Church and hoped its apology would serve as a model for other French institutions whose complicity in the wartime persecution of Jews had yet to be acknowledged.[45] As if on cue, a few days after the Church's statement of repentance, the National Union of Uniformed Police gathered at the Tomb of the Unknown Jewish Martyr and asked to be pardoned for "the active collaboration of a not negligible part of the active police in the deportation of Jews from France." French doctors and then French lawyers offered their mea culpas a short time later. In the apparent rush to dissociate from Vichy, contrition for wartime anti-Semitism was all the rage.

Still, while apologies abounded, public attention remained fixed on a formal condemnation of the French state: the Vichy state during the war and the Paris state that followed. Papon, like Mitterrand, had worked for both. After his Vichy tenure, Papon had served in de Gaulle's postwar government and in several key administrative posts in the Fourth Republic. He then was Paris chief of police under de Gaulle and a Gaullist representative in the National Assembly before becoming budget minister under Raymond Barre during the Giscard presidency. At Vichy, wrote historian Marc Olivier Baruch, author of the recently published *Servir l'Etat française: L'administration en France de 1940 à 1944* (*To Serve the French State: Administration in France from 1940 to 1944*), "the culture of a state official [was] to obey without asking questions." And during his tenure as police chief, Papon had indicated a continued commitment to this bureaucratic ethos. "There is no crisis of conscience," he had written, "when one obeys the orders of the government." Radical under Léon Blum, Pétainist under Vichy, socialist during the Fourth Republic, Gaullist then Giscardist under the Fifth, Papon seemed less committed to republican government than to serving the state, whoever was in power and whatever the nature of the regime. As *L'Express*'s Eric Conan remarked, he was not a pariah fleeing justice, like Touvier, or someone excluded from public service after the war, like Bousquet. Rather, he was a symbol of the "administrative continuity" between Vichy and successive postwar governments. And although he was surely not the only Vichy functionary still alive, his illustrious government career after the war had made him a relatively high-profile target.[46]

Like Mitterrand before him, Papon personified a morally bankrupt and anachronistic French state, one that had endured long after World War II. As Pierre Nora, editor of the monumental *Les lieux de mémoire* (*Sites of memory*), a multi-volume study of French sites of memory, said shortly before the trial began, Papon represented precisely what younger generations most despised: "a sort of technocratic *nomenklatura*," the kind of "apolitical" domination of politics about which so many had expressed concern after the Carpentras desecration. Chirac's assumption of Vichy guilt on behalf of the current state, clearly designed to distinguish his administration from earlier postwar governments, nonetheless had failed to provide a perpetrator, someone on whom the public could unload its vexation. It was a pronouncement of guilt without a living guilty party to assume it, and in that sense it exacerbated public frustration with the current nameless and faceless technocracy. In the trial of Papon, both the Vichy regime and the "aseptic, technocratic" state would be implicated, and civil servants would learn the imperative of personal responsibility. According to one poll, furthermore, sixty percent of the French agreed that the trial would show that during World War II, "France was not only Vichy but especially resisters and those who aided Jews." For over half the population, Papon was to take the blame, the population were to be exonerated, and the distinction between the state and the people—between "official France" and "true was to be upheld.[47]

The proceedings began on October 8, 1997, and just over a week later the state was on the stand. October 17 was the anniversary of a 1961 demonstration held in Paris by the French branch of the Algerian National Liberation Front. At the time, the war for Algerian independence was raging, and the violence extended to the streets of France. To protest a curfew that Papon, in his capacity as Paris police chief, had instituted less than two weeks earlier, tens of thousands of Algerians walked peacefully together through the streets of Paris. Under Papon's orders, the police responded by rounding up, beating, and shooting anyone who looked Algerian. Some were strangled, others drowned in the Seine. Official records indicate that three were killed; conservative scholarly estimates put the number closer to fifty and suggest that as many as 300 Algerians died in Paris throughout the year. To mark the thirty-sixth anniversary of the violence, protesters demonstrated in Paris and Bordeaux carrying signs reading "October 17, 1961, Papon guilty." No sooner had the trial begun, in other words, than Papon found himself in the dock for his conduct under de Gaulle as well as Vichy. While Pierre Messmer, army minister in 1961, testified on Papon's behalf, historian Jean-Luc Einaudi testified that Papon's personal responsibility for the murders was "direct and overwhelming."[48]

According to a *Le Monde* editorial, the October 1961 bloodshed showed the extent to which the misdeeds of the French state, including the massacre of Commune participants in 1871, the 1945 murders at Sétif, and repression of the Madagascar riots in 1947, had been treated with silence by French officialdom. It demonstrated the "French exception," which dictated that "a law of silence cover up the bloody consequences of politics led by authorities benefiting from a kind of national consensus. . . . " The violence and killings, the editorial continued, were without doubt one of the most effectively concealed episodes of state injustice. They were proof, concurred *Libération*, of the state's obstinate refusal under the Fourth and Fifth Republics to be held in the least bit accountable for either Vichy or the "dark hours" of colonialism. A petition circulated much later by scholars and other public figures called the October 17 assassinations "a crime against humanity committed by the State." As the controversy intensified, Jean-Marc Varaut, Papon's chief attorney, admitted that he had not grasped the magnitude of "the trial within the trial."[49]

In the meantime, former de Gaulle cabinet chief Olivier Guichard reiterated in his testimony that de Gaulle had been concerned primarily with establishing national unity, that Papon's tenure at Vichy had not been unknown to the general, and that certain of de Gaulle's prime ministers also had served Vichy. Le Pen then quipped that it had been "more comfortable to resist in London than in Paris." All of this was too much for Philippe Séguin, president of the Gaullist RPR, who complained on television that the Papon proceedings had become a pretext for the trial of de Gaulle, Gaullism, and France. He denounced Chirac's 1995 pronouncement of national guilt and criticized France's "permanent climate of collective expiation and masochism." A few days later, in a *Le Figaro* opinion entitled "Enough! Enough! Enough!", Séguin accused the Socialist Party of encouraging support for the FN in an effort to discredit the republican Right, a charge that also had been leveled at Mitterrand. Socialist Prime Minister Lionel Jospin, who had condemned the roundups of Jews only a few months earlier, during the fifty-fifth Vél d'Hiv commemoration, quickly responded that neither his government nor his party intended to conduct a trial of Gaullism, however much that might be the goal of Le Pen. It was necessary to prosecute Papon, he added, but France could not be guilty of Vichy crimes because Vichy was "the negation of France and in any case the negation of the Republic." In his July speech, he noted, he had not "employed the same terms" as Chirac's apology and had not "personally used the word 'France.'" At a Haute-Savoie ceremony honoring righteous French people who had hidden and rescued Jews, a message read on the president's behalf reiterated that World War II exhibited the best and worst of France and that the nation "must assume its whole history."[50]

The state, France, and the Republic: assessing responsibility continued to be, in the words of Laurent Joffrin, "a delicate semantic question." And after the Touvier trial, polemics about Mitterrand, and over sixteen years of controversy surrounding Papon, the nation remained far from consensus on who was "guilty" for Vichy. On the one hand were people like Séguin, many of whom had distanced themselves from Chirac's public atonement a few years earlier. For them, any suggestion that Vichy was France delegitimated de Gaulle, the Resistance, and righteous French citizens. Vichy, as de Gaulle had proclaimed in 1944, was "null and void," a parenthesis in the history of France. On the other hand were those who recognized Vichy as an authentic French regime but who nonetheless struggled to determine accountability. The Republic is certainly not culpable, argued Joffrin, but as for the nation, or "France," both acquittal and condemnation are equally contestable. To exonerate France is to forget the degree and pervasiveness of collaboration, but to declare the nation guilty is to repudiate the Resistance and legitimize Pétain. Alain Duhamel concurred in *Libération*, suggesting that France was "both victim and accomplice, defeated and victorious, resistant and Marshalist." Its best part was in London, its "black soul" at Vichy. "The France that we [*on*] love can demand pardon," concluded Joffrin. "But for the faults of the France that we do not love."[51]

While Joffrin and Duhamel acknowledged the complexity of determining France's responsibility for Vichy crimes, they and many others, including Chirac, were unequivocal about the guilt of the French state. By many accounts, in fact, the trial was more a vehicle to condemn the state and government functionaries than to convict Papon, whose guilt was assumed. No doubt motivated by a concern to preserve de Gaulle's stature and the viability of the Gaullist party, Séguin's outburst also reflected a desire to protect the autonomy of France and the authority of the French state in a consolidating and non-state-centric Europe. For many in the RPR, the very idea of France depended on national independence and a powerful state. De Gaulle's singular strength, his legacy, wrote Alain Peyrefitte, former de Gaulle minister and spokesperson, was his "idea of France": the affirmation of France's survival—its independence as a nation and the sovereignty of its state—in 1940, 1944, and 1958, moments when no one else had the courage to insist that only national interest could define legitimacy. To acknowledge that a reprehensible but no less legitimate regime had governed France would call to question the moral authority of the French state, whose sovereignty and independence were pillars of "the idea of France" that de Gaulle and his disciples had worked so hard to realize and that the latter feared would be buried in the new European Union. With France in such disarray, asked Peyrefitte, is it any wonder that de Gaulle's message seems "absolutely current?" Citing many examples of "diminished state prerogative," RPR senator and former interior minister Charles Pasqua, a critic of European unification, argued in a front-page *Le Monde* letter to his "comrades" that "the weakening of state authority threatens to tear apart national cohesion and the Republic itself." In the new Europe, he stressed, any meaningful notion of France rested with the fundamental principles of the national community: "national sovereignty, republican values, and state authority."[52]

The trial, in other words, served as a battleground for partisans and critics of the French state. "Functionary you were, functionary you will remain. A functionary who functions," wrote journalist and author Daniel Schneiderman in an open letter to Papon. If nothing else, "your trial at least will have had the benefit of opening my eyes to the administration of my country." There were those who argued that Papon was a scapegoat, a stand-in for the dead Bousquet and Leguay, administrators whose connection to the state and responsibility for Jewish deportations were more direct and difficult to dispute. But even many who acknowledged that Papon had become a sort of sacrificial lamb for Vichy argued that he was "a scapegoat and guilty."[53] After the October 17 and Séguin controversies, the deportation of Bordeaux Jews—the crimes for which Papon was on trial—appeared more peripheral than central. When survivors and families of the victims took the stand in December, seemingly rote phrases about the "overwhelming" testimony sounded empty, almost forced, as though journalists had turned to Barbie and Touvier trial commentary for copy. It was the deportation of Jews, a crime against humanity, that made possible a trial over fifty years after the alleged offenses had been committed. But it was not the crime against Jews, the details of which had pervaded public discourse at least since the Barbie trial, that galvanized public interest. The Holocaust had been repeatedly deplored, its executors had been found guilty, and the specifics of Papon's misdeeds were not in themselves particularly interesting. The possibility of condemning the state through one of its administrators, however, provoked passionate debate.

In the end, nearly six months after the trial had begun, Papon was found guilty on two counts of having helped organize the arrest and deportation of Jews from Bordeaux. The jury acquitted him, however, of complicity in their murder at Auschwitz. The prosecutor-general had asked that Papon be sentenced to twenty years in prison, but the jury had cut the term in half. Both the verdict and sentence raised disturbing questions about the legal contortions marking the Papon case. Was there not something incongruous about guilt for crimes against humanity, the only offenses serious enough not to be subject to a statute of limitations, and a ten-year sentence? Could there be degrees of crimes against humanity? Even Papon had argued in his own defense that he was either innocent or guilty. "This crime cannot be chopped up," he had told the jury. "It's all or nothing. I am guilty or innocent." But the court handed down what the press called "a mixed verdict":

Papon was guilty of the deportation of Jews from Bordeaux to French concentration camps, which in itself constituted a crime against humanity, but it had not been proven that Papon "knew" that the deportees faced certain death at Auschwitz. The decision, therefore, satisfied much of the public for whom a guilty verdict was symbolically required; at the same time, it stopped short of categorizing Papon, a career government administrator, with Barbie and Touvier, witting killers of Jews.

Papon was found guilty not of complicity in the Final Solution but of implementing the Vichy regime's policies of anti-Semitism and collaboration. He was condemned, wrote Serge July in *Libération*, not for having been a partisan of the National Revolution, a militant for collaboration, or even an anti-Semite but for having been a functionary, "efficient and indifferent to the consequences of his actions." The verdict, he went on, could provoke "a healthy shakeup" in France,

where civil service is a religion, where lawyers, engineers, and technocrats constitute an all-powerful State bourgeoisie, conceived by every regime as the veritable backbone of the nation, [a bourgeoisie] which for centuries played an active role in its own grandeur. But that history also has black pages. Until now, these were inaccessible . . . Until now, it was unimaginable to ask senior officials in France to account for their administrative doings. The Bordeaux verdict put an end to the untouchables, possibly responsible but never guilty.

For *Libération*'s Gérard Dupuy, the trial challenged "the *a priori* absolution of state servants" and reinforced "the accountability of the French state." It brought to light an "office crime," wrote *Le Monde*'s Jean-Marie Colombani, and refused the automatic exculpation of high-ranking officials.

If there is only one lesson in the trial for the present and the future, it would be this: in a country where the State remains an object of worship, the Bordeaux verdict signifies for all civil servants that conforming to administrative policy does not relieve them, should the case arise, from having to answer personally for their actions.[54]

Lawyers for the civil parties, however, were unimpressed with the verdict's lessons for contemporary government functionaries. With the exception of Arno Klarsfeld, who along with his father had argued before the trial began for a sentence that distinguished Papon from Barbie and Touvier, the civil parties expressed irritation that Papon had been found guilty only for contributing to arrest and deportation. "The Final Solution was in the trains: those that went from Drancy to Auschwitz, but also those from Bordeaux to Drancy," argued Maurice-David Matisson, a plaintiff. Said Raymond Blet, a civil party attorney, "this verdict is a sanction of Vichy laws, but it does not go beyond that. It clears Vichy of knowing about the concentration camps." Victims who had testified said they were "disgusted" by a "preposterous, incomplete" verdict. "Ten years is what they [*on*] give people for theft . . . It's half a victory." Even the normally moderate Jewish leadership could not hide its disappointment. In an official statement, the CRIF said that the sentence, "disproportionate to the facts, leaves a certain bitterness," while Jean Kahn, then president of the Central Consistory, was unusually acerbic. "For principle, for the memory of nearly 1,650 murdered women, men, and children, for so much suffering, torture, death, and pain, we would have hoped for a less symbolic sentence."[55]

The Papon verdict demonstrated that the convergence of opinion on Vichy's guilt masked divergent understandings of what that guilt represented. For many Jews, the establishment of Vichy culpability separated the French state from the citizenry: Vichy was "official France," an aberration, a regime whose hostility to the Jews distinguished it from "true France," embodied by the French people. As Hajdenberg had said after the French Church's apology, it was important to differentiate between "the government of Vichy, which failed, and the soul of France, which remained intact." Throughout the trial, national sentiment actually seemed to be largely congruent with the dominant Jewish opinion, expressed as early as the Six-Day War, that the French people could not be confounded with the Vichy state. But whereas most Jews suggested that the state was guilty for having contributed to the Final Solution, for having betrayed the ideals embodied by the Revolution and Jewish emancipation, the dominant national position was that Vichy stood less for the Holocaust, for betrayal of the revolutionary promise and Jewish citizenship, than for collaboration, French suffering during World War II, and state malfeasance. Papon, as July pointed out, had been found guilty as a government administrator, a cog in the vast machinery of the state. He was condemned not for acts contributing to the Holocaust but for having served Vichy, a collaborationist and undemocratic regime. The accent in most public discourse, in other words, was not on Vichy's contributions to the Final Solution, of which Papon's actions were only one example, but on the misdeeds of the French state, represented by Papon's complicity in the arrest and deportation of Jews.

While many Jews and non-Jews seemed united in their appraisal of Vichy, they continued to be divided by a broad gulf in the *meaning* of the Holocaust for France. Little wonder, then, that so many Jews expressed disappointment in the verdict. From their perspective, as had been true with the Barbie and Touvier proceedings, Papon's crimes against humanity trial seemed to have slipped away. Still, many who criticized the dismissal of the murder charge conveyed gratitude that the court, speaking for the French people, had found Papon guilty of crimes against humanity. This appreciation was due in part to the fear of acquittal that had begun to develop as the prosecution struggled to present its case, and lawyers Alain Lévy and

Michel Zaoui denounced the "shared relief" of those who dreaded Papon's exoneration and those who feared the effect of a life sentence as "a shocking consensus in what it hides of the ruling's real content." If nothing else, they wrote in a *Libération* opinion, "appearances are saved . . . Saturated by commentary, public opinion will remember that a representative of the Vichy regime was condemned for crimes against humanity. The sentence as well as the breakdown of charges retained against Papon already seem secondary."[56] For Lévy and Zaoui, it was the Holocaust, ostensibly central to the trial, that had become peripheral.

But many Jews' seemingly conflicted reaction betrayed more than simple relief. It also reflected a longing to experience the trial not simply as Jews but as members of the national community. On the one hand, they were pleased that their country had declared a Frenchman's guilt for Jewish persecution, and they refused to conflate "France" with Vichy. "This trial should not overshadow that most true France," said Grand Rabbi Sitruk, "the France of the Resistance, of courage, of anonymous men and women who saved and protected Jews during the war." Even the trial's critics, such as Kahn and Marek Halter, made sure to salute "the righteous of all walks of life . . . those French people who by the thousands saved persecuted Jews in our country while men like Papon sent them to Drancy."[57] On the other hand, many Jews felt that the jury's dismissal of the third charge and the ten-year sentence trivialized Jewish suffering. The sum of Jewish responses revealed a long-standing desire to be both distinct and unmarked, to foreground Jewish identity and at the same time participate as indistinguishable French citizens in the institutions of secular, national society. They also betrayed a simultaneous longing to share the Holocaust and to protect its singularity, or the dialectic of trauma. As the genocide became national heritage and was interpreted by groups of people with widely varying experiences and frames of reference (including younger generations of Jews), it lost the element of uniqueness, of incommensurableness, that so many Jews saw as its very essence. It became a means by which a variety of thematically related concerns could be expressed, much as emancipation, the Dreyfus Affair, and Vichy anti-Semitism had served as a screen for other national concerns. In that sense, the conflict between Jewish and French identity, initiated during the Revolution and first articulated publicly during the Six-Day War, remained unresolved.

On the morning of October 11, 1999, with his appeal still pending, Papon fled France for Switzerland. In a widely quoted letter published in *Sud-Ouest*, Papon swore that he had not "fought against Nazi violence to beg for liberty from the judiciary" and claimed that it was impossible for justice to be served in a country where "the Klarsfelds speak in the name of the president of the Republic." Under the headlines "Wanted" (in English) and

"Papon: The Hunt," *Libération* and the rest of the French press reported daily on the search for the convicted criminal against humanity.[58] Papon managed to elude French authorities for ten dramatic days before being arrested in Bern the evening of October 21. The public was then treated to the spectacle of an eighty-nine-year-old former government minister with a failing heart being led back to France in police custody. Maurice Papon: the last, it seemed to many observers, in a long line of pathetic old men called upon to account for the Holocaust in France.[59]

## CHAPTER EIGHT

# Conclusion
## Judeocentrism? The Holocaust and Political Identity in France

Public discourse, where the loudest voice or cleverest prose is regularly mistaken for the most compelling point of view, is perhaps the last place to look for nuance. Any trace of concession, any intimation that the opinion being expressed is less than completely irrefutable, can appear as a sign of its ultimate falsehood. Thus the ambiguity at the heart of most politics is transformed for the sake of rhetoric into clarity. Complexity turns into simplicity, what is confusing becomes clear, and the messiness of trying to make sense of human behavior is reduced to a series of either/or propositions that are most often presented as mutually exclusive. At least since "The Sorrow and the Pity," France has struggled to reconcile the Janus-faced national portrait, at once defiant and compliant, that emerged from the war. Indeed, the antithesis between the Resistance and collaboration, de Gaulle and Vichy, has been a defining characteristic of French public conversations about the Holocaust. In the early years after the war, de Gaulle and others deliberately suppressed the extent of collaboration in an effort to rebuild a deeply fractured nation. This refusal to acknowledge more than a handful of traitors in the Vichy regime, however politically expedient, paved the way for a backlash, and Ophuls's film not only refuted the notion that France had been comprised entirely of resisters but suggested the opposite: that most of the French had been anti-Semitic supporters of Vichy and the Nazis. By challenging the legend of national heroism, the Gaullist myth, in such a polemical fashion, the movie helped frame public debates about both World War II and the Holocaust in binary terms: the French had been either resisters or collaborators, and France had been either valiant or cowardly. That *both* the Resistance and Vichy had generated support was impossible to reconcile in a discourse that recognized only grandeur or disgrace.

Historian Henry Rousso has been the most outspoken critic of the public's tendency to reduce history to simple categories like "innocent" and "guilty."[1] Incapable of extricating itself from the present, he has argued, the nation has mistaken memory for history and has failed repeatedly in its impossible quest to satisfy contemporary political needs, remember the past, apply the law, and provide an accurate rendering of history, all at the same time. After the Touvier trial and the controversies surrounding Mitterrand, during which Vichy was in the news every day, Rousso and journalist Eric Conan lamented that the nation was "obsessed" with the past and that memory of Vichy had turned into a "Judeocentric" misrepresentation of World War II, an "anachronistic" and exaggerated emphasis on the Holocaust that overstated its significance to both the Vichy regime and the rest of France during the war. Anti-Semitism appeared as the centerpiece of Vichy ideology when in fact it was only one component of a much more comprehensive agenda designed to erase the accomplishments of the Revolution and to ensure a prominent place for France in a German-dominated Europe. An epoch cannot be judged with the hindsight and moral standards of the current generation, they contended, without distorting history.[2]

The acerbity of their tone notwithstanding, it is difficult to contest the substance of Conan and Rousso's critique. Public discourse on World War II has been dominated by Holocaust rhetoric. The absence of a statute of limitations on crimes against humanity facilitated the prosecution not of war criminals but of those alleged to have participated in the persecution and deportation of Jews, while the emergence of non-national identities and the associated attention to oppression and victimization made the Holocaust the most palpable representation of the war. The "Judeocentrism" about which Conan and Rousso complained stemmed from a conjuncture of legal and social forces that made the Holocaust a resonant parable, and history was often misrepresented in the process. Yet by suggesting that memory of the Holocaust overshadowed memory of Vichy, the authors overlooked a crucial nuance. For both practical and symbolic reasons, the Holocaust was called upon to address a range of issues that had little to do with the genocide itself. In fact, it was a preoccupation with collaboration and French guilt that was expressed through memory of the Holocaust, which functioned in public discourse largely to deflect contemporary anxieties about Vichy and national identity. To be sure, much information about Vichy anti-Semitism and Jewish suffering was unearthed in the process, and the public is no doubt better informed about the experiences of Jews in World War II France. But while the authors rightly pointed out the disproportionate attention paid to the Holocaust in public debate, they failed to recognize the degree to which it served as a trope: a route rather than a destination, a means rather than an end.

It has likewise been true throughout modern French history that ostensibly Jewish issues have served as a screen onto which have been projected concerns that are only marginally about Jews. During emancipation debates, the Dreyfus Affair, and the Vichy regime, discussions about Jews reflected opposing visions of national identity, a pattern that has continued in public discourse where the Holocaust is a central theme. The rue Copernic bombing, for example, was portrayed as an attack on France, a battle in the country's enduring war against fascism, while the pillage at Carpentras's Jewish cemetery highlighted the nation's failure to combat racism and discredit Le Pen. The Holocaust became a metaphor for social subjugation, and by the time of the Barbie trial, it stood as much for oppression and the victimization of the French Resistance as for the Nazi genocide of the Jews. Crimes contributing to the Holocaust, which made possible trials forty to fifty years after the facts, became in the Touvier and Papon disputes a vehicle through which the nation could transmit its sense of having been victimized by the Vichy regime and its disillusion with the French state. In these trials, and especially in the Mitterrand affair, the Holocaust served as a point of departure for debates about the past, present, and future identity of France.

Jews and the Nazi genocide were neither irrelevant nor a source of indifference during these controversies. But while both were rhetorically at the center of public discourse, they were peripheral in the overall meaning of debates in much the same way that Jewish welfare was incidental in 1790–91, at the turn of the nineteenth century, and during Vichy rule. During the Revolution, most Jews believed that they could become citizens and maintain their Jewish identity; in the prevailing non-Jewish vision, emancipation meant the disappearance of Jewishness. Citizenship, therefore, was not denied to Jews as people but *as Jews*. After the Six-Day War, Jews adopted a narrative of trauma to justify their allegiance to both Jewishness and Frenchness, to demonstrate their particularity *and* their connection to others; in response, the rest of the nation denied the genocide not as an atrocity but as a trauma, or as *Jewish*. Thus the postwar saga of the Holocaust has demonstrated less the appropriation of Jews' experience than its integration, or its narrative assimilation into national discourse. Of course there have been and continue to be people motivated primarily by anti-Semitism, philo-Semitism, or some notion of social justice. But for most others, Jews and/or the Holocaust seemed more a pretext for than the object of national debate. In that sense, public discourse is hardly "Judeocentric," as Conan and Rousso claimed, even if the vocabulary and imagery that characterize debates have focused on the Holocaust.

But what explains the insatiable desire to talk about World War II and the repeated admonition, even after the Papon trial and years of virtually daily public debate, that France refused to face its past? As Barbie, Le Pen, Touvier, Mitterrand, Papon (and Bousquet and Leguay) were pronounced guilty, there seemed to be a frenetic desire to find someone else to condemn, as though France had not really grappled with the issues raised by Vichy and therefore had not really censured the past. The nation's confrontation with its history seemed partial or unresolved because the incessant renunciation of Vichy often bypassed the complexities of the epoch that could be most thorny in the present. Perhaps, therefore, the insistence that France had not yet contended with the past reflected an unconscious sense that the voluminous public discourse on the war had not addressed the most pressing question: what did Vichy reveal about national history and identity? As Pierre Nora and other contributors to the magisterial *Les Lieux de mémoire* contend, "memory" becomes most conscious or deliberate when one's connection to the past seems most remote. And as Rousso has suggested, France's problem has not been facing up to the past, which younger generations who bear no direct responsibility have done with relative ease. Instead, "the problem lies in integrating this past into the national narrative, and, even more, into the image we wish to fashion of our country's history." The history of Vichy, he argued, "contains an 'overflow' of past and memory that demonstrates our difficulty in confronting the future, and no doubt a far deeper crisis of national identity than we care to admit." If the French have had difficulty "coming to terms with the past," in other words, it is because their relationship to this past weighs heavily on the present and future, on contemporary and projected notions of what it means to be French.[3]

For many Jews, the Holocaust was also about identity, or the contradictions between being Jewish and French, and in his discussion of the "reawakening" of Jewish memory and Jews' "obsession" with the Holocaust, Rousso fails to appreciate the centrality of this identity dissonance.[4] It was in demanding for the first time that their particularity as Jews be publicly acknowledged and that their allegiance to France not be correspondingly challenged—in articulating the Holocaust as trauma—that Jews breached the terms of the long-standing citizenship compact and set in motion a narrative politics of the Holocaust. As the Holocaust came to symbolize oppression, the victimization of the Resistance, and the perfidy of the French state, it lost its traumatic element, and in that sense, the evolution of Holocaust consciousness in France demonstrates well the inability of public discourse to resolve the dialectic of trauma, the simultaneous desire for and refusal of empathy. But for younger Jews, both the Holocaust and the philosophy of assimilation that stemmed from the Revolution seemed remote. In the late 1970s and early 1980s, the rhetoric behind the violence and Zionism of many Jewish youth bespoke a conscious repudiation of the assimilationist ideal. And when students and young Jewish activists asserted themselves with neither apology nor defensiveness in the 1990s, the old model of assimilation no longer even needed to be rejected.

The progression of Holocaust discourse and the dissipation of the trauma make clear that the very notion of political identity in France has undergone a seismic shift since the end of World War II. While far from dead, the idea of the pure citizen, unfettered by competing loyalties and in an unmediated relationship with the state, hardly inspires the consensus it once did. Certainly Jews' new public confidence and the prominence of the Holocaust after the Six-Day War did not cause a transformation in civic life; but the evolution of Jewish identity and Holocaust symbolism both shaped and reflected changing attitudes about the role of politics and the nature of political discourse. And while the new pluralism in France has not reached the fever-pitch of American multiculturalism, it has dramatically altered the rules of civil engagement. For younger Jews, more comfortable in a France that seemed willing both to recognize Jewish suffering during World War II and to tolerate particularist loyalties, the trauma was less compelling. To be sure, the Holocaust anchored their Jewish identity; in an age where suffering and oppression were badges of honor, and in the absence of a sustained anti-Semitic threat, the genocide served as the foundation for their ethnic claims. They continued to make pilgrimages to eastern Europe and were vocal during debates regarding the Holocaust. But, as the statements of UEJF members during the Touvier and Mitterrand controversies reveal, they did not seek to justify their public presence as Jews, and they spoke on behalf of all of Hitler's victims, including Gypsies and members of the Resistance. It was the Holocaust as an emblem of perennial anti-Semitism, as an episode of mass suffering that *joined* them with oppressed others, and not the Holocaust as trauma—as unfathomable and incommensurable—that informed their Jewishness.

The story of the Holocaust's integration into national consciousness is not without irony. In declaring their distinctiveness, for example, Jews turn out to be not all that special, and the trauma that grounded their assertion becomes a representation of difference broadly defined. What was once radical and revolutionary—public affirmation of corporate loyalty—approaches conventional, and Jews' particularity, paradoxically, becomes a metaphor for difference. The singularity of the Holocaust, moreover, is lost in the proliferation of particularisms often expressed via metaphors of the genocide, or in the dialectic of trauma. Myriad subjects claim their own holocaust, and for some Jews, this is intolerable. But this identification with the Holocaust also enables the genocide to become part of mass consciousness. It is ironic, in this respect, that Jews become integrated into the nation as difference becomes normative, that in an effort to demonstrate their particularity, Jews are once again subsumed by the nation. The relative indifference that most younger Jews convey regarding the symbolic uses of the Holocaust is one indication of this normalization of diversity. Like many non-Jewish groups, they express themselves publicly with little hint of self-consciousness because it is no longer traumatic to recognize multiple identities and conflict between them. The trauma fades with the passing of time, the waning of the assimilationist ideal, and the advent of a more differentiated form of political identity.

While the postwar story of the Holocaust sheds light on the unfolding of trauma in a social context, it also reveals a nation in flux, struggling to understand French history and identity in the past, present, and future. Here again, the limits of public discourse become apparent. That Vichy might have participated in but not endorsed the Final Solution; that the Republic might have been absent from and yet responsible for Vichy crimes; that some French people had denounced Jews while others had risked their lives to save them (and that most had done neither)—in short, that "France" could incarnate both the acme of universalism and the abyss of exclusionary nationalism—these were inconsistencies that were impossible to grasp in the context of public debate, inhospitable terrain for moral complexity and the intricacies of history. Judgments about the past could not but have an impact on current disputes surrounding immigration, citizenship, and the role of France in a new Europe, and the paradoxes of the war era confounded a people enmeshed in the politics of the present and concerned about the consequences of interpretation. After the Barbie trial, moreover, once public discussions began to focus on Vichy and the Holocaust, other historical controversies raised further questions about French national character. In 1989, for example, a long-standing debate among historians about the founding of the Republic filtered into the mainstream media, and on the occasion of its 200th anniversary, the Revolution appeared not as a radical break with the old regime but as its continuation, not as a popular revolt against monarchy but as an example of democracy's congenitally tyrannical impulses. Like the heroism of World War II France, the great innovation of the Revolution now appeared to be tainted, and as was true in discussions of Vichy and the Holocaust, this ambiguity cast a shadow over the past while provoking debates about what, if anything, was to be celebrated about France and French identity.

The opacity of national history, however, was most anguishing during the controversy surrounding the Touvier *non-lieu*. As the court effectively pronounced not only Touvier but France innocent of crimes against humanity, the evidence seemed overwhelming that the past was being manipulated, rewritten to create an image of a France that had been essentially hostile to Nazi Germany and utterly peripheral to the Holocaust. As it was, the court's decision backfired, and a starkly different portrait, one of a stubbornly xenophobic country that refused to confront its dark past, dominated public discourse. The painstaking attempt to differentiate between the state, the Republic, and "France" a few months later, after the Vél d'Hiv controversy, reflected a desire to navigate between these two extremes, to discern who, exactly, was responsible for Vichy misdeeds and what, precisely, was their relationship to contemporary France. What seemed like a hopelessly semantic analysis was an effort to untangle the nation's heritage, to decipher what it meant to be French at present and what it would mean in the future. The almost frenetic endeavor to distance the nation from Touvier and the "Vichy" judges and to link a rejection of Vichy to a repudiation of Le Pen made clear that the past and present were inextricably linked. And the distinction repeatedly drawn between the population under Vichy and the Vichy regime, between the French people and the French state, suggested that the nation was beginning to be defined as a distinct entity, one detached from the central government of France. As Oliver Mongin wrote during the uproar surrounding *A French Youth*, French elites continued to see the nation only through its monarchy and failed to realize that society "no longer lives only by the rhythm of its king."[5]

Indeed, after the Barbie trial, all the personalities implicated in public discourse were, to varying degrees, associated with the French state. Bousquet, Leguay, Touvier, Mitterrand, and Papon, not to mention Pétain—all were pilloried for their seemingly blind allegiance to the state, for having served the state rather than the principles for which France purportedly stood: in short, for having placed the state as an institution above France as a nation. These men seemed to prove, indeed to epitomize, what the Revolution's detractors had argued: that the modern French state, the Republic, was no more a guarantee against tyranny than the one it had replaced. What better proof than Mitterrand and Papon, both of whom had turned from the Republic to Vichy and back to the Republic without any apparent *crise de conscience*, each of whom seemed utterly incapable of grasping why he was being criticized. When Mitterrand said that his conscience was clear because he had "always acted the same way," when Papon explained that he had cried for the Jews after authorizing their deportation, both were trying to convey what they believed to be an irreproachable loyalty to France by way of service to the state. It was this unabashed commitment to amoral leadership, this apparently cynical attachment to power whatever the nature of the regime, that diminished the nation's trust in the state and from which much of the public sought to distance itself in the 1990s. "Everything today indicates that the French prefer a relative to an absolute presidency," wrote Alain Duhamel in 1999, remarking on the new popularity of governments of cohabitation.[6] In March 2000, the National Assembly passed a law creating "a national holiday in memory of the victims of racist and anti-Semitic crimes committed by the French State and in homage to the 'Just' of France." Whereas the holiday instituted by Mitterrand in February 1993 had referred only to "the de facto authority of the so-called 'government of the French State'" and had made no mention of the righteous French, the new commemoration simultaneously condemned the state and honored the people. At the same time, it legitimated a narrative that many Jews had conveyed since the end of the Six-Day War: the enemy had been the French state and the heroes the French people.

Still, this was complicated, as the republican state had long been revered as the embodiment of popular will and one of France's most significant contributions to the world. It and its leaders were at the center of modern national history, of what defined France as France, and to suggest that they were essentially without principle was to upset one of the foundations of national identity. Dimitri Nicolaïdis, editor of a recently published book on national identity, argued during the Péan controversy that the nation had forever been identified with the state, that national unity and state continuity were co-constitutive, and that the Mitterrand controversy created a malaise because it revealed this relationship and made it problematic. It challenged "the landmarks of our identity," he contended, and the country's obsession with Vichy masked its inability to confront directly the centrality of the state to the nation's self-understanding.[7] From the old regime and continuing through the Revolution, empires, restorations, republics, Vichy, and republics again, the French people had shown great enthusiasm for the head of state, a certain reverence for and deference toward the central authority, whether it was a king, a radical revolutionary, a prince, head of the French state, or a president. This explains at least in part the ease with which much of the nation converted from the Republic to Pétain in 1940 and then from the French state to de Gaulle in 1944. For some observers, Mitterrand marked the end of the state's hegemony in national identity.

For others, however, the state was too entrenched in the minds of the French to be dismissed so easily. While *Maréchal, nous voilà* (Marshal, here we are) was the rallying cry of Pétain enthusiasts, for example, *Président, nous voilà* (President, here we are) was the headline of a *Libération* opinion, written by psychoanalyst Michel Schneider, after Mitterrand's television debacle. He argued that the nation had enabled and even encouraged Mitterrand's deception by treating him like a father. When we told him "tell me the truth," Schneider suggested, what we were really saying was "say it isn't true"; when we joined Elkabbach in admonishing Mitterrand, "we are going to tell the whole story, right?" what we really meant was "tell me you love me." And by refusing to condemn Bousquet or his own past, Mitterrand told us he loved us. Because the subject in our imaginary—the father, the king, the president—whom we believe to be all-knowing is also, in the imaginary, the guarantor of meaning. For Schneider, the French were more attached to the paternal authority of their leader than even they understood. Mitterrand was steadfast in his convictions, and it was the nation's "transferential illusion" to believe that it expected or wanted him to be otherwise. All of our criticism, our sense of betrayal, Schneider contended, is "tinged with the mark of love." To whom can we complain that the loved one no longer loves us if not the loved one himself? "President, here we are."[8]

In the anger expressed toward Mitterrand was a mixture of affection, betrayal, and relief, a complex of emotions that simultaneously condemned the state and revealed its continued omnipotence. "We are an old country which has astonished the world by our influence," said Gaullist deputy Patrick Devedjian, "but we continue to devour ourselves to the point at which we imagine that our future depends on the power of state. A state to which we confide our soul and which we prefer to the rule of law."[9] The state, in fact, exemplified a fundamental contradiction inherent in shifting notions of French identity since the Revolution: namely, the tension between the pioneering universalism of revolutionary ideology and the glorification of France itself. Even Michelet, as Suzanne Citron pointed out in her work on the French "national myth," had tended both to promote universalism and to admire France as the only nation inherently capable of transmitting universal ideals.[10] The state, in all of its historical incarnations, was actually a potent symbol of these competing national impulses. The hero of Verdun and the villain of Vichy, Pétain epitomized the best and worst of France; the Vichy apologist and the Socialist savior, Mitterrand presented a similar contradiction. It was fitting that Mitterrand's insistence on honoring Pétain's tomb was one of the defining moments in the evolution of Holocaust discourse.

It is ironic, moreover, that amidst widespread criticism of the state it is de Gaulle, the architect of the presidential republic, who emerges all the greater. In embodying the falsity of the Resistance myth, Mitterrand ennobled its creator and magnified the greatness of his choice. And in their feebleness, Mitterrand and Papon immortalized the general as the savior of the good France. Of course de Gaulle had inspired both praise and contempt as a general and then as president of the Republic. But his memory was exalted in later discussions of World War II because the contrast between him and those implicated in Vichy scandals was so stark. Memory of de Gaulle, in other words, was no more nuanced than it was for the Resistance, collaboration, and the Holocaust. It was no more a confrontation with the complexity of the general's political career than had been any of the other debates about which critics such as Rousso had complained. Nonetheless, public discourse about Vichy undoubtedly challenged the integrity of the national past. "We no longer know of which history we are the children," remarked Nora in 1997. Confronted with an ambiguous historical legacy, a socially heterogeneous present, and an uncertain European future, the French—"orphans of time" in the words of historian Jean Chesneaux—could still turn to a hero, someone in the past who could ground their identity and provide evidence of their virtue. As Elizabeth Bellamy has argued, memory serves primarily to create subjective continuity where none exists, and it makes possible a lasting idealization of the lost loved one. During debates about Vichy, true France could be found in the memory of de Gaulle. And not unlike the way Jews had functioned during the Revolution, Dreyfus Affair, and Vichy regime, the Holocaust served as a theater for various scripts about national identity.[11]

## Chapter 1

1. Lanzmann quoted in *Le Monde*, June 2, 1967.

2. Jean-Marie Charon, *La Presse en France de 1945 à nos jours*, 1991, 134.

3. In the early 1970s, circulation was as follows: *Tribune Juive*, 15,000; *L'Arche*, 20,000; *Information Juive*, 23,000; *Cahiers Bernard Lazare*, 2,000. By 2000, readership for *Tribune Juive* and *L'Arche* had remained steady, *Information Juive* had dropped to around 10,000, and 18,000 subscribed to *Actualité Juive*. See Josef Fraenkel, *The Jewish Press of the World*, 1972, 16–18, and Valérie Rouvière, "La presse juive en France," http://www.france5.fr (December 8, 2001).

4. Cathy Caruth, "Unclaimed Experience: Trauma and the Possibility of History," 1991, 181; Judith Herman, *Trauma and Recovery*, 1992, 33.

5. Kirby Farrell, *Post-traumatic Culture: Injury and Interpretation in the Nineties*, 1998, 3, 7; Gay Becker, *Disrupted Lives: How People Create Meaning in a Chaotic World*, 1997, 2, 4; Cathy Caruth, *Trauma: Explorations in Memory*, 1995, 152–53.

6. I understand narrative as a form of discourse where the details or truth of individual statements are less important than their sequentiality, or the overall meaning that a story is meant to convey. Situated storytelling means "situated in a cultural setting" where implicit agreements on social meaning govern what particular actors say and do in given circumstances. See Jerome Bruner, *Acts of Meaning*, 1990, 19, 43–45.

7. Farrell, *Post-Traumatic Culture*, 7, 18; Becker, *Disrupted Lives*, 15. Bruner, *Acts of Meaning*, 47.

8. Michael S. Roth, *The Ironist's Cage: Memory, Trauma, and the Construction of History*, 1995, 13.

9. Bruner, *Acts of Meaning*, 59.

10. Lawrence L. Langer, *Preempting the Holocaust*, 1998, 59–60; Lawrence L.

Langer, *Admitting the Holocaust*, 1995, 4, 10; Claude Lanzmann, "The Obscenity of Understanding: An Evening with Claude Lanzmann," in Cathy Caruth (ed.), *Trauma: Explorations in Memory*, 1995, 206–7; Michael André Bernstein, *Foregone Conclusions: Against Apocalyptic History*, 1994, 13; Jean-François Lyotard, *Le Différend*, 1988, and Sande Cohen, "Between Image and Phrase: Progressive History and the 'Final Solution' as Dispossession," in Saul Friedlander (ed.), *Probing the Limits of Representation: Nazism and the Final Solution*, 1992, 171–84.

11. On Lanzmann's "Shoah," see Omer Bartov, "Spielberg's Oskar: Hollywood Tries Evil," Miriam Bratu Hansen, "'Schindler's List' is not 'Shoah': Second Commandment, Popular Modernism, and Public Memory," and "Holocaust Others: Spielberg's 'Schindler's List' versus Lanzmann's 'Shoah,'" in Yosefa Loshitzky (ed.), *Spielberg's Holocaust: Critical Perspectives on Schindler's List*, 1997, 54–56; Ilan Avisar, "Holocaust Movies and the Politics of Collective Memory," in Alvin Rosenfeld (ed.), *Thinking About the Holocaust: After Half a Century*, 1997, 39–44; and James Young, *Writing and Rewriting the Holocaust: Narrative and the Consequences of Interpretation*, 1988, 160–68. Roth, *The Ironist's Cage*, 205; Herman, *Trauma and Recovery*, 1.

12. Elizabeth J. Bellamy, *Affective Genealogies: Psychoanalysis, Postmodernism, and the "Jewish Question" after Auschwitz*, 1997, 8; Herman, *Trauma and Recovery*, 181, 175, 177–78.

13. See Elizabeth Spelman, *Fruits of Sorrow: Framing Our Attention to Suffering*, 1997, 113–32.

14. The Declaration of the Rights of Man, which decreed that all men were born free and equal, was voted into law in August 1789. Jews were not included in its purview. Initial debates about non-Catholics, dominated by the question of Jewish citizenship, resulted in the formal granting of equality to Protestants and the explicit exclusion of Jews. It was not until January 1790 that the largely assimilated Sephardi Jews were emancipated, and only in September 1791 did the National Assembly bestow citizenship on the Ashkenazi Jews of the east. Women were constitutionally accorded full political rights only in 1946. See Arthur Hertzberg, *The French Enlightenment and the Jews: The Origins of Modern Anti-Semitism*, 1968, 339–49.

15. Nancy Green in André Kaspi (ed.), *La Révolution française et l'émancipation des Juifs de France*, 1989, 86–88. See also Nancy Green, "La Révolution dans l'imaginaire des immigrants juifs," in Pierre Birnbaum (ed.), *Histoire politique des juifs de France*, 1990, 153–62, and *The Pletzl of Paris*, 1986.

16. Michael R. Marrus, *The Politics of Assimilation: The French Jewish Community at the Time of the Dreyfus Affair*, 1971, 196–231; Jean-Denis Bredin, *The Affair: The Case of Alfred Dreyfus*, [1983] 1986, 297–99, 527–29; Paula Hyman, *The Jews of Modern France*, 1998, 111. Léon Blum, himself an active Dreyfusard, harshly judged the response of the Jewish community, especially Jewish elites. See Blum, *Souvenirs sur l'Affaire*, 1982. On Durkheim and the affair, see Pierre Birnbaum, *Jewish Destinies: Citizenship, State, and Community in Modern France*, [1995] 2000, 64–98.

17. Michael R. Marrus and Robert O. Paxton, *Vichy France and the Jews*, 1983, 109–12, 336; Hyman, *The Jews of Modern France*, 183–84. See also Jacques Adler, *The Jews of Paris and the Final Solution*, [1985] 1987, and Renée Poznanski, *Être juif en*

*France pendant la Seconde Guerre Mondiale*, 1994, 94–102, 143–67, 202–12, 246–55, 478–518, 619–33, 698–705.

18. Hertzberg, *The French Enlightenment and the Jews*, 339.

19. Thus, moreover, was it plausible for French Jews to understand their particular predicament in the broad context of French politics. "They could see their victimization," writes Hyman, "as merely an unfortunate part of the general assault on the Republic and on capitalism" (*The Jews of Modern France*, 111).

20. In *Le mythe national: l'histoire de France en question* (1991), Suzanne Citron shows how French history books have presented "France" as a subject, a "living organism," long before it actually existed as a country. A 1985 textbook explains that in feudal times, "France was divided into a number of independent domains," which implies that a sovereign France actually predated a partition. Another textbook illustrates the Norman invasions on a map which situates Nantes, Bordeaux, Paris, and Rouen in a perfect (and anachronistic) hexagon. "'History' is the history of France," she writes. "The history of 'others' does not exist" (85–87).

21. See Pierre Birnbaum, *Les Fous de la République: Histoire des Juifs d'état, de Gambetta à Vichy*, 1994, and Birnbaum, *Jewish Destinies*, 4.

22. Hertzberg, *The French Enlightenment and the Jews*, 347.

23. Shmuel Trigano argues that "the Jews *qua* Jews were *collectively* deprived of their citizenship and collectively removed from the French nation" and that this "left indelible marks . . . on the Jews who had been singled out as Jews" ("The Rebirth of the 'Jewish Nation' in France," 1985, 254). While this might have been the case, it was no less true for groups as diverse as nobles, the clergy, and workers, all of whom were targeted by revolutionary anti-corporatism and some of whom found ways to mold the new rhetoric to their own needs. Still, as Trigano contends, Jews were not included in the category of "men," and their emancipation was uniquely contested. See also Trigano, *La nouvelle question juive: l'avenir d'un espoir*, 1979, and Stanley Hoffmann, "Remarks on Trigano," 1985.

24. Hyman, *The Jews of Modern France*, 43, 183.

25. See Doris Bensimon and Sergio Della Pergola, *La population Juive de France: socio-démographie et identité*, 1984, and Claude Tapia, "Religion et politique: interférence dans le judaïsme français après l'immigration judéo-maghrébine," 1989.

26. Sarah Farmer, *Martyred Village: Commemorating the 1944 Massacre at Oradour-sur-Glane*, 1999, 58; Henry Rousso, *The Vichy Syndrome: History and Memory in France Since 1944*, 1991.

27. See Eric Conan and Henry Rousso, *Vichy: An Ever-Present Past*, 1998, *passim*. I will consider Conan and Rousso's critique of memory more fully in the conclusion.

## Chapter 2

1. *On* is a particularly "slippery" word in French and can be translated to mean "we," "they," "one," "you," or even "I." It is an especially elusive construction in conversations about moral responsibility. In certain quotations, including this one, the

English word selected as translation can dramatically alter the tone and meaning. When I have not translated it as "one," I have followed the translation with "[*on*]."

2. Sperber in *L'Arche*, June 1967; Nollier in *Le Monde*, June 3, 1967.

3. Though the word "Holocaust" did not appear with frequency in French public discourse until the 1979 broadcast of the film "Holocaust" on French television, 1967 marks the first moment when the annihilation of over five million European Jews began to be portrayed as conceptually autonomous, or as an event with parameters distinct from those of World War II. I use the term, therefore, to describe discussions that focus on the Nazi genocide of the Jews.

4. As late as May 18, after Egyptian president Gamal Abdul Nasser had demanded the withdrawal of UN forces from Egypt and Jordanian and Syrian forces had joined Egyptian troops in a state of alert, *Le Figaro* suggested that Cairo's gesture seemed destined more to impress Arab opinion than to be a prelude to massive action. *Le Monde* argued on May 20 that war was far from imminent: Israel was not prepared to battle both Egypt and Syria, and Egyptian troops were already committed in Yemen. *La Croix* also argued on May 21 that Egyptian troops were too strained to open another front. The Jewish *L'Arche* had not run a cover story on Israel since May 1966, when it had reported on the country's water problem; its May 1967 issue expressed no noticeably elevated concern about the conflict in the Middle East. *Bulletin de nos communautés* marked Israel's nineteenth anniversary in its May 5 issue and also featured an article titled "The Crisis," which explored Israeli economic concerns; and *UNIR*, the monthly journal of the Jewish community in Strasbourg, had included during the first five months of the year only passing references to tensions in Israel.

5. Annette Wieviorka, *Déportation et génocide*, 1992, 279, 282, 322, 351. See parts two and three of the text for further discussion of Jews in the first decade after the war, as well as David Weinberg, "The Reconstruction of the French Jewish Community after World War II," in *She'erit Hapletah, 1944–48: Rehabilitation and Political Struggle*, 1990, 168–86. See also Gérard Namer, *La Commémoration en France: de 1945 à nos jours*, 1987, for an analysis of French commemoration ceremonies immediately following the war.

6. Muriel Klein-Zolty, "La perception du génocide dans la presse française en 1946," *Le Monde Juif* (January 1994), 109–20.

7. See André Kaspi, "L'Affaire des enfants Finaly," 1985, and Henry Rousso, *The Vichy Syndrome*, 1991, 54–55.

8. None of this support was without qualification, and cold war politics usually guided how people perceived the Middle East. Pro-Israel sentiment, furthermore, was much stronger when Israel was in danger, a fact not lost on many Jews in 1967 (see discussion below). Citing surveys administered in the years surrounding the Suez crisis, Jean-William Lapierre notes that "sympathy for Israel" rose from 11% in December 1955 to 40% in December 1956 and 43% in May 1957. Those with no opinion hovered around 50% in similar surveys (Lapierre, *Information sur l'État d'Israél dans les grands quotidiens français en 1958*, 1968). It is precisely the fact that both indifference and lukewarm backing transformed into a solid endorsement of the state of Israel in times of crisis that bolstered Jewish confidence.

9.  Before the Six-Day War, covers of Jewish publications such as *Cahiers Bernard Lazare* and *L'Arche* were more frequently devoted to Israel than to any other issue. Stories about Israel constituted the overwhelming majority of overall coverage, and those discussions centered on other aspects of Jewish life were also presented in ways that emphasized the centrality of Israel.

10.  *Information Juive*, April 1952; *Cahiers Bernard Lazare*, June 1957. The Uprising began on April 19, 1943, in response to the Nazi plan to liquidate the Warsaw Ghetto and deport all Jews to the Treblinka extermination camp. Though the Ghetto was ultimately destroyed, the Jewish underground resisted for nearly a month, killing several German soldiers and forcing the Nazis to divert precious material and human resources to the Ghetto in the process.

11.  *Information Juive*, May 1954. "Hatikvah (The Hope)" is the Israeli national anthem.

12.  *Cahiers Bernard Lazare*, April 1961. In the 1950s, the Tomb of the Unknown Jewish Martyr came into being in ways that facilitated its absorption into both the history of French martyrdom and the landscape of French memorials. At the October 1956 inauguration, Vichy was not discussed. Heroic France was contrasted with evil Germany, and the ceremony closed with a singing of both the *Marseillaise* and the Israeli national anthem, thereby enabling participants to focus on a hopeful future. See Annette Wieviorka, "Un lieu de mémoire: Le Mémorial du martyr juif inconnu," 1985, and *Le Monde Juif*, December 1956, 26–53.

13.  According to Heinz Kohut (*The Analysis of the Self*, 1971, 176–86), disavowal characterizes not the painful events buried in the unconscious, as in repression, but instead those that are held in abeyance in consciousness. A segment of consciousness is split off from the rest of the ego, and it is here that the event remains: unassimilated, consciously avoided, and at times forcefully suppressed by the dominant ego.

14.  De Gaulle had declared that France would not be officially aligned with either Israel or the Arabs and that whoever "fired the first shot" would not receive French support.

15.  Neher in *L'Arche*, June 1967. See also *Information Juive*, which claimed in June 1967 that Israeli Jews were "at the front lines of Judaism."

16.  *UNIR*, June 2, 1967.

17.  A group of leftist intellectuals, many not Jewish, issued a public statement expressing support for Israel. Among the signatories were Jean-Paul Sartre, Pablo Picasso, Marguerite Duras, Simone de Beauvoir, Jean-François Lyotard, Daniel Mayer, Pierre Vidal-Naquet, and Vladimir Jankelevitch. They claimed to be "friends of the Arab peoples and adversaries of American imperialism" who considered "incomprehensible the identification of Israel with an imperialist, aggressive camp." The statement was printed in several newspapers, including *Le Figaro*, May 29, 1967, and *Le Monde*, June 1, 1967.

18.  Daniel in *Le Nouvel Observateur*, May 31 and June 7, 1967; Lanzmann quoted in *Le Monde*, June 2, 1967; Mayer quoted in *Le Figaro*, June 6, 1967.

19.  According to historian Annette Wieviorka, Mayer had supported the Tomb of the Unknown Jewish Martyr only after making it clear that he did so as an antiracist (and not as a Jew). Mayer contended that he had told Isaac Schneerson, a Jew-

ish community activist trying to galvanize support for the project, that he was "not at all in favor of a special monument for an unknown Jewish martyr. If he is unknown, how do you prove he is Jewish? And how do you prove that the Unknown Soldier is not Jewish?" When Schneerson returned with the backing of all other government ministers, Mayer claimed in 1985, he felt obliged to add his support. See Wieviorka, "Un lieu de mémoire: le mémorial du martyr juif inconnu," 1985, 84, 97n.14.

20. Institut français de l'opinion publique, *Sondages*, 2 (1967). The last response indicated that despite broad support for de Gaulle's professed neutrality (fifty-nine percent), fewer French endorsed his plan to establish closer ties both to the Arabs and to the Soviet Union, a goal which had been frequently remarked upon in French debates. The total exceeds 100 percent in the last question because of multiple responses.

21. Many opinion letters in *Le Monde*, however, consistently linked the Holocaust and the Six-Day War and gave *Le Monde* a decidedly pro-Israel slant.

22. On one occasion, however, just after the war had begun, Pierre Limagne argued on the front page of *La Croix* that while it was difficult to know who had started this war, "we feel compelled to argue that many of the most influential Arab voices have proclaimed their intention to massacre to the very end the members of a nation principally founded under the auspices of the United Nations and with the survivors of Nazi persecution—to carry out, if possible, a carefully orchestrated genocide" (*La Croix*, June 7, 1967). With this exception, the newspaper made little connection between the Holocaust and the present conflict.

23. Montaron in *Témoignage Chrétien*, June 1, 1967; *L'Humanité*, May 30, 1967.

24. Cuau in *Le Figaro*, May 24, 1967; Massip in *Le Figaro*, June 1, 1967; *Le Monde*, June 1, 1967; and Ionesco in *Combat*, quoted in *Le Monde*, June 2, 1967.

25. *Bulletin de nos communautés*, June 2, 1967; *Information Juive*, June 2, 1967. The rabbis were quoted in several papers, including *Le Figaro*, June 6, 1967.

26. See, for example, *Le Figaro* on June 1, 1967, which reported that over 20,000 protestors had marched and chanted in front of the Israeli embassy in Paris while carrying signs reading "Down with Arab Nazism!"

27. Monteil in *Le Monde*, June 8, 1967. Monteil was referring to the 1948 attack on the Palestinian village of Deir Yassin, during which members of the Irgun, an Israeli right-wing paramilitary organization, had massacred over 250 men, women, and children, and also to Oradour-sur-Glane, the small French village whose inhabitants had been brutally murdered by SS soldiers at the end of World War II. The comparison was meant to equate Israelis and Nazi soldiers. See also the opinion of Maxime Rodinson, a scholar of Islamic Studies and one of the only Jews to publicly oppose Israel, in *Le Monde*, June 4, 1967.

28. *Le Nouvel Observateur*, June 14 and June 21, 1967.

29. Comité de soutien à la révolution arabe, *Juin 1967: Le conflit Israëlo-Arabe. Études et Positions*, (n.d.).

30. Wegner in *La Croix*, June 13, 1967. This sentiment was echoed throughout the non-Jewish press. See, for example, *Le Nouvel Observateur*, June 14 and June 21, 1967, as well as *Le Monde*, June 10, 1967, where Robert Escarpit suggested that "Israel evokes a culpability, more or less latent, in every European . . . It would be re-

grettable if instead of disappearing, racism only changed its target, if for an anti-Jewish anti-Semitism we only knew how to substitute an anti-Arab anti-Semitism."

31. Duquesne in *La Croix*, June 14, 1967. Two days later, a front-page article criticized Russian poet Yevgeny Yevtushenko's "Babi Yar" because "it suggested that Jews were the only victims of the Nazis in Ukraine."

32. The Franco-Prussian War ended in 1871 with France's bitter defeat; June 1940 marked French capitulation to the Nazis. Both losses were accompanied by extensive territorial and administrative violations of French national sovereignty.

33. Pierre Déméron, *Contre Israël*, 1968, 39, 43, 45, 52, 63.

34. Givet, *La Gauche contre Israël*, 68, 89, 102, 119, 124. The Givet and Déméron books were both published in a series entitled "New Liberties," edited by Jean-François Revel, who later went on to be editor of the popular news magazine *L'Express*. In a preface to *Contre Israël*, Revel wrote that "given the passions provoked by the 1967 Arab-Israeli conflict and the moral weight of the questions associated with it," he felt compelled to break with editorial practice and to state his preference, "from a purely personal perspective," for the "pro-Israel arguments of Givet." Though exact readership for the texts is difficult to establish, the polemic between Déméron and Givet manifested the themes and emotional rhetoric that characterized debates surrounding the War.

35. See Jacques Sabbath in *L'Arche*, August 1967. Although the Israeli occupation of Arab lands did produce dissent from Jews on the Left, the rhetoric that assimilated Israelis and Nazis provoked universal Jewish opprobrium.

36. Givet, *La Gauche contre Israël*, 133, 147, 152.

37. Mandel in *L'Arche*, July 1967; Lévy-Valensi in *L'Arche*, August 1967; Touati in *Information Juive*, December 1967.

38. De Gaulle's remarks were cited in several French newspapers and magazines. See, for example, *Le Figaro*, November 28, 1967, where his speech was reproduced in its entirety.

39. Daniel in *Le Nouvel Observateur*, December 6, 1967; Mayer in *Témoignage Chrétien*, December 7, 1967.

40. See especially the series of articles Aron wrote on Jews and Israel in *Le Figaro Littéraire*, February 24, March 3, and March 10, 1962. See also Aline Benain, "L'Itinéraire juif de Raymond Aron: hasard, déchirement et dialectique de l'appartenance," *Pardès* 11 (1990).

41. Raymond Aron, *De Gaulle, Israël, et les juifs*, reprinted in Raymond Aron, *Essais sur la condition juive contemporaine*, 1989, 47, 50, 49, 72, 51, 64, 67, 49.

42. Aron, *Le Figaro Littéraire*, 1962, and *Essais sur la condition juive contemporaine*, *passim*.

43. Many on the Left who were unequivocal in their anti-Zionism complained that they were being unfairly attacked as anti-Semitic; many Jews and other supporters of Israel, on the other hand, contended that anti-Zionism was really anti-Semitism in disguise. As editor of *Les Temps Modernes*, for example, Jean-Paul Sartre published a special edition on the Middle East conflict, over 1,000 pages divided into pro-Israel and pro-Arab sections (May 1967). In the preface, Sartre wrote that he and many others on the Left were "allergic to everything that even remotely resembles anti-Semitism. To which many Arabs will respond: 'We are not

anti-Semites but anti-Israel.' They are undoubtedly right: but can they change the fact that these Israelis, for us, are also Jews?"

44. Montaron in *Témoignage Chrétien*, December 7, 1967.

45. James Young writes of a similar conflict between poet Sylvia Plath and those who criticized her for using the Holocaust as a metaphor for suffering. "[I]f Plath's pain is not perceived literally to be part of the larger pain of Jewish suffering," he argued, "then even the figurative force of her metonymical connection loses its authority" (*Writing and Rewriting the Holocaust: Narrative and the Consequences of Interpretation*, 1988, 132).

46. André Neher in *L'Arche*, June 1967; *Bulletin de nos communautés*, May 19 and May 26, 1967; *Information Juive*, June 1967.

## Chapter 3

1. *Bulletin de nos communautés*, September 1967. This magazine would become *Tribune Juive* in 1968.

2. A poll conducted February 26–March 2, 1971, and published in *L'Arche*, June 26, 1971, reported that sixty-nine percent of the French answered yes to the following question: "Does a Jew feel Jewish before feeling French?" Fifty-five percent believed that Jews were "closer to Jews living in Israel," while twenty-one percent thought they were "closer to other French." Whereas sixty-nine percent were "rather in agreement" with the statement "It is normal that French Jews actively demonstrate their sympathy for Israel," fifty-three percent were "rather in agreement" that "If French Jews want to actively demonstrate their sympathy for Israel, all they have to do is go live there."

3. See especially *Le Figaro Littéraire*, February 24, 1962, where Aron remarked, *inter alia*, that "[a] European Jew experiences no conscience of ethnic unity with a Yemenite Jew (even when both are citizens of the State of Israel)."

4. Aron and Bloch-Michel in *L'Arche*, April 1968.

5. Morin in *L'Arche*, April 1968. See also the roundtable discussion "Qu'est-ce qu'un Juif?" between Albert Memmi, Roger Ikor, Armand Lanoux, and Léon Poliakov, published in *Combat*, January 22, 1969.

6. Touati and Neher in *Information Juive*, September 1969. This marriage between French and Israeli ideals characterized the earliest and most radical Zionist discourse following the Holocaust. For example, an image on the front page of *La Riposte* (December 29, 1948), a French Zionist newspaper published in the years surrounding the 1948 war over Palestine, shows Jewish World War II veterans welcoming Menachem Begin, "the liberator of Palestine." Begin stands in a light of glory in front of the Israeli flag, while the revolutionary symbol Marianne, flanked by a group of Jewish resisters, welcomes him with outstretched arms. Though most Jewish resisters had been members of the FTP (Francs-Tireurs-Partisans), the Resistance branch made up largely of Jews, immigrants, and communists, this image shows them wearing the armbands of the FFI (Forces Françaises de l'Intérieur), the section comprised of more "French" resisters. The caption reads: "The France of the Resistance salutes the Liberator of Palestine."

7.  The debate between Rabi and his critics was published in *Les nouveaux cahiers*, Spring 1972. Rabi's primary targets were André Neher and Robert Misrahi, both of whom he already had taken to task in *L'Arche*, February 26, 1968. There he had challenged Neher's statement that "Israel is truly innocent, innocent on the same order of innocence as the Jewish people across history . . . Israel is absolutely innocent," and Misrahi's argument that "Israel is absolutely innocent, Israel is perfection incarnate."

8.  The 1967 manifesto was published in *L'Arche*, January 26, 1968.

9.  Cercle Gaston Crémieux, "Historique et Principes Généraux," n.d.

10.  Richard Marienstras, "Israël n'est pas négociable" (July 1967) and "Les grandes lignes d'une politique culturelle de la Diaspora," address presented to the general assembly of the Fonds social juif unifié (November 1970), reprinted in Marienstras, *Être un peuple en diaspora*, 1975, 159–70, 198, 200, 201.

11.  Maurice Szafran, *Les juifs dans la politique française*, 1990, 184, 181, 187, 185. See also Yaïr Auron, *Les Juifs d'extrême gauche en Mai 1968*, 1998. Jean Moulin was a Resistance hero tortured and murdered by the Nazis.

12.  Pierre Goldman, *Souvenirs obscurs d'un Juif polonais né en France*, 1975, 33, 46, 56, 62, 34, 59, 70–71, 124–25.

13.  For criticism of Pompidou, see the editorials in *Les nouveaux cahiers*, Spring 1969 and Autumn 1969, and Daniel Amson, "De Gaulle n'aurait jamais fait çela," *Les nouveaux cahiers*, Autumn 1971. On the charge of "double loyalty," see René Massigli, "Double appartenance," in *Le Monde*, February 27, 1970.

14.  Wladimir Rabi in *L'Arche*, February 26, 1973.

15.  *Information Juive*, May 1969. The reference to decisions of "flagrant injustice" concerned de Gaulle's recent decision to impose an embargo on arms to Israel, weaponry for which the Israelis had already paid.

16.  Sabbath and Rabi in *L'Arche*, February 26, 1973.

17.  Quoted in Szafran, *Les juifs dans la politique française*, 219.

18.  Maurice Szafran, *Simone Veil: Destin*, 1994, 214, 215.

19.  The Holocaust-abortion analogy was commonly employed by many opposed to the abortion project, and often in ways that did not criticize either Jews or Veil and which would be difficult to classify as explicitly anti-Semitic. See, for example, Georges Naughton, *Le choc du passé: avortement, néo-Nazisme, nouvelle morale*, 1974.

20.  Szafran, *Simone Veil*, 217, 209–10.

21.  Veil and Vidal-Naquet quoted in Szafran, *Les Juifs dans la politique française*, 218, 227–28.

22.  See Henry Rousso, *The Vichy Syndrome: History and Memory in France since 1944*, 1991, especially 100–114.

23.  Rousso, *The Vichy Syndrome*, 10, 101; Stanley Hoffmann, "In the Looking Glass: Sorrow and Pity?" 1972, in *Decline or Renewal? France Since the 1930s*, 1974, 56.

24.  John F. Sweets, "Hold that Pendulum! Redefining Fascism, Collaborationism and Resistance in France," 1988, argues that this is precisely what began to happen in the 1980s.

25.  Fabre-Luce in *Le Monde*, May 13 and June 8, 1971.

26.  Lévy and Bulawko in *Le Monde*, June 8, 1971.

27. "Pardonner?" originally published in 1971 and reprinted in Vladimir Jankelevitch, *L'imprescriptible*, 1986.

28. *L'Arche*, June 26, 1971.

29. Jacques Derogy, "*L'Express* a retrouvé le bourreau de Lyon," *L'Express*, June 5, 1972; Rousso, *The Vichy Syndrome*, 117.

30. Mayer in *Tribune Juive*, June 16, 1972. In its July 7 edition, *Tribune Juive* reported that "a few dozen" people had met to protest the government's failure to obtain Barbie's extradition. Barbie was tried for crimes against humanity in France in 1987 (see chapter five).

31. See Sarah Fishman et al. (eds.), *France at War: Vichy and the Historians*, 2000, especially John F. Sweets, "*Chaque livre un événement*: Robert Paxton and the French, from *briseur de glace* to *iconoclaste tranquille*," 21–34, and Henry Rousso, "The Historian, a Site of Memory," 285–302, for an analysis of the role of *La France de Vichy* in the development of French historiography on World War II.

32. Rousso suggests that French Jews "commended the book warmly, clearly satisfied that an American scholar had lent authoritative support to their relentless criticism of Vichy" (*The Vichy Syndrome*, 254). But he provides evidence for neither this warm commendation nor Jews' "relentless" critique of Vichy. Rabi wrote a brief and positive but not unequivocal review in the back pages of *L'Arche*'s book section (March 1973), but *La France de Vichy* does not appear to have inspired the reaction Rousso attributes to French Jews.

33. On March 12, 1979, Jean Leguay, Bousquet's assistant in the occupied zone, was indicted, and Nazi hunter Serge Klarsfeld announced his intention to pursue Bousquet.

34. *L'Express*, October 28, 1978.

35. Daniel in *Le Nouvel Observateur*, November 6, 1978.

36. Socialist Gilles Martinet in *Le Matin*, November 1, 1978. Far from the dangerous violation of a taboo, countered writer Edgar Morin, Darquier had provoked a "political re-vaccination."

37. Veil in *Le Matin*, October 30, 1978; Jankelevitch in *Le Matin*, November 1, 1978; *L'Express*, November 4 and November 11, 1978. Darquier had been born at Cahors.

38. Pilhes in *Le Monde*, November 4, 1978; *L'Express*, November 11, 1978; Montaron in *Témoignage Chrétien*, November 9, 1978.

39. Daniel in *Le Nouvel Observateur*, November 6, 1978; Aron in *L'Express*, November 11, 1978.

40. *Figaro Magazine*, February 10, 1979.

41. Jacquot Grunewald in *Tribune Juive*, December 1, 1978.

42. Praise for "Holocaust" was so widespread that Serge July, in severely criticizing the film, remarked sarcastically that "if my reaction was so clearly in the minority, it was quite simply because anti-Semitism lurked within me" (*Libération*, March 12, 1979).

43. *Le Monde*, February 11–12 and February 14, 1979; *Le Matin*, February 15, 1979; *Le Point*, February 12, 1979; Jamet in *L'Aurore*, February 14, 1979.

44. *Le Monde*, February 15 and February 16, 1979; *La Lettre de la nation*, February 15, 1979; *L'Humanité* quoted in *Le Monde*, February 16, 1979. In an effort to bol-

ster Franco-German cooperation, Giscard had canceled the national celebration of May 8, or V-E Day, in 1975. The Socialist government of Pierre Mauroy then reinstated May 8 as a national holiday in September 1981. See Gérard Namer, *La Commémoration en France: de 1945 à nos jours*, 1987, for the politics surrounding the celebration of V-E Day in France.

45. *Le Matin*, February 15, 1979.

46. *Le Point*, February 12, 1979.

47. See, for example, Alfred Grosser in *Le Matin*, February 15, 1979. When the press brought attention to Vichy's contributions to the Holocaust, they were most often either ignorant of or flagrantly careless with the details. The total number of Jews deported from France, for example, ranged in the press from 90,000 to 117,000. Most scholars (see, for example, Serge Klarsfeld, *Vichy-Auschwitz: Le rôle de Vichy dans la question juive en France*, 1983, 1985, and Michael R. Marrus and Robert O. Paxton, *Vichy France and the Jews*, 1983) agree that roughly 78,000 Jews were deported, of whom fewer than 3,000 returned at the end of the war. By the time of the Barbie trial, these numbers were widely and consistently reported in public discourse, a measure of the nation's more informed consciousness of Jewish deportations from France.

48. Soliman in *Le Matin*, February 17, 1979; *Rouge*, February 15, 1979; Ben Jelloun and Giniewski in *Le Monde*, February 27, 1979.

49. Passages from Beullac's message were published in *Le Figaro*, February 14, 1979. *L'Agence Télégraphic Juive*'s response of February 15, 1979, was partially reprinted in *Le Monde*, February 16, 1979. For Jewish responses to the film, see *Tribune Juive*, February 9, 1979, and *L'Arche*, March 1979 and April 1979.

50. *Le Nouvel Observateur*, February 19, 1979. Jankelevitch's remarks about the singularity of Nazi anti-Semitism were first elaborated in "Dans l'honneur et la dignité" (1948) and "Pardonner?" (1971), both reprinted in *L'imprescriptible*, 1986.

51. Lanzmann in *L'Arche*, March 1979, and *Le Matin*, February 17, 1979. His "Shoah" was released in 1985.

52. Faurisson and Wellers in *Le Monde*, December 29, 1978; Wurmser in *Le Monde*, December 30, 1978. The historians' declaration was printed in *Le Monde*, February 21, 1979. For a history of revisionism in France, see Nadine Fresco, "Parcours du ressentiment: pseudo-histoire et théorie sur mesure dans le 'révisionnisme' française," 1989. For the Chomsky preface, see Faurisson, *Mémoire en défense. Contre ceux qui m'accusent de falsifier l'histoire. La question des chambres de gaz*, 1980.

53. Pierre Goldman in *L'Arche*, December 1978.

54. Shmuel Trigano, *La nouvelle question juive: l'avenir d'un espoir*, 1979, 23, 46–47, 95–110; *L'Arche*, December 1978.

55. *Le Monde*, March 7, 1979.

## Chapter 4

1. Poliakov in *Le Quotidien de Paris*, October 3, 1980. The most prominent of earlier anti-Semitic attacks was the 1979 bombing of a kosher university cafeteria on rue Médicis in Paris.

2. Finkielkraut in *Libération*, September 30, 1980, and *Le Juif imaginaire*, 1980.

3. July in *Libération*, October 6, 1980; Kahn in *Le Matin*, October 6, 1980; *Le Monde*, October 5/6, 1980; *Le Quotidien de Paris*, October 6, 1980. A few years later, Giscard acknowledged that he had been wrong not to respond immediately. See Claude Tapia, "Religion et politique: Interférence dans le judaïsme français après l'immigration judéo-maghrébine," 1989, 223 n. 9.

4. Former FANE leader Mark Frederiksen, who since the group's dissolution had organized another openly fascist organization, was sentenced in mid-October to eighteen months in prison for racial defamation and provocation to discrimination and racial hatred in an incident unrelated to the Copernic attack.

5. *Libération*, October 7, 1980; *Le Monde*, October 7, 1980; Bernard-Henri Lévy in *Le Quotidien de Paris*, October 6, 1980; *L'Express*, October 11, 1980; Grunewald in *Tribune Juive*, October 10, 1980.

6. Robert Pagès in *Libération*, October 7, 1980; *Esprit* editor Paul Thibaud in *Le Matin*, October 13, 1980; Jean Potin in *La Croix*, October 7, 1980; Touraine in *Le Matin*, October 6, 1980; Jamet in *Le Quotidien de Paris*, October 7, 1980; Rollin in *Libération*, October 7, 1980.

7. July in *Libération*, October 6, 1980. The statements of both Giscard and Mitterrand were widely reproduced (i.e. *Le Monde*, October 10, 1980).

8. For example, Chirac delivered a long speech on July 18, 1986, during the inauguration of a plaque marking the Vélodrome d'Hiver, the bicycle stadium where Paris Jews had been sent before being deported in July 1942. See the program by the Commission du Souvenir du CRIF, *Inauguration de la Place des Martyrs Juifs au Vélodrome d'Hiver: Grande Rafle des 16 et 17 juillet 1942*, July 18, 1986.

9. Rabi in *Le Monde*, October 17, 1980.

10. *Le Matin*, October 6, 1980; *Libération*, October 6, 1980; *Le Monde*, October 5/6, 1980; Kagan quoted in *Témoignage Chrétien*, October 13, 1980. In fact, Pétain had refused to mandate the yellow star in the Vichy zone. Only those in Nazi-occupied France were obligated to wear it.

11. *Le Monde*, October 7, 1980.

12. Grunewald in *Tribune Juive*, November 7, 1980; Grynfogel quoted in *Tribune Juive*, December 5, 1980; *Libération*, October 6, 1980.

13. July in *Libération*, October 4 and October 7, 1980; Dominique Pouchin in *Le Monde*, October 19, 1980.

14. Daoud, the alleged mastermind behind the murder of Israeli athletes at the 1972 Olympics, had been arrested by French authorities in 1977. Despite Israeli and German requests for his extradition, French authorities enabled him to leave for Algeria.

15. The statement was widely and variably quoted and is reprinted in its entirety in Alain de Rothschild, *Le Juif dans la cité: Discours et conférences*, Paris, 1984.

16. Guy de Rothschild's speech was reprinted in *L'Arche*, June 1967. See chapter two.

17. Recounted in *Le Point*, October 13, 1980.

18. *Le Matin*, October 4/5, 1980; *Le Monde*, October 5/6, 1980.

19. *Le Monde*, October 18 and October 19/20, 1980.

20. *L'Arche*, June 1980, reprinted in Annie Kriegel, *Réflexion sur les questions juives*, 1984, 188.

21. Quoted in Henry Weinberg, *The Myth of the Jew in France*, 1987, 150.

22. For an analysis of the immediate post-Holocaust generation of French Jews, see Finkielkraut, *Le juif imaginaire*, especially 103–15. See also Yaïr Auron, *Les juifs d'extrême gauche en mai 68*, 1998, especially 90–115.

23. Alexandre Adler and Bernard Cohen, *Juif & Juif: Ashkénazes et sépharades aujourd'hui*, 1985, 162; Tapia, "Religion et politique," 214–15, and Claude Tapia, *Juifs sépharades en France*, 1986, especially 232–43. Despite constituting some of the best doctors in French medicine, wrote Cohen, Sephardi Jews were rarely psychoanalysts, "without doubt because their history did not immerse them enough in the neuroses of Western societies" (106).

24. *Le Monde*, October 15, 1980.

25. Grunewald in *Tribune Juive*, November 7, 1980.

26. Quoted by Pouchin in *Le Monde*, October 18, 1980.

27. See Suzanne Citron, *Le mythe national*, Paris, 1989, especially 27–50, 103–14, 140–49.

28. *Le Monde*, October 26/27, 1980. At the time, Hajdenberg also served on the "official" CRIF.

29. The community appeal was reprinted in Rothschild, *Le Juif dans la cité*.

30. Hermier in *Révolution*, October 10, 1980; Ledure in *La Croix*, October 12, 1980.

31. Pujo in *Aspects de la France*, October 9, 1980; Mitterrand quoted in *Le Monde*, October 19, 1980.

32. *Le Matin*, October 7, 1980.

33. Until 1974, MRAP had stood for Movement Against Racism, Anti-Semitism and for Peace (Mouvement contre le racisme, l'antisémitisme et pour la paix). This communist-initiated group then dropped the reference to anti-Semitism and changed the acronym's denotation to Movement Against Racism and for Friendship Among People (Mouvement contre le racisme et pour l'amitié entre les peuples). The non-communist LICRA also had changed its name from LICA, the International League Against Anti-Semitism (Ligue internationale contre l'antisémitisme), to LICRA, the International League Against Racism and Anti-Semitism (Ligue internationale contre le racisme et l'antisémitisme).

34. *Tribune Juive*, October 10, 1980; *Libération*, October 6, 1980.

35. Montaron in *Témoignage Chrétien*, October 13, 1980; Pagès in *Libération*, October 7, 1980; Pihan in *La Croix*, October 8, 1980.

36. *Le Matin*, October 8, 1980.

37. *Le Monde*, October 9, 1980.

38. Halter in *Le Monde*, October 7, 1980; Mandel in *Le Quotidien de Paris*, October 9, 1980.

39. Goldman quoted in *Le Monde*, October 11, 1980. Elisabeth Domansky makes a similar argument about post-Holocaust generations in Germany. She suggests that anniversaries of Kristallnacht, the November 9, 1938, evening when Nazis looted and burned Jewish property, provide an opportunity for young Germans to separate

themselves from their parents without examining contemporary forms of anti-Semitism and their own potential "guilt." See her "'Kristallnacht,' the Holocaust, and German Unity: The Meaning of November 9 as an Anniversary in Germany," 1992.

40. A cartoon in *Témoignage Chrétien* (October 13, 1980) humorously depicted Interior Minister Bonnet, flanked by four police officers wearing swastikas and Hitler buttons, explaining that "the investigation seems difficult because we lack information on the Far Right."

41. *Le Monde*, October 9, 1980.

42. Finkielkraut, *Le Juif imaginaire*, 44, 52, 76–77, 121.

43. Finkielkraut, *Le Juif imaginaire*, 45, 51.

44. Trigano, *La République et les Juifs après Copernic*, 1982, 21–22, 26, 179, 246–47.

45. Paupert in *Le Monde*, January 4/5, 1981; de Beauvoir in *Le Nouvel Observateur*, January 12, 1981.

46. Halter, quoted in *Le Quotidien de Paris*, August 10, 1992; Sollers in *Le Quotidien de Paris*, August 13, 1992; Finkielkraut in *Le Matin*, August 16, 1982.

47. "Oradour" was a reference to the SS massacre of virtually the entire village of Oradour-sur-Glane at the end of World War II. Both Mitterrand and Begin's remarks were widely quoted, including *Libération*, August 11, 1982.

48. Sirat in *Le Matin*, August 13, 1982.

49. *Le Matin*, August 11, 1982.

50. *Le Monde*, August 13, 1982.

51. Dupuy in *Libération*, September 20, 1982; July in *Libération*, September 21, 1982.

52. Finkielkraut in *Libération*, September 24, 1982. See also Pierre Vidal-Naquet, *Libération*, September 20, 1982; Daniel Amson, *Le Quotidien de Paris*, September 20, 1982; Finkielkraut and Blandine Barrett-Kriegel, *Libération*, September 21, 1982; Jean Daniel and Jean-François Kahn, *Le Matin*, September 21, 1982; Georges Kiejman, *Le Matin*, September 22, 1982; and Claude Lanzmann, *Le Matin*, September 23, 1982.

53. Finkielkraut, *La Réprobation d'Israël*, 1983, 59, 68–69, 122–23, 142–43.

54. Finkielkraut, *Le Juif imaginaire*, 50.


## Chapter 5

1. See the results of a poll conducted February 5–7 and published in *VSD*, February 10, 1983.

2. See Henry Rousso, *The Vichy Syndrome: History and Memory in France since 1944*, 1991, 203–4.

3. The Front de Libération Nationale was the revolutionary body, comprised of various nationalist organizations, that led the Algerian war for independence against France between 1954–62.

4. Vergès attributed the omission of Moulin's death from the original indictment to Badinter's "Jewish sensibility." Badinter's father had been deported in the liquidation of the Lyon UGIF, one of the crimes for which Barbie was originally indicted. See *Pour en finir avec Ponce Pilate* (1983), in which Vergès also outlined a series of crimes perpetrated by the colonial west.

5. See Rousso, *The Vichy Syndrome*, 199–216.

6. Lévy had relied heavily on the work of Zeëv Sternhell, whose *La droite révolutionnaire, 1885–1914: Les origines françaises du fascisme* (1978) and later *Ni droite ni gauche: L'idéologie fasciste en France* (1983) contended that French fascism was a peculiar amalgam of right- and left-wing ideology. Lévy was among the country's "new philosophers" who argued that communism and fascism were equally pernicious forms of totalitarianism. For responses to Lévy, see Jean-François Kahn in *Les nouvelles littéraires*, January 15, 1981; Philippe Sollers in *Le Matin*, January 15, 1981; Raymond Aron and Jean-François Revel in *L'Express*, February 7, 1981; Paul Thibaud in *Esprit*, May 1981; and Emmanuel Le Roy Ladurie, Pierre Nora, and Léon Poliakov in *Le débat*, June 1981.

7. The ruling is quoted in David Ruzie, "The Klaus Barbie Case: War Crimes Versus Crimes Against Humanity," 1986, 31.

8. Faurisson partisans attacked the court ruling, Barbie's indictment, and crimes against humanity charges against former Vichy functionary Maurice Papon in Le Citoyen, *L'Affaire Papie-Barbon et l'arrêt du 26 avril 1983: contribution de la jurisprudence française au concept de génocide*, 1983.

9. Vidal-Naquet in *Le Nouvel Observateur*, May 30, 1986. "Un Eichmann de papier" was first published in *Esprit* (September 1980) and then included in *Assassins of Memory: Essays on the Denial of the Holocaust*, [1987] 1992. See also Michèle Cointet and Rainer Riemenschneider, "Histoire, déontologie, médias: à propos de l'affaire Roques," March 1987.

10. Variations on Faurisson's name appeared throughout the trial. See, for example, *Le Quotidien de Paris*, May 16, 1987; *L'Humanité*, June 10, 1987; *Le Progrès*, July 2, 1987; *Lyon Libération*, July 2, 1987; *La Croix*, July 3, 1987.

11. Pierre Chaunu in Reynald Sécher, *Le Génocide franco-français: le Vendée vengé*, 1986, 24. In 1991, Sécher published a second book, *Juifs et Vendéens: d'un génocide à l'autre*. Here he attempted to identify the similarities between massacres in the Vendée and the Holocaust in order, he wrote, to prevent the "official revisionism" that characterized the former's history from being applied to the latter.

12. *Le Figaro*, June 30, 1987. The resolution passed by only eight votes, with forty-two members abstaining.

13. Steg's remarks were cited in *Le Monde* and reprinted in their entirety in *Tribune Juive*, February 26, 1987.

14. Potin in *La Croix*, May 5, 1987; Smolarski in *Tribune Juive*, May 8, 1987. See also *Rencontre Chrétiens et Juifs*, 1981, which advised gentiles not to "Christianize" the Holocaust by transforming it into "a demonstration of Christian evangelicalism." Several years later, *Les Temps Modernes* criticized *Le Grand Larousse Universel* for describing the Holocaust as "of the same nature as the crucifixion of Jesus" (April 1993).

15. *Le Monde*, May 17/18, 1987; *Lyon Libération*, June 23, 1987; Maurice Szafran in *L'Événement du Jeudi*, May 14, 1987; *Le Figaro*, May 13, 1987. In this chapter, references to Lyon and other local publications are from articles reprinted in Paul Gauthier (ed.), *Chronique du procès Barbie: pour servir la mémoire*, 1988. Only two articles from Jewish magazines, both from *Tribune Juive*, appeared in this enormous compilation of press coverage from the Barbie trial.

16. Théolleyre in *Le Monde*, May 6, 1987; Dumas quoted in *Le Progrès*, June 26, 1987.

17. Bois in *Le Figaro*, June 4, 1987; Klarsfeld in *Le Progrès*, May 7, 1987; Jakubowicz in *Lyon Figaro*, June 20, 1987.

18. Lucie Aubrac, who with her husband Raymond had been an active member in the Resistance, also maintained throughout the trial that crimes against Jews were qualitatively different from those committed against resisters. Despite the horror of torture and murder in both contexts, she argued, only Nazi treatment of Jews could be meaningfully considered a crime against humanity. Raymond, on the other hand, endorsed the more expansive law. See Raymond and Lucie Aubrac, "Les Français sont capables de comprendre ce qui s'est passé dans leur pays," in Bernard-Henri Lévy (ed.), *Archives d'un procès: Klaus Barbie*, 1986, 205–19.

19. Frossard in *Lyon Figaro*, May 13, 1987. His testimony was partially reprinted in *Lyon Libération*, May 26, 1987. See also André Frossard, *Le crime contre l'humanité*, 1987.

20. Filippi in *Rivarol*, June 19, 1987.

21. Portions of Iannucci's remarks were published in *Le Figaro*, June 23, 1987, and *Lyon Matin*, June 23, 1987. *L'Événement du Jeudi*, June 4, 1987. Dumas' address to the jury was partially reprinted in *Le Progrès*, June 26, 1987, and *Le Monde*, June 28, 1987.

22. July in *Libération*, May 12, 1987. Le Pen recently had made several disparaging remarks, including referring to people with AIDS, or "SIDA" in French, as "sidaïques," a play on the French word "judaïque." Laborde in *Le Quotidien de Paris*, May 11, 1987.

23. Besson in *L'Humanité*, May 14, 1987; Besançon in *L'Express*, July 3, 1987.

24. *L'Humanité*, June 2, June 12, June 17, June 13, July 1, 1987.

25. Jakubowicz in *Lyon Figaro*, June 20, 1987, and quoted in *Le Monde*, June 28, 1987; Zelmati quoted in *Le Progrès*, June 23, 1987.

26. Smolarski in *Tribune Juive*, May 8, 1987. Wiesel's primary testimony was in a prepared statement, read by attorney Alain Jakubowicz, because French law forbade witnesses to read from written remarks. The testimony was also reprinted in *Libération*, June 3, 1987, *Tribune Juive*, June 12, 1987, and in Pierre Mérindol, *Barbie: le procès*, 1987, 371–78.

27. Wiesel, quoted in *Le Progrès*, June 3, 1987.

28. Portions of Klarsfeld's statement were reprinted across the French press. These remarks appeared in *Lyon Libération*, June 18, 1987. On "Shoah," see *Le Monde*, July 2, 1987, and *L'Humanité*, June 29, 1987.

29. Lanzmann in *Le Monde*, June 28/29, 1987, and *Lyon Figaro*, May 23, 1987.

30. Maurice Szafran, *Simone Veil*, 1994, 14–15; Halter in *Le Quotidien de Paris*, May 11, 1987. Halter had created a memorial that traveled from city to city across France in an effort to inform the country about the Holocaust. According to *Le Figaro* on July 3, over 230,000 visitors, mostly young and non-Jewish, had come to the memorial in Lyon since the trial began. In the gold books where visitors wrote their impressions, testimonies of deportees and Holocaust survivors were intermingled with messages about Sabra and Shatilla, the Gulag, and apartheid.

31. Lévy quoted in *Nice-Matin*, May 11, 1987; Antoine Spire in *Tribune Juive*, July 3, 1987.

32. The proposal for the 1964 law had been put forth by several communist members of the National Assembly in response to debates in Germany about the statute of limitations on German war crimes.

33. Excerpts of Vergès's remarks were published in *Lyon Libération*, July 3, 1987, and *Le Matin*, July 4, 1987.

34. Rappaport in *Le Progrès*, June 18, 1987; Vidal-Naquet in *Le Monde*, June 16, 1987; Daniel in *Le Nouvel Observateur*, June 19, 1987.

35. Excerpts from Mbemba's statement were quoted in *Lyon Libération*, July 3, 1987, and *Le Matin*, July 4, 1987. Bouaïta's remarks were partially reprinted in *Le Monde*, July 3, 1987, and *La Croix*, July 3, 1987. The Zaoui and La Phuong statements were printed in *Lyon Libération*, July 2, 1987. The lawyers' statements were quoted in *La Croix*, July 3, 1987, and *Le Progrès*, July 2, 1987.

36. Halter quoted in *Le Progrès*, July 3, 1987; Finkielkraut quoted in *Le Progrès*, July 2, 1987; Finkielkraut, *La mémoire vaine: du crime contre l'humanité*, 1989, 76–77.

37. Jamet in *Le Quotidien de Paris*, July 4, 1987; Finkielkraut, *La mémoire vaine*, 62–64.

38. *Le Patriote Résistant*, July 1987; *La Croix*, July 21, 1987.

39. *Tribune Juive*, May 17, 1985, March 14, 1986, June 12, 1987, and July 10, 1987.

40. *Le Nouvel Observateur*, May 15, 1987; Chalandon in *Lyon Libération*, June 12, 1987; Théolleyre in *Le Monde*, June 17, 1987; *Le Canard enchaîné*, May 6, 1987.

41. *Esprit*, July 1987.

42. Chalandon in *Libération*, May 27, 1987.

43. Chambraud in *L'Événement du Jeudi*, May 14, 1987; *Esprit*, July 1987.

## *Chapter 6*

1. Shortly after the Darquier controversy, in November 1978, Serge Klarsfeld filed crimes against humanity charges against Jean Leguay, allegedly responsible for the deportation of Jews from the occupied zone. Indicted a few months later, Leguay died of natural causes in July 1989, just after Touvier's arrest and following ten years of protracted legal maneuvering. In a break with precedent, the examining court simultaneously closed the case and declared Leguay guilty of crimes against humanity. A short time later, Klarsfeld filed charges against René Bousquet, who was indicted in March 1991. Meanwhile, in 1981, on the heels of the controversy surrounding Bernard-Henri Lévy's *L'idéologie française*, *Le Canard enchaîné* accused Maurice Papon, former prefect of Paris police and finance minister in the Giscard government, of having authorized the deportation of thousands of Jews from Bordeaux during the occupation. Papon, who had served during the war as general secretary of the Gironde prefecture, was indicted in 1983. Charges were dismissed in 1987 but filed again in 1988.

2. Pierre Birnbaum, *Jewish Destinies: Citizenship, State, and Community in Modern France*, 2000, 184–85. Chirac and Pasqua in *Libération*, April 27, 1988, and *Le*

*Monde*, May 2, 1988, quoted in Martin A. Schain, "Toward a Centrist Democracy? The Fate of the French Right," 1991, 78.

3. *Tribune Juive*, July 19, 1990. See also Frank Eskenazi and Edouard Waintrop, *Le Talmud et la République: Enquête sur les Juifs français à l'heure des renouveaux religieux*, 1991. The Carpentras affair is discussed below.

4. See Birnbaum, *Jewish Destinies*, especially 205–10.

5. In 1998, under investigation in the European Parliament for breaking laws that made trivializing the Holocaust a crime, Le Pen modified his original comments by calling the genocide "a scandalous detail, an essential detail."

6. Autant-Lara was quoted in several newspapers, including *Libération*, September 8, 1989. A few months later, Le Pen was denounced again after asking Lionel Stoléru, secretary of state for planning, whether he was of Israeli or French nationality.

7. Joffrin in *Le Nouvel Observateur*, September 14, 1989. The survey was published in a special edition of *Tribune Juive*, December 1987, and also reported in *Le Monde*, December 15, 1987.

8. An agreement between Jews and Catholics in 1987 had stipulated that the convent would move within two years. But by 1989, the building of new facilities had yet to begin, and a controversial demonstration by American Jews at the convent triggered new confrontations. Construction on the new Catholic center was completed in early 1993, but the nuns remained at Auschwitz. A personal intervention from the Pope persuaded them to leave later that year.

9. More likely, they argued, the attack had been orchestrated by extremists on the Far Right in order to make Jews look violent. See *Le Quotidien de Paris*, September 18, 1989, and *Tribune Juive*, September 22, 1989.

10. *Le Nouvel Observateur*, September 14, 1989.

11. Birnbaum, *Jewish Destinies*, 187.

12. Daniel in *Le Nouvel Observateur*, September 21, 1989.

13. Serge July in *Libération*, May 25, 1989; Veil in *Le Figaro*, May 26, 1989; Chenu in *La Croix*, May 26, 1989.

14. Boucher in *Le Monde*, June 3, 1989; Vergès quoted in *Le Figaro*, May 26, 1989. Headlines in *Rouge*, July 18, 1989; *Libération*, May 31, 1989; and *Le Figaro*, May 29, 1989. Frossard in *La Croix*, June 8, 1989; Guérin in *L'Humanité*, May 25, 1989.

15. The letter to Mitterrand was published in *Le Monde*, April 19, 1989. *Aspects de la France*, June 1, 1989. Many Jews had been openly critical of the Pope's cordial relationship with Arafat and Austrian premier Kurt Waldheim, suspected of having participated in the deportation of Jews from Austria during the war. They also criticized the Pope's response to the Carmelite affair and the Vatican's continued nonrecognition of Israel. See, for example, Jacquot Grunewald in *Tribune Juive*, September 11, 1987.

16. Kriegel in *Le Figaro*, May 29, 1989.

17. See her collected essays in Kriegel, *Réflexion sur les questions juives*, 1984, especially 109–268.

18. *La Croix*, July 8, 1989.

19. Kahn quoted in Birnbaum, *Jewish Destinies*, 242; *Le Monde*, May 16, 1990.

20. "Night and Fog" showed horrifying pictures of deportation and mass death but did not address the specifically Jewish dimension of Nazi atrocities.

21. Lévy and Noir in *L'Express*, May 18, 1990; Touraine in *Le Nouvel Observateur*, May 24, 1990; Marchais quoted in *Libération*, May 14, 1990; July in *Libération*, May 26, 1990; Winock in *Le Quotidien de Paris*, May 16, 1990; Bredin in *Le Monde*, May 29, 1990; Veil in *Le Quotidien de Paris*, May 15, 1990. See also Paul Yonnet, "La machine Carpentras: Histoire et sociologie d'un syndrome d'épuration," 1990, which charged that the cemetery defilement was being manipulated to make it look like Le Pen was responsible. It was not until April 1997 that four "skin-heads" were found guilty of the Carpentras profanation (an alleged fifth accomplice had already died).

22. Finkielkraut in *Les nouveaux cahiers*, Summer 1990; Taguieff in *Le Quotidien de Paris*, May 16, 1990. See also Yonnet, "La machine Carpentras," who argued that Carpentras helped fill the Left's need for an adversary.

23. Sitruk, Lévy, and Frossard in *Le Monde*, May 27, 1990; Bredin in *Le Monde*, May 29, 1990; Badinter in *Le Monde*, May 15, 1990; Domenach in *Le Quotidien de Paris*, May 14, 1990; Hamon in *Libération*, May 21, 1990.

24. Bredin in *Le Monde*, May 29, 1990. Winock in *Le Quotidien de Paris*, May 16, 1990; Sibony in *Libération*, May 26, 1990; Halter in *Libération*, May 26, 1990.

25. July in *Libération*, May 26, 1990.

26. Roy in *Le Monde*, May 19, 1990.

27. *Le Monde*, May 19, 1990.

28. In December 1992, after much investigation, confusion, and controversy, Minister of Culture Jack Lang issued an official communiqué indicating that the card file was in fact not from the 1940 census. While it was clear that the file had been created by Vichy, its exact contents were impossible to identify, though it later appeared to be a disparate collection of different files used by Vichy police services. In debates over where the documents should be housed, several historians argued that as part of the national patrimony, they belonged in the National Archives (see, for example, the opinion by Jean-Pierre Azéma, François Bédarida, and Henry Rousso in *Le Monde*, November 6, 1996). President Jacques Chirac, however, sided with those who wanted the files kept at the CDJC, where they were deposited in December 1997.

29. The historians' report was published in René Remond et al., *Touvier et l'Eglise*, 1992. The first poll, originally published by *Le Parisien*, was reported in *Le Monde*, April 17, 1992. The second, commissioned by *L'Événement du Jeudi* and Channel 2, was reported by Laurent Greilsamer in *Le Monde*, May 5, 1992. The petition was published in *Le Monde*, April 29, 1992.

30. On the broadcast of "Night and Fog," see *Le Monde*, April 29, 1992. Like the film, the Paris Memorial does not mention Jews.

31. *L'Humanité*, April 16, 1992; Frappat in *Le Monde*, April 15, 1992.

32. Portions of the 213-page ruling were reprinted throughout the French press. See also François Bédarida, *Touvier, Vichy, et le crime contre l'humanité: le dossier de l'accusation*, 1996, 314–21. Rousso in *Le Nouvel Observateur*, April 23, 1992. Todorov and Bredin in Golsan, ed., *Memory, the Holocaust, and French Justice*, 1996, 119–20, 113; Frappat in *Le Monde*, April 15, 1992.

33. For criticism of the court's writing of history, see Larivière in *Témoignage Chrétien*, April 25, 1992; Jean-Noël Jouanneau in *Le Monde*, June 20, 1992; Plenel in *Le Monde*, April 22, 1992. Conan in *L'Express*, April 23, 1992.

34. Chouraqui in *Tribune Juive*, June 23, 1989; Antoine Pelletier in *Tribune Juive*, May 29, 1992.

35. Théo Klein, *Oublier Vichy? À propos de l'arrêt Touvier*, 1992, 11–12, 26–28.

36. Similarly, the CRIF held its first demonstration against the *non-lieu* at the Memorial to the Deportation on the Ile de la Cité, where inscriptions speak of deportees from France but never of Jews in particular. There they were joined by members of the National Assembly from all the major parties. The next day, the CRIF sponsored a ceremony at theTomb of the Unknown Jewish Martyr in the Marais.

37. Klein, *Oublier Vichy?*, 41–42, 84, 24, 90–91.

38. The petition appeared in *L'Événement du Jeudi*, May 7, 1992; Ferenczi in *Le Monde*, April 16, 1992. Todorov in Golsan, ed., *Memory, the Holocaust, and French Justice*, 120–21.

39. Coubard in *L'Humanité*, April 15, 1992; Griotteray in *Le Figaro*, April 16, 1992, and *Figaro Magazine*, April 25, 1992.

40. Ferenczi in *Le Monde*, April 16, 1992; *Le Nouvel Observateur*, July 9, 1992; Toubon in *Le Quotidien de Paris*, April 15, 1992; Baumel in *Figaro Magazine*, April 16, 1992; Varaut in *Le Quotidien de Paris*, March 24, 1992.

41. Klein, *Oublier Vichy?*, 36–37, 22–23; Klarsfeld in Serge Klarsfeld and Henry Rousso, "Histoire et justice," *Esprit*, 1992.

42. Bérégovoy's remarks were quoted in *Le Figaro*, April 16, 1992; Revel in *Le Point*, April 17, 1992.

43. Frossard in *Le Nouvel Observateur*, April 16, 1992. Scholars and critics of the period debated the extent to which the French population had collaborated with the Nazis and the Vichy regime. While Maurice Rajsfus went so far as to accuse the Jews of the UGIF of having collaborated with Vichy, Serge Klarsfeld and historians Asher Cohen and Susan Zuccotti emphasized the fact that large segments of the French population and clergy had hidden and provided for Jews in occupied and unoccupied France. Historians Michael Marrus and Robert Paxton argued that French Jews' relatively high survival rate had several causes, including the fact that they were highly assimilated, widely dispersed, and difficult to identify. See Rajsfus, *Des juifs dans la collaboration*, 1980; Klarsfeld and Rousso, "Histoire et justice," 26–28, 31; Asher Cohen, *Persécutions et sauvetages: Juifs et Français sous l'Occupation et sous Vichy*, 1993; Susan Zuccotti, *The Holocaust, the French, and the Jews*, 1993; and Michael R. Marrus and Robert O. Paxton, *Vichy et les juifs*, 1981, translated as *Vichy France and the Jews*, 1983, especially 256–72.

44. In fact, the Nazi party actually had lost votes in the November 1932 elections, and Hitler was appointed chancellor of Germany by President Paul von Hindenburg in January 1933. In France, on the other hand, democratically elected members of the National Assembly in July 1940 voted to grant full power over the French government to Pétain, effectively putting an end to the Republic.

45. Frossard in *Le Figaro*, January 27, 1992.

46. On "La Marche du Siècle," see Eric Conan and Henry Rousso, *Vichy, un*

*passé qui ne passe pas*, 1994, 26. The *Esprit* issues were "Que faire de Vichy?" (May 1992); "Le poids de la mémoire" (July 1993); and "Que reste-t-il de la Résistance?" (January 1994).

47. Survey results were published in *Globe Hebdo*, March 22, 1994, and reprinted throughout the French press.

48. Sitruk quoted in Birnbaum, *Jewish Destinies*, 223; *Libération*, April 26, 1994; *Le Monde*, March 19, 1994; *Le Nouvel Observateur*, June 9, 1994. Said to be concerned about how the FN would respond, Interior Minister Charles Pasqua refused to make alternate arrangements for Jews to vote.

49. Klein, Drai, and Finkielkraut in *Libération*, April 26, 1994; Bernheim quoted in *Le Nouvel Observateur*, June 9, 1994.

50. *Actualité Juive*, April 7, 1994; Elkana in *Le Monde*, April 8, 1994.

51. *Événement Junior*, March 17, 1994; *Infos Junior*, March 19, 1994; Nicolaïdis in *Actualité Juive*, March 10, 1994; Vidal-Naquet in *Globe Hebdo*, March 30, 1994; Wieviorka in *Le Monde*, March 18, 1994. For Grosser's remarks, see François Bédarida, Alfred Grosser, and Pierre Vidal-Naquet, "La morale de l'histoire," in Dimitri Nicolaïdis (ed.), *Oublier nos crimes: L'Amnésie nationale, une spécificité française?*, 1994, 215–16. Gallo in *L'Événement du Jeudi*, March 24, 1994.

52. Poirot-Delpech in *Le Monde*, March 23, 1994; Rousso in *Libération*, April 20 and April 13, 1994, reprinted in Golsan (ed.), *Memory, the Holocaust, and French Justice*, 169, 157.

53. Christian Didier, his assassin, had tried to kill Klaus Barbie in 1987 and was apparently mentally ill. His connection to the Jewish community and the Holocaust and his motivation for the assassination remain unclear.

54. Variations on these headlines from *Le Figaro*, March 18, 1994, *Rivarol*, March 18, 1994, and *Action Française*, March 24, 1994, blanketed the national press throughout the trial.

55. Rousso in *Libération*, April 3, 1994. See also *La Hantise du passé*, 1998, especially 49–84, for Rousso on the "judicialization" of the past.

56. Nicolaïdis in *Actualité Juive*, March 10, 1994; *L'Événement du Jeudi*, March 31, 1994; Pierre Pujo in *Action Française*, March 24, 1994; *Rivarol*, March 18, 1994; Varaut in *Le Quotidien de Paris*, March 24, 1994.

57. Amouroux in *Tribune Juive*, January 13, 1994.

58. On "Tzedek" and French heroes, see *Tribune Juive*, January 21, 1993, *Le Nouvel Observateur*, November 24 and December 15, 1994, and *Le Point*, November 26, 1994. Marcel Ophuls dedicated his 1988 film about Klaus Barbie, "Hotel Terminus," to a certain Madame Bontout, "a good neighbor," who had tried to save a young Jewish girl from deportation. Historical texts also emphasized the resistance of righteous French citizens. See, for example, Cohen, *Persécutions et sauvetages: Juifs et Français sous l'occupation*.

59. Poirot-Delpech in *Le Monde*, March 30, 1994. See also Jean-Michel Chaumont, *La Concurrence des victimes: génocide, identité, reconnaissance*, 1997, who argues that claims about the Holocaust's uniqueness have led to a competition among victims.

60. *Le Progrès*, March 15, 1994; Chalandon in *Libération*, March 17, 1994; Sorman in *L'Événement du Jeudi*, March 24, 1994.

## Chapter 7

1. Plenel in *Le Monde*, April 22, 1992.
2. The appeal was published in *Le Monde*, June 17, 1992.
3. Daniel in *Le Nouvel Observateur*, July 19, 1992.
4. For example, "Les Guichets du Louvre," a film critical of Vichy's role in Jewish deportations, and "Night and Fog" were shown that night in Saint-Germain, and demonstrations were held in the provinces.
5. See the Appeal's letter to *Le Monde*, July 24, 1992.
6. This account is based on the report in *Le Monde*, July 18, 1992.
7. *Le Monde*, July 18 and July 19/20, 1992.
8. Kravetz in *Libération*, July 16, 1992; Rochette in *Libération*, July 31, 1992; Hamon in *Le Quotidien de Paris*, July 17, 1992; Plenel in *Le Monde*, July 19/20, 1992. For a discussion of the legality of the parliament vote, see Vivian Grosswald Curran, "The Legalization of Racism in a Constitutional State: Democracy's Suicide in Vichy France," 1998, especially 24–30.
9. Pierre-Bloch in *Le Monde*, July 23, 1992; Lanzmann in *Le Monde*, July 17, 1992.
10. Plenel in *Le Monde*, July 19/20, 1992; Sitruk quoted in *Libération*, July 18, 1992; Dujardin in *Le Monde*, July 17, 1992; *La Croix*, July 18, 1992.
11. Frappat and Dujardin in *Le Monde*, July 17, 1992; Paxton in *Libération*, July 16, 1992.
12. Lanzmann in *Le Monde*, July 17, 1992, and *Libération*, August 26, 1992; Kahn quoted in *Le Monde*, July 18, 1992; Hamon in *Le Quotidien de Paris*, July 17, 1992.
13. Badinter's remarks were widely quoted. Lanzmann in *Libération*, August 26, 1992. On "Shoah," see chapter five.
14. *Le Monde*, July 18, 1992.
15. *Libération*, July 18, 1992. That December, CRIF president Jean Kahn faulted Klarsfeld and claimed that Mitterrand would not have continued to decorate the tomb if he had not been provoked by Klarsfeld's announcement (*Tribune Juive*, December 10, 1992). Kahn had just returned from accompanying Mitterrand on a trip to Israel. Klarsfeld later confirmed that he had concocted the leak in an effort to spare the president precisely the scandal that ensued. See his letter to Mitterrand in *Libération*, September 12, 1994, and his interview with *Actualité Juive* journalist Claude Bochurberg in Bochurberg, *Entretiens avec Serge Klarsfeld*, 1997, 193.
16. Journalist Eric Conan later revealed that each of the Fifth Republic's previous presidents had laid a wreath on Pétain's tomb only one time: de Gaulle, in November 1968, to mark the fiftieth anniversary of the World War I victory; Pompidou, in February 1973, when the ex-marshal's remains were re-interred after his stolen coffin turned up in a Paris suburb; and Giscard, on the sixtieth anniversary of the end of World War I. It was Mitterrand who had made the act an annual ritual. See *L'Express*, November 19, 1992.
17. Conan and Plantu in *L'Express*, November 19, 1992; Jewish responses quoted in *Le Quotidien de Paris*, November 13, 1992, *Le Figaro*, November 13, 1992, and *Tribune Juive*, December 3, 1992.
18. Duquesne in *La Croix*, December 2, 1992; Griotteray in *Figaro Magazine*, December 5, 1992; Ferenczi in *Le Monde*, November 15, 1992; Bensaïd in *Le Monde*,

December 31, 1992. Excerpts from the radio interview were printed in *Le Quotidien de Paris*, November 14, 1992, and *Le Monde*, November 15/16, 1992.

19. *Action Française*, November 19, 1992.

20. Some Jews, such as Henri Bulawko, thought that Mitterrand's decree should be rescinded. Endorsing a proposal by Théo Klein, Bulawko asked that the National Assembly, "the elected representatives of the French Republic," acknowledge Vichy's crimes and that Jews be left to organize the Vél d'Hiv commemoration on their own, as they had in the past (*Tribune Juive*, September 8, 1994). See also Caroline Wiedmer, *The Claims of Memory: Representations of the Holocaust in Contemporary Germany and France*, 1999, 51–53, 71, on the "nationalization" of the Vél d'Hiv commemoration.

21. 1994 was the centennial of the Dreyfus Affair, and that February, a weekly army journal published an error-filled article written by the head of the ground army's historical division. In what was perceived to be a rather tendentious phrase, Colonel Paul Gaujac suggested that "Dreyfus' innocence is a thesis generally accepted by historians." He was immediately fired by Defense Minister François Léotard, and throughout the controversy that ensued, discussions of "the new Dreyfus Affair" led almost invariably to debates about anti-Semitism in contemporary France and the country's inability to confront its complicity in the Nazi Holocaust.

22. Wieviorka, *Nous entrerons dans la carrière*, 1994, 350. The interviews were conducted in April 1990, January 1991, and January 1993, but are presented in the text as one continuous conversation. Thus it is difficult to gauge the evolution of Mitterrand's thought, especially how it might have been shaped by specific events, such as the Carpentras desecration and the controversies of 1992.

23. See especially Jean-Marie Colombani in *Le Monde*, September 9, 1994; Pierre Birnbaum in *Le Monde*, October 21, 1994; and Daniel Bensaïd in *Le Monde des débats*, October 1994.

24. All references are to the extended excerpts of the interview printed in *Le Monde*, September 14, 1994.

25. In a conversation published in 1995, when Elie Wiesel asked the president whether he felt sorry about his relationship with Bousquet, Mitterrand was unequivocal. "There is no regret or remorse to have. None. Why? The accusations against me are infuriating . . . I am at peace with myself." See Mitterrand and Wiesel, *Mémoire à deux voix*, 1995, especially 105–6.

26. The cartoon was reprinted in Plantu, *Le petit Mitterrand illustré*, 1995.

27. Mongin in *Esprit*, November 1994.

28. Moscovici in *Tribune Juive*, September 29, 1994. On Mitterrand during the Carpentras demonstration, see "Un président de la République dans la rue," *Libération*, May 15, 1990. Letter from Yvonne Lecat-Dijan in *Tribune Juive*, October 20, 1994; Derai in *Tribune Juive*, September 15, 1994; Kahn in *Le Monde*, September 23, 1994.

29. Kiejman in *Le Monde*, September 11/12, 1994; Klarsfeld in *Libération*, September 12, 1994. For Klarsfeld's perspective, see Bochurberg, *Entretiens avec Serge Klarsfeld*, 1997, especially 188–92.

30. Bensaïd in *Le Monde des débats*, October 1994; Movement of Young Socialists in *Le Monde*, September 8, 1994; Martinet in *Le Monde*, September 14, 1994;

Rousso in *Libération*, September 14, 1994, and *Tribune Juive*, September 29, 1994; Szafran in *L'Événement du Jeudi*, September 22, 1994.

31. Bouthors in *Esprit*, November 1994.

32. See Ronald Tiersky, *François Mitterrand: The Last French President*, 2000.

33. See Jean Daniel's discussion of Mitterrand and de Gaulle in *Le Nouvel Observateur*, September 22, 1994.

34. Duhamel in *Libération*, November 12, 1993.

35. Mongin in *Esprit*, November 1994. The poll and Devedjian were cited in Jonathan Fenby, *France on the Brink*, 1998, 280.

36. Plenel in *Le Monde*, September 14, 1994.

37. Baumont in *Libération*, September 9, 1994.

38. Mongin in *Esprit*, November 1994.

39. Attali in *Le Monde*, January 10, 1996.

40. Chirac's speech is reprinted in its entirety in Conan and Rousso, *Vichy: An Ever-Present Past*, 1998, 39–42.

41. Esther Benbassa, *The Jews of France: A History from Antiquity to the Present*, 1999, 193. Le Pen complained that the president was "paying his electoral debt to the Jewish community," while other critics, including Socialist Mitterrand stalwarts, challenged what they called the "fishy business" of the Republic apologizing for Vichy. Claude Bartolone went so far as to label Chirac's "clever" declaration an attack on Mitterrand and the Socialist Party, a charge bolstered by Mitterrand arch-enemy Michel Rocard's front-page opinion in *Le Monde* praising the new president's initiative (*Le Monde*, July 19, 1995). Though they did not strenuously dissent, moreover, several members of Chirac's party did not support official sentiment that broke so definitively with the Gaullist legend.

42. LévyWillard in *Libération*, July 17, 1995. See also Henry Rousso on Chirac's break with de Gaulle in the same edition.

43. *Libération*, September 21, 1995; *L'Equipe*, June 1996.

44. The poll was conducted by and published in *L'Express*, October 2, 1997.

45. See *Le Monde*, October 1, 1997, for extended excerpts of the Church's apology and Jewish reactions. See also *Tribune Juive*, November 13, 1997.

46. Baruch in *Le Monde*, October 1, 1997; Conan in *L'Express*, October 2, 1997.

47. Nora in *Le Monde*, October 1, 1997. The poll was conducted by the Institut CSA and published in *Tribune Juive*, November 13, 1997.

48. See Richard J. Golsan, *Vichy's Afterlife: History and Counterhistory in Postwar France*, 2000, 156–80, for an analysis of the Papon trial and the Algerian War.

49. *Le Monde*, October 18, 1997; Varaut in *Libération*, October 22, 1997. The petition called for a place to be established in memory of the victims and was published in *Libération*, October 19, 1999.

50. Séguin's initial comments were quoted in *Le Monde*, October 21, 1997; *Le Figaro*, October 21, 1997. Jospin's remarks, presented before the National Assembly, were quoted in *Le Monde*, October 23, 1997.

51. Joffrin in *Libération*, October 22, 1997; Duhamel in *Libération*, October 24, 1997.

52. Peyrefitte in *Figaro Magazine*, January 24, 1998; Pasqua in *Le Monde*, October 21, 1997. *Compagnon* generally translates as "comrade," "companion," or "friend."

It also designates a Resistance fighter, as in *Compagnon de la Libération*, a nuance Pasqua could not have failed to appreciate in the midst of a trial about Vichy.

53. Schneidermann, *L'Etrange procès*, 1998, 45–46; Jean Daniel in *Le Nouvel Observateur*, October 23, 1997.

54. July in *Libération*, April 3, 1998; Dupuy in *Libération*, April 2, 1998; Colombani in *Le Monde*, April 4, 1998.

55. See *Libération*, April 3, 1998; *Le Monde*, April 3, 1998; and *L'Humanité*, April 2, 1998.

56. Lévy and Zaoui in *Libération*, April 16, 1998. Long after the verdict, FNDIRP lawyer Lévy unsuccessfully lobbied Interior Minister Jean-Pierre Chevènement for symbolic damages of one franc in order that "the responsibility of the State for the office crimes committed in its name against the Jews during the Second World War be recognized for the first and last time." See *Le Monde* and *Libération*, March 7, 2000.

57. Sitruk quoted in *L'Humanité*, April 3, 1998; Kahn in *Libération*, April 3, 1998; Halter in *Libération*, April 1, 1998.

58. See, for example, *Libération*, October 21 and October 22, 1999.

59. After Chirac denied three appeals for clemency, Papon was released from prison in September 2002 under the terms of an amendment, passed earlier that year, that allowed for the discharge of gravely ill inmates. Widespread outrage followed, with many pointing to Papon's apparent good health and the continued imprisonment of numerous criminals with cancer and AIDS. The government of Jean-Pierre Rafferin distanced itself from the decision, though others, including Badinter, argued that "humanity should triumph over crime."

## Chapter 8

1. Rousso, *La hantise du passé*, 1998, 90 and *passim*.

2. Eric Conan and Henry Rousso, *Vichy: An Ever-Present Past*, 1998, 75, 269, and *passim*. See also Rousso, *The Vichy Syndrome*, 1991, and "The Historian, a Site of Memory," 2000.

3. Pierre Nora, "Between Memory and History: *Les Lieux de Mémoire*," Spring 1989, and *Les Lieux de mémoire*, 1984–1992; Rousso, "The Historian, a Site of Memory," 300.

4. Henry Rousso, *The Vichy Syndrome*, 132.

5. Mongin in *Esprit*, November 1994.

6. Duhamel in *Libération*, May 7, 1999.

7. Nicolaïdis in *Libération*, October 6, 1994. See also Nicolaïdis (ed.), *Oublier nos crimes: L'Amnésie nationale, une spécificité française?*, 1994.

8. Schneider in *Libération*, October 12, 1994.

9. Devedjian quoted in Fenby, *France on the Brink*, 1998, 280.

10. Suzanne Citron, *Le mythe national*, 1989, 78.

11. Nora in *La Croix*, June 24, 1997; Chesneaux in *Le Monde*, August 15, 1996; Elizabeth Bellamy, *Affective Genealogies: Psychoanalysis, Postmodernism, and "the Jewish Question" after Auschwitz*, 1997, 9.

Adler, Alexandre and Bernard Cohen, *Juif & Juif: Ashkénazes et Sépharades aujour-d'hui*, Paris: Autrement, 1985.

Adler, Jacques, *The Jews of Paris and the Final Solution*, Oxford: Oxford University Press, 1987.

Adorno, Theodor, "What Does Coming to Terms With the Past Mean?" in Hartman (ed.), 1986, 114–29.

Alexander, Philippe, *Plaidoyer impossible pour un vieux président abandonné par les siens*, Paris: Albin Michel, 1994.

Amery, Jean, *At the Mind's Limits: Contemplations by a Survivor on Auschwitz and Its Realities*, New York: Schocken, 1980.

Antelme, Robert, *L'Espèce humaine*, Paris: Gallimard, 1957.

Antze, Paul and Michael Lambek (eds.), *Tense Past: Cultural Essays in Trauma and Memory*, New York: Routledge, 1996.

Arendt, Hannah, *Eichmann in Jerusalem: A Report on the Banality of Evil*, New York: The Viking Press, 1964.

——, *The Origins of Totalitarianism*, New York: Harcourt Brace Jovanovich, 1951.

Aron, Raymond, *Mémoires*, New York: Holmes and Meier, 1990.

——, *Essais sur la condition juive contemporaine*, Paris: Editions de Fallois, 1989.

Ascot, Roger, *Le sionisme trahi ou les Israéliens du dimanche*, Paris: Editions Balland, 1991.

Auron, Yaïr, *Les Juifs d'extrême gauche en mai 1968*, Paris: Albin Michel, 1998.

Azéma, Jean-Pierre, *From Munich to the Liberation, 1938–1944*, Cambridge: Cambridge University Press, 1984.

Azéma, Jean-Pierre and François Bédarida (eds.), *Le Régime de Vichy et les français*, Paris: Fayard, 1992.

Badinter, Robert, *Libres et égaux: L'émancipation des Juifs, 1789–1791*, Paris: Fayard, 1989.

Baldwin, Peter, *Reworking the Past: Hitler, the Holocaust, and the Historians' Debate*, Boston: Beacon Press, 1990.

Barcellini, Serge and Annette Wieviorka, *Passant, souviens-toi!* Paris: Plon, 1995.

Bartov, Omer, "Intellectuals on Auschwitz: Memory, History and Truth," *History and Memory*, 5:1 (Spring/Summer 1993), 87–129.

Baruch, Marc Olivier, *Servir l'Etat française: L'administration en France de 1940 à 1944*, Paris: Fayard, 1997.

——, "A propos du procès Papon," *French Politics and Society*, 16:3 (Summer 1998), 38–45.

Bauman, Zygmunt, *Modernity and the Holocaust*, Ithaca: Cornell University Press, 1989.

Becker, Gay, *Disrupted Lives: How People Create Meaning in a Chaotic World*, Berkeley: University of California Press, 1997.

Becker, Jean-Jacques and Annette Wieviorka (eds.), *Les Juifs de France de la Révolution française à nos jours*, Paris: Editions Liana Levi, 1998.

Bédarida, François (ed.), *Touvier, Vichy et le crime contre l'humanité: le dossier de l'accusation*, Paris: Seuil, 1996.

——, (ed.), *La Politique nazi d'extermination*, Paris: IHTP/Albin Michel, 1989.

Bédarida, François, Alfred Grosser, and Pierre Vidal-Naquet (roundtable), "La morale de l'histoire," in Nicolaïdis (ed.), 1994, 208–26.

Bellamy, Elizabeth J., *Affective Genealogies: Psychoanalysis, Postmodernism, and "the Jewish Question" after Auschwitz*, Lincoln: University of Nebraska Press, 1997.

Benain, Aline, "L'Itinéraire juif de Raymond Aron: hasard, déchirement et dialectique de l'appartenance," *Pardès*, 11 (1990), 161–77.

Benbassa, Esther, *The Jews of France: A History From Antiquity to the Present*, Princeton: Princeton University Press, 1999.

Bensaïd, Daniel, *Qui est le juge? Pour en finir avec le tribunal d'histoire*, Paris: Fayard, 1999.

Bensimon, Doris and Sergio Della Pergola, *La population juive de France: socio-démographie et identité*, Jerusalem: Hebrew University of Jerusalem, 1984.

Bernstein, Michael André, *Foregone Conclusions: Against Apocalyptic History*, Berkeley: University of California Press, 1994.

Besançon, Alain, *Le malheur du siècle: sur le communisme, le nazisme et l'unicité de la Shoah*, Paris: Fayard, 1998.

Birnbaum, Pierre, *Jewish Destinies: Citizenship, State, and Community in Modern France*, New York: Hill and Wang, 2000.

——, "Between Social and Political Assimilation: Remarks on the History of Jews in France," in Birnbaum and Katznelson (eds.), 1995, 94–127.

——, *Les Fous de la République: Histoire Politique des Juifs d'état, de Gambetta à Vichy*, Paris: Editions du Seuil, 1994.

——, *Histoire politique des juifs de France*, Paris: Presses de la Fondation nationale des Sciences politiques, 1990.

——, *Un mythe politique: la "République juive,"* Paris: Fayard, 1988.

Birnbaum, Pierre and Ira Katznelson (eds.), *Paths of Emancipation: Jews, States, and Citizenship*, Princeton: Princeton University Press, 1995.

Blum, Léon, *Souvenirs sur l'affaire*, Paris: Gallimard, 1982.

Blumenkranz, Bernhard and Albert Soboul, *Les juifs et la Révolution française*, Paris: Franco-Judaica 4, 1989.

Bochurberg, Claude, *Entretiens avec Serge Klarsfeld*, Paris: Stock, 1997.

——, *Mémoire et vigilance*, Paris: Editions Le Lisere Bleu, 1986.

Boulanger, Gerard, *Maurice Papon: un technocrate français dans la Collaboration*, Paris: Le Seuil, 1994.

Bower, Tom, *Klaus Barbie: The Butcher of Lyons*, New York: Pantheon, 1984.

Bracher, Nathan, "The Trial of Papon and the Tribulations of Gaullism," in Golsan (ed.), 2000, 115–30.

——, "Memory Null and Void? The Broken Record of Vichy Polemics in the Papon Case," *Contemporary French Civilization*, 23:1 (Winter 1998), 65–80.

Brayard, Florent (ed.), *Le Génocide des Juifs: entre procès et histoire, 1943–2000*, Paris: Editions Complexe/IHTP, 2001.

Bredin, Jean-Denis, *The Affair: The Case of Alfred Dreyfus*, New York: George Braziller, 1986.

Bruckner, Pascal, *La tentation de l'innocence*, Paris: Grasset, 1995.

Bruner, Jerome, *Acts of Meaning*, Cambridge: Harvard University Press, 1990.

Burrin, Philippe, *La France à l'heure allemande*, Paris: Seuil, 1995.

Byrnes, Robert, *Anti-Semitism in Modern France*, New Brunswick: Rutgers University Press, 1950.

Carr, David, *Time, Narrative, and History*, Bloomington: Indiana University Press, 1986.

Carroll, David, *French Literary Fascism*, Princeton: Princeton University Press, 1995.

Caruth, Cathy (ed.), *Trauma: Explorations in Memory*, Baltimore: The Johns Hopkins University Press, 1995.

——, "Unclaimed Experience: Trauma and the Possibility of History," *Yale French Studies*, 79 (1991), 181–92.

Centre de documentation juive contemporaine, *Le procès de Jérusalem: jugement—documents*, Paris: Calmann-Lévy, 1963.

Charon, Jean-Marie, *La Presse en France de 1945 à nos jours*, Paris: Editions du Seuil, 1991.

Chaumont, Jean-Michel, *La Concurrence des victimes: génocide, identité, reconnaissance*, Paris: Éditions La Découverte, 1997.

Chelain, André, *Le procès Barbie: ou le Shoah-Business à Lyon*, Paris: Polémiques, 1987.

Chevalier, Yves, "Mutations de la communauté juive de France," *Yod*, 3:2 (1978), 42–54.

Le Citoyen, *L'Affaire Papie-Barbon et l'arrêt du 26 avril 1983: contribution de la jurisprudence française au concept de génocide*, Paris: La Vieille Taupe, 1983.

Citron, Suzanne, *Le mythe national: l'histoire de France en question*, Paris: Les éditions ouvrières/Études et documentations internationales, 1991.

Cochet, François, *Les exclus de la victoire: histoire des prisonniers de guerre, deportés, et STO (1945–1985)*, Paris: Kronos, 1992.

Cohen, Asher, *Persécutions et sauvetages: Juifs et Français sous l'Occupation et sous Vichy*, Paris: Cerf, 1993.

Cohen, Richard I., *The Burden of Conscience*, Bloomington: Indiana University Press, 1987.

Cohen, Sande, "Between Image and Phrase: Progressive History and the 'Final So-lution' as Dispossession," in Friedlander (ed.), 1992, 171–84.

Cointet, Jean-Paul, *Pierre Laval*, Paris: Fayard, 1993.

Cointet, Michèle and Rainer Riemenschneider, "Histoire, déontologie, médias: à propos de l'affaire Roques," *Revue d'histoire moderne et contemporaine* (March 1987), 174–84.

Combe, Sonia, *Archives interdites: les peurs françaises face à l'Histoire contemporaine*, Paris: Albin Michel, 1994.

Conan, Eric, *Le Procès Papon: un journal d'audience*, Paris: Gallimard, 1998.

——, *Sans oublier les enfants: les camps de Pithiviers et Beaune-la-Rolande, 19 juillet en 16 septembre 1942*, Paris: Grasset, 1991.

Conan, Eric, and Henry Rousso, *Vichy: An Ever-Present Past*, Hanover: University Press of New England, 1998.

——, *Vichy, un passé qui ne passe pas*, Paris: Fayard, 1994.

Connerton, Paul, *How Societies Remember*, Cambridge: Cambridge University Press, 1989.

Courtois, Stéphane, Nicolas Werth, Jean-Louis Panne, Andrzej Packowski, and Jean-Louis Margolis, *Le Livre noir du communisme: crimes, terreurs, répressions*, Paris: Robert Laffont, 1997.

Crews, Frederick, et al., *The Memory Wars: Freud's Legacy in Dispute*, New York: *The New York Review of Books*, 1995.

Curran, Vivian Grosswald, "The Legalization of Racism in a Constitutional State: Democracy's Suicide in Vichy France," *Hastings Law Journal*, 50:1 (November 1998), 1–96.

Déméron, Pierre, *Contre Israël*, Paris: Libertés nouvelles, 1968.

Diner, Dan, "European Counterimages: Problems of Periodization and Historical Memory," *New German Critique*, 53 (Spring/Summer 1991), 163–74.

——, "Israel and the Trauma of Mass Extermination," *Telos*, 57 (Fall 1983), 41–52.

Domansky, Elisabeth, "A Lost War: World War II in Postwar German History," in Rosenfeld (ed.), 1997, 233–72.

——, "'Kristallnacht,' the Holocaust, and German Unity: The Meaning of November 9 as an Anniversary in Germany," *History and Memory*, 4:1 (Spring/Summer 1992), 60–94.

Drai, Raphael, *Identité juive, identité humaine*, Paris: Armand Colin, 1995.

Eskenazi, Frank and Edouard Waintrop, *Le Talmud et la République: enquête sur les Juifs français à l'heure des renouveaux religieux*, Paris: Grasset, 1991.

*Esprit*, "Le président, Vichy, la France, et la mort," special issue, November 1994.

——, "Que reste-t-il de la Résistance?" special issue, January 1994.

——, "Le poids de la mémoire," special issue, July 1993.

——, "Que faire de Vichy?" special issue, May 1992.

Evans, Richard J., *In Hitler's Shadow: West German Historians and the Attempt to Escape from the Nazi Past*, New York: Pantheon Books, 1989.

Farmer, Sarah, *Martyred Village: Commemorating the 1944 Massacre at Oradour-sur-Glane*, Berkeley: University of California Press, 1999.

Farrell, Kirby, *Post-Traumatic Culture: Injury and Interpretation in the Nineties*, Baltimore: The Johns Hopkins University Press, 1998.

Faurisson, Robert, *Mémoire en défense. Contre ceux qui m'accusent de falsifier l'histoire. La Question des chambres de gaz*, Paris: La Vieille Taupe, 1980.

Faux, Emmanuel, Thomas Legrand, and Gilles Perez, *La main droite de Dieu*, Paris: Le Seuil, 1994.

Felman, Shoshana, "In an Era of Testimony: Claude Lanzmann's *Shoah*," *Yale French Studies*, 79 (1991), 39–81.

Fenby, Jonathan, *France on the Brink*, New York: Arcade, 1998.

Fentress, James and Chris Wickham, *Social Memory*, Oxford: Basil Blackwell, 1992.

Finkielkraut, Alain, *La mémoire vaine: du crime contre l'humanité*, Paris: Gallimard, 1989.

——, *L'Avenir d'une négation: réflexions sur la question du génocide*, Paris: Seuil, 1983.

——, *La Réprobation d'Israël*, Paris: Denoël, 1983.

——, *Le juif imaginaire*, Paris: Editions du Seuil, 1980.

Fishman, Sarah, Laura Lee Downs, Ioannis Sinanoglou, Leonard V. Smith, Robert Zaretsky (eds.), *France at War: Vichy and the Historians*, New York: Berg, 2000.

Fraenkel, Josef, *The Jewish Press of the World*, London: The World Jewish Congress, 1972.

Fredj, Jacques, *La création du CRIF: 1943 à 1966*, mémoire de maïtrise, Université de Paris IV, 1988.

Fresco, Nadine, "Parcours du ressentiment," *History and Theory*, 28:2 (1989), 173–97.

——, "La diaspora des cendres," *Nouvelle Revue de Psychanalyse*, 24 (1981), 206–20.

Freud, Sigmund, *The Standard Edition of the Complete Psychological Works of Sigmund Freud*, edited by James Strachey, London: Hogarth Press, 1953–74.

Friedlander, Judith, *Vilna on the Seine: Jewish Intellectuals in France Since 1968*, New Haven: Yale University Press, 1990.

Friedlander, Saul (ed.), *Probing the Limits of Representation: Nazism and the Final Solution*, Cambridge: Harvard University Press, 1992.

——, "Trauma, Transference, and 'Working Through' in Writing the History of the 'Shoah,'" *History and Memory*, 4:1 (Spring/Summer 1992), 39–59.

——, *Réflexions sur l'avenir d'Israël*, Paris: Editions du Seuil, 1969.

Froment, Pascal, *René Bousquet*, Paris: Stock, 1994.

Frossard, André, *Le crime contre l'humanité*, Paris: Laffont, 1987.

Funkenstein, Amos, "Collective Memory and Historical Consciousness," *History and Memory*, 1 (1989), 5–26.

Ganier Raymond, Philippe, *Une certaine France: L'antisémitisme, 40–44*, Paris: Balland, 1975.

Gauthier, Paul (ed.), *Chronique du procès Barbie: pour servir la mémoire*, Normandie Cerf, 1988.

Geertz, Clifford, *The Interpretation of Cultures*, New York: Basic Books, 1973.

Gillis, John R. (ed.), *Commemorations: The Politics of National Identity*, Princeton: Princeton University Press, 1994.

Girard, Patrick, *La Révolution française et les Juifs*, Paris: Robert Laffont, 1989.

Givet, Jacques, *La Gauche contre Israël*, Paris: Libertés nouvelles, 1968.

Glucksmann, André, *De Gaulle, ou es-tu?* Paris: Jean-Claude Lattes, 1995.

Goldman, Pierre, *Souvenirs obscurs d'un Juif polonais né en France*, Paris: Seuil, 1975.

Golsan, Richard J. (ed.), *The Papon Affair: Memory and Justice on Trial*, New York: Routledge, 2000.

——, *Vichy's Afterlife: History and Counterhistory in Postwar France*, Lincoln: University of Nebraska Press, 2000.

——, (ed.), *Memory, the Holocaust, and French Justice: The Bousquet and Touvier Affairs*, Hanover: University Press of New England, 1996.

Green, Nancy L., "La Révolution dans l'imaginaire des immigrants juifs," in Birnbaum (ed.), 1990, 153–62.

——, *The Pletzl of Paris: Jewish Immigrant Workers in the "Belle Epoque,"* New York: Holmes and Meier, 1986.

Greilsamer, Laurent and Daniel Schneiderman, *Un certain Monsieur Paul: L'Affaire Touvier*, Paris: Fayard, 1994.

Grosser, Alfred, *Le crime et la mémoire*, Paris: Flammarion, 1989.

Guillauma, Yves, *La presse en France*, Paris: Editions La Découverte, 1990.

Hadas-Lebel, Mireille and Evelyne Oliel-Grausz, *Les juifs et la Révolution française: Histoire et mentalités*, Louvain: Editions Peeters, 1992.

Halbwachs, Maurice, *On Collective Memory*, Chicago: University of Chicago Press, 1992.

——, *Les Cadres sociaux de la mémoire*, Paris: Mouton-LaHaye, [1925] 1976.

Halter, Marek, *La mémoire inquiétante: il y a cinquante ans, le ghetto de Varsovie*, Paris: Laffont, 1993.

Hamon, Hervé and Patrick Rotman, *Génération*, 2 volumes, Paris: Seuil, 1987, 1988.

Hartman, Geoffrey (ed.), *The Longest Shadow: In the Aftermath of the Holocaust*, Bloomington: Indiana University Press, 1996.

——, *Holocaust Remembrance: The Shapes of Memory*, Cambridge: Basil Blackwell, 1994.

——, *Bitburg in Moral and Political Perspective*, Bloomington: Indiana University Press, 1986.

Hayes, Peter (ed.), *Lessons and Legacies: The Meaning of the Holocaust in a Changing World*, Evanston: Northwestern University Press, 1991.

Hazan, Katy, *La persécution des Juifs dans quelques procès d'épuration et de collaboration*, mémoire, DEA, Institut des Etudes Politiques, 1993.

Herman, Judith Lewis, *Trauma and Recovery: The Aftermath of Violence—From Domestic Abuse to Political Terror*, New York: Basic Books, 1992.

Hertzberg, Arthur, *The French Enlightenment and the Jews: The Origins of Modern Anti-Semitism*, New York: Columbia University Press, 1968.

Hoffmann, Stanley, "Histoire et mémoire," *Commentaire*, 52 (Winter 1990–91), 808–11.

——, "Remarks on Trigano," in Malino and Wasserstein (eds.), 1985, 282–87.

——, *Decline or Renewal? France Since the 1930s*, New York: Viking, 1974.

Hollifield, James F., and George Ross (eds.), *Searching for the New France*, London: Routledge, 1991.

Hunt, Lynn (ed.), *The New Cultural History*, Berkeley: University of California Press, 1989.

Hutton, Patrick H., *History as an Art of Memory*, Hanover: University Press of New England, 1993.

——, "Sigmund Freud and Maurice Halbwachs: The Problem of Memory in Historical Psychology," *Historical Reflections*, 19:1 (1993), 1–16.

Huyssen, Andreas, *Twilight Memories: Marking Time in a Culture of Amnesia*, New York: Routledge, 1995.

Hyman, Paula, *The Jews of Modern France*, Berkeley: University of California Press, 1998.

Institut d'histoire du temps présent, *La mémoire des Français: Quarante ans de commémorations de la Seconde Guerre mondiale*, Paris: Editions du CNRS, 1986.

Irwin-Zarecka, Iwona, *Neutralizing Memory: The Jew in Contemporary Poland*, New Brunswick: Transaction Publishers, 1989.

Jakubowicz, Alain, *Touvier: histoire du procès*, Paris: Editions Julliard, 1995.

Jankelevitch, Vladimir, *L'imprescriptible*, Paris: Editions du Seuil, 1986.

Jeanneney, Jean-Noël, *Le Passé dans le prétoire: l'historien, le juge et le journaliste*, Paris: Seuil, 1998.

Judt, Tony, "Moving Pictures" (review of "The Sorrow and the Pity," "Shoah," and "Heimat"), *Radical History Review*, 41 (1988), 129–44.

Kahn, Annette, *Personne ne voudra nous croire*, Paris: Payot, 1991.

Kantin, Georges and Gilles Manceron (eds.), *Les échos de la mémoire: tabous et enseignements de la Seconde Guerre mondiale*, Paris: *Le Monde* Editions, 1991.

Karal, William and Blanche Finger, *Opération Vent Printanier*, Paris: La Découverte, 1992.

Kaspi, André (ed.), *La Révolution française et l'émancipation des Juifs de France*, Paris: Hamoré, 1989.

——, "L'Affaire des enfants Finaly," *L'Histoire*, 76 (March 1985), 40–53.

Khouri, Fred J., *The Arab-Israeli Dilemma*, Syracuse: Syracuse University Press, 1985.

Klarsfeld, Arno, *Papon: un verdict française*, Paris: Ramsay, 1998.

——, *Touvier, un crime français*, Paris: Fayard, 1994.

Klarsfeld, Serge, *Vichy-Auschwitz: le rôle de Vichy dans la question juive en France*, 2 volumes, Paris: Fayard, 1983, 1985.

Kleeblatt, Norman L. (ed.), *The Dreyfus Affair: Art, Truth, and Justice*, Berkeley: University of California Press, 1987.

Klein, Théo, *Oublier Vichy? À propos de l'arrêt Touvier*, Paris: Criterion, 1992.

Kohut, Heinz, *The Analysis of the Self*, New York: International Universities Press, Inc., 1971.

Kramer, Jane, *Europeans*, New York: Viking, 1988.

Kriegel, Annie, "Les intermittances de la mémoire: de l'histoire immédiate à l'Histoire," *Pardès*, 9–10 (1989), 248–58.

——, *Réflexion sur les questions juives*, Paris: Hachette, 1984.

——, *Israël, est-il coupable?* Paris: Robert Laffont, 1982.

——, "Une communauté à double foyer," *H-Histoire*, 3 (1979), 161–69.

Kritzman, Laurence D. (ed.), *Auschwitz and After: Race, Culture, and "the Jewish Question" in France*, New York: Routledge, 1995.

Laborie, Pierre, *L'Opinion française sous Vichy*, Paris: Editions du Seuil, 1990.

LaCapra, Dominick, "Trauma, Absence, Loss," *Critical Inquiry*, 25 (Summer 1999), 696–s727.

——, *History and Memory after Auschwitz*, Ithaca: Cornell University Press, 1998.

——, *Representing the Holocaust: History, Theory, Trauma*, Ithaca: Cornell University Press, 1994.

——, *History and Criticism*, Ithaca: Cornell University Press, 1985.

Lacouture, Jean, *De Gaulle: The Ruler, 1945–1970*, New York: Norton, 1991.

Lagrou, Pieter, *The Legacy of Nazi Occupation: Patriotic Memory and National Recovery in Western Europe, 1945–1965*, Cambridge: Cambridge University Press, 2000.

Lalieu, Olivier, *La déportation fragmentée: les anciens déportés parlent de politique, 1945–1980*, Paris: La Boutique de l'Histoire, 1994.

Lambert, Bernard, *Dossiers d'accusation: Bousquet, Papon, Touvier*, Paris: Editions de la Fédération nationale des déportés et internés résistants et patriots, 1991.

Langer, Lawrence L., *Preempting the Holocaust*, New Haven: Yale University Press, 1998.

——, *Admitting the Holocaust*, New York: Oxford University Press, 1995.

Lanzmann, Claude, "The Obscenity of Understanding: An Evening with Claude Lanzmann," in Caruth (ed.), 1995, 200–220.

——, "Seminar With Claude Lanzmann, 11 April 1990," *Yale French Studies*, 79 (1991), 82–99.

——, *Shoah: An Oral History of the Holocaust*, New York: Pantheon, 1985.

——, "De l'Holocauste à 'Holocauste,' ou comment s'en débarrasser," *Les Temps Modernes* (June 1979), 1897–1909.

Lapierre, Jean-William, *Information sur l'Etat d'Israél dans les grands quotidiens français en 1958*, Paris: Editions du CNRS, 1968.

Lasry, Jean-Claude and Claude Tapia (eds.), *Les Juifs du maghreb: diasporas contemporaines*, Paris: Éditions l'Harmattan, 1989.

Laughland, John, *The Death of Politics: France Under Mitterrand*, London: Michael Joseph, 1994.

Lavabre, Marie-Claire, "Usages du passé, usages de la mémoire," *Revue française de science politique*, 44:3 (June 1994), 480–93.

——, "Du poids du passé. Lecture critique du *Syndrome de Vichy*," *IHTP Cahiers*, 18 (June 1991), 177–85.

Lazar, David, *L'Opinion française et la naissance de l'Etat d'Israél, 1945–1949*, Paris: Calmann-Lévy, 1972.

Levy, Benny, "Today's Hope: Conversations with Sartre," *Telos*, 44 (Summer 1980), 155–81.

Lévy, Bernard-Henry, *Les adventures de la liberté*, Paris: Editions Grasset et Fasquelle, 1991.

——, *Archives d'un procès: Klaus Barbie*, Paris: Le Livre de poche, 1986.

——, *L'idéologie française*, Paris: Bernard Grasset, 1981.

Lévy, Claude and Paul Tillard, *La grand rafle de Vél d'Hiv*, Paris: Laffont, 1992.

Lewis, Bernard S., *History: Remembered, Recovered, Invented*, New York: Touchstone, 1975.

Lindenberg, Daniel, "Guerres de mémoire en France," *Vingtième Siècle*, 42 (April 1994), 77–95.

Loshitzky, Yosefa (ed.), *Spielberg's Holocaust: Critical Perspectives on Schindler's List*, Bloomington: Indiana University Press, 1997.

Lyotard, Jean-François, "Discussing, or Phrasing 'after Auschwitz,'" in Kritzman (ed.), 1995, 149–79.

——, *Le Différend*, Paris: Les éditions de minuit, 1988.

——, *The Postmodern Condition*, Minneapolis: University of Minnesota Press, 1984.

Maier, Charles S., "A Surfeit of Memory: Reflections on History, Melancholy and Denial," *History and Memory*, 5:2 (Fall/Winter 1993), 136–52.

——, *The Unmasterable Past: History, Holocaust, and German National Identity*, Cambridge: Harvard University Press, 1988.

Malino, Francis and Bernard Wasserstein (eds.), *The Jews in Modern France*, Hanover: University Press of New England, 1985.

Malka, Victor, *Aujourd'hui être Juif*, Paris: Cerf, 1984.

Mandel, Arnold, *Nous autres Juifs*, Paris: Hachette, 1978.

Marienstras, Richard, *Être un peuple en diaspora*, Paris: François Maspero, 1975.

Marrus, Michael R., *The Politics of Assimilation: The French Jewish Community at the Time of the Dreyfus Affair*, Oxford: Clarendon Press, 1971.

Marrus, Michael R. and Robert O. Paxton, *Vichy France and the Jews*, New York: Schocken Books, 1983.

Mbemba, Jean-Martin, *L'autre mémoire du crime contre l'humanité*, Paris: Présence africaine, 1990.

Memmi, Albert, *Portrait d'un Juif*, Paris: Gallimard, 1962.

——, *La libération du Juif*, Paris: Gallimard, 1966.

Merindol, Pierre, *Barbie: le procès*, Lyon: La manufacture, 1987.

Merle, Marcel, "Le procès Barbie, ou la fin du droit de la guerre?" *Études*, 367:5 (November 1987), 459–67.

Middleton, David and Derek Edwards (eds.), *Collective Remembering*, Newbury Park: Sage, 1990.

Miller, Alice, *Thou Shalt Not Be Aware*, New York: Meridian, 1984.

Miller, Judith, *One, By One, By One: Facing the Holocaust*, New York: Simon and Schuster, 1990.

Minow, Martha, *Between Vengeance and Forgiveness: Facing History after Genocide and Mass Violence*, Boston: Beacon Press, 1998.

Mitchell, W.T.J. (ed.), *On Narrative*, Chicago: University of Chicago Press, 1981.

Mitscherlich, Alexander and Margarete, *The Inability to Mourn: Principles of Collective Behavior*, New York: Grove Press, Inc., [1967] 1975.

Mitterrand, François, and Elie Wiesel, *Mémoire à deux voix*, Paris: Editions Odile Jacob, 1995.

Modiano, Patrick, *La Place de l'étoile*, Paris: Gallimard, 1968.

Moniquet, Claude, *Touvier, un milicien à l'ombre de l'église*, Paris: Orban, 1989.

Morel, Guy, *Barbie: pour mémoire*, Paris: Editions Fédération nationale des déportés et internés résistants et patriots, 1986.

Morgan, Ted, *An Uncertain Hour*, New York: Arbor House/William Morrow, 1990.

Morray, Joseph P., *Grand Disillusion: François Mitterrand and the French Left*, Westport: Praeger, 1997.

Mosse, George L., *Toward the Final Solution: A History of European Racism*, Madison: University of Wisconsin Press, 1985.

Namer, Gérard, *La Commémoration en France: de 1945 à nos jours*, Paris: L'Harmattan, 1987.

Naughton, Georges, *Le choc du passé: avortement, néo-nazisme, nouvelle morale*, La Celle Saint Cloud: Group d'action et de recherches pour l'avenir de l'homme, 1974.

Nettlebeck, Colin, "Getting the Story Right: Narratives of World War II in Post-1968 France," *Journal of European Studies*, 15 (1985), 77–116.

Nicault, Catherine, *La France et le sionisme, 1897–1948: une rencontre manquée?* Paris: Calmann-Lévy, 1992.

Nicolaïdis, Dimitri (ed.), *Oublier nos crimes: L'Amnésie nationale, une spécificité française?* Paris: Editions Autrement, 1994.

Noguerès, Henri, *La vérité aura le dernier mot*, Paris: Seuil, 1985.

Nora, Pierre, "Between Memory and History: *Les Lieux de Mémoire*," *Representations*, 26 (Spring 1989).

——, *Les lieux de Mémoire*, 3 vols., Paris: Gallimard, 1984–1992.

Novick, Peter, *The Resistance Versus Vichy*, New York: Columbia University Press, 1968.

Ophuls, Marcel, *Le chagrin et la pitié*, Paris: Editions Alain Moreau, 1980.

Paxton, Robert O., *Vichy France: Old Guard and New Order, 1940–1944*, New York: Columbia University Press, 1972.

Paris, Erna, *Unhealed Wounds: France and the Klaus Barbie Affair*, New York: Grove Press, 1985.

Péan, Pierre, *Une jeunesse française: François Mitterrand, 1934–1947*, Paris: Fayard, 1994.

Peschanski, Denis, *Les Tsiganes en France, 1939–1946*, Paris: Editions du CNRS, 1994.

Pisar, Samuel, *Le sang de l'espoir*, Paris: Robert Laffont, 1979.

Plantu, *Le petit Mitterrand illustré*, Paris: Seuil, 1995.

Poirot-Delpech, Bertrand, *Monsieur Barbie n'a rien à dire*, Paris: Gallimard, 1987.

Poliakov, Léon, *Histoire de l'antisémitisme*, 3 volumes, Paris: Calmann-Lévy, 1956–68.

Poznanski, Renée, *Être Juif en France pendant la Seconde Guerre mondiale*, Paris: Hachette, 1994.

Pulzer, Peter, *The Rise of Political Anti-Semitism in Germany and Austria*, Cambridge: Harvard University Press, 1988.

Rabinbach, Anson and Jack Zipes (eds.), *Germans and Jews Since the Holocaust: The Changing Situation in West Germany*, New York: Holmes and Meier, 1986.

Rajsfus, Maurice, *Identité à la carte: le judaïsme français en questions*, Paris: Arcantere, 1989.

——, *Des juifs dans la collaboration: l'Union générale des israélites de France*, Paris: EDI, 1980.

Rayski, Adam, *Le choix des juifs sous Vichy*, Paris: La Découverte, 1992.

Reid, Donald, "The Trial of Maurice Papon: History on Trial?" *French Historical Studies*, 16:4 (Fall 1998), 62–79.

Remond, René, Jean-Pierre Azéma, François Bédarida, Gérard Cholvy, Bernard Comte, Jean Dyandin, Jean-Dominique Durand, and Yves-Marie Hilaire, *Touvier et l'église*, Paris: Fayard, 1992.

Ricoeur, Paul, *La Mémoire, l'histoire, l'oubli*, Paris: Editions du Seuil, 2000.

———, *Time and Narrative*, volume 1, Chicago: University of Chicago Press, 1984.

———, *Le conflit des interprétations*, Paris: Seuil, 1969.

———, *De l'interprétation: essai sur Freud*, Paris: Editions du Seuil, 1965.

Rioux, Jean-Pierre, *The Fourth Republic, 1944–1958*, Cambridge: Cambridge University Press, 1987.

Rodinson, Maxime, *Israël et le refus arabe*, Paris: Editions du Seuil, 1968.

Rondeau, Daniel, *Mitterrand et nous*, Paris: Grasset, 1994.

Rosenfeld, Alvin (ed.), *Thinking About the Holocaust: After Half a Century*, Bloomington: Indiana University Press, 1997.

Rosenzweig, Luc, *La jeune France juive: conversations avec des juifs d'aujourd'hui*, Paris: Editions Libres-Hallier, 1980.

Roth, Michael S., *The Ironist's Cage: Memory, Trauma, and the Construction of History*, New York: Columbia University Press, 1995.

Rothschild, Alain, *Le Juif dans la cité: discours et conférences*, Paris, 1984.

Rousso, Henry, *Vichy: L'Événement, la mémoire, l'histoire*, Paris: Gallimard, 2001.

———, "The Historian, a Site of Memory," in Fishman et al. (eds.), *France at War*, 2000, 285–301.

———, *La hantise du passé*, Paris: Les éditions Textuel, 1998.

———, *The Vichy Syndrome: History and Memory in France Since 1944*, Cambridge: Harvard University Press, 1991.

———, "Pour une histoire de la mémoire collective: l'après-Vichy," *IHTP Cahiers*, 18 (June 1991), 163–76.

Rutkoff, Peter M., *Revanche and Revision: The Ligue des Patriots and the Origins of the Radical Right in France*, Athens: Ohio University Press, 1981.

Ruzie, David, "The Klaus Barbie Case: War Crimes Versus Crimes Against Humanity," *Patterns of Prejudice*, 20:3 (1986), 27–33.

Sadat, Leila Nadya, "The Legal Legacy of Maurice Papon," in Golsan (ed.), 2000, 131–60.

Santner, Eric, "History Beyond the Pleasure Principle: Some Thoughts on the Representation of Trauma," in Friedlander (ed.), 1992, 143–54.

Schafer, Roy, "Narration in the Psychoanalytic Dialogue," in Mitchell (ed.), 1981, 25–49.

Schain, Martin A., "Toward a Centrist Democracy? The Fate of the French Right," in Hollifield and Ross (eds.), 1991, 57–84.

Schnapper, Dominique, "The Politics of French Intellectuals," *Partisan Review*, 55 (Spring 1988), 219–37.

———, "Les jeunes générations juives dans la société française," *Etudes*, 358:3 (March 1983), 323–37.

———, *Jewish Identities in France*, Chicago: University of Chicago Press, 1983.

Schneiderman, Daniel, *L'étrange procès*, Paris: Fayard, 1998.

Schor, Ralph, *L'antisémitisme en France pendant les années trente*, Brussels: Editions Complexe, 1992.

Schuman, Howard and Jacqueline Scott, "Generations and Collective Memories," *American Sociological Review*, 54 (1989), 359–81.

Schwartz, Barry, Yael Zerubavel, and Bernice M. Barnett, "The Recovery of Masada: A Study in Collective Memory," *The Sociological Quarterly*, 27:2 (1986), 147–64.

Schwartz-Bart, André, *The Last of the Just*, New York: Atheneum, 1960.

Schwarzfuchs, Simon, *Du Juif à l'israélite: Histoire d'une mutation, 1770–1870*, Paris: Fayard, 1989.

Seager, Frederic H., *The Boulanger Affair: Political Crossroad of France, 1886–1889*, Ithaca: Cornell University Press, 1969.

Sécher, Reynald, *Juifs et Vendéens: d'un génocide à l'autre*, Paris: Olivier Orban, 1991.

——, *Le génocide franco-français: le Vendée vengé*, Paris: Presses universitaires de France, 1986.

Segev, Tom, *The Seventh Million: The Israelis and the Holocaust*, New York: Hill and Wang, 1993.

Slitinsky, Michel, *L'Affaire Papon*, Paris: Alain Moreau, 1983.

Sommet, Jacques, "Justice et mémoire: à propos du procès Barbie," *Études*, 366:5 (May 1987), 591–96.

Spelman, Elizabeth V., *Fruits of Sorrow: Framing Our Attention to Suffering*, Boston: Beacon Press, 1997.

Spence, Donald, *Narrative Truth and Historical Truth: Meaning and Interpretation in Psychoanalysis*, New York: Norton, 1982.

Spiegelman, Art, *Maus: A Survivor's Tale*, 2 volumes, New York: Pantheon, 1986, 1991.

Springer, Anne, "The Return of the Repressed in the Mask of the Victim," *The Journal of Psychohistory*, 17:3 (Winter 1990), 237–56.

Stein, Arlene, "Whose Memories? Whose Victimhood? Contests for the Holocaust Frame in Recent Social Movement Discourse," *Sociological Perspectives*, 41:3 (1998), 519–40.

Sternhell, Zeëv, *Neither Right nor Left: Fascist Ideology in France*, Berkeley: University of California Press, 1986.

——, *Ni Droite ni gauche: l'idéologie fasciste en France*, Paris: Le Seuil, 1983.

——, *La droite révolutionnaire, 1885–1914: Les origines françaises du fascisme*, Paris: Seuil, 1978.

Sweets, John F., "Hold that Pendulum! Redefining Fascism, Collaborationism and Resistance in France," *French Historical Studies*, 15:4 (Fall 1988), 731–58.

——, *Choices in Vichy France*, Oxford: Oxford University Press, 1986.

Swidler, Ann, "Culture in Action: Symbols and Strategies," *American Sociological Review*, 51 (April 1986), 273–86.

Szafran, Maurice, *Simone Veil: Destin*, Paris: Flammarion, 1994.

——, *Les Juifs dans la politique française*, Paris: Flammarion, 1990.

Taguieff, Pierre-André, "La nouvelle judéophobie: antisionisme, antiracisme, et anti-imperialisme," *Les Temps Modernes* (November 1989).

Tapia, Claude, "Religion et politique: interférence dans le judaïsme français après l'immigration judéo-maghrébine," in Lasry and Tapia (eds.), *Les Juifs du Maghreb*, 1989, 207–23.

——, *Les Juifs sépharades en France, 1965–1985*, Paris: Éditions L'Harmattan, 1986.

Terdiman, Richard, "Deconstructing Memory: On Representing the Past and Theorizing Culture in France Since the Revolution," *diacritics*, 15:4 (Winter 1985), 13–36.

Tiersky, Ronald, *François Mitterrand: The Last French President*, New York: St. Martin's Press, 2000.

Todorov, Tzvetan, "Letter from Paris: The Touvier Affair," *Salmagundi* (Winter 1993), reprinted in Golsan (ed.), 1996, 114–21.

——, *Les Abus de la mémoire*, Paris: Seuil/Arlea, 1995.

——, *Face à l'extrême*, Paris: Editions du Seuil, 1991.

Touraine, Alain, *The May Movement: Revolt and Reform*, New York: Random House, 1971.

Trigano, Shmuel, "From Individual to Collectivity: The Rebirth of the 'Jewish Nation' in France," in Malino and Wasserstein (eds.), 1985, 245–81.

——, *La République et les Juifs après Copernic*, Paris: Les presses d'aujourd'hui, 1982.

——, *La Nouvelle question juive, l'avenir d'un espoir*, Paris: Gallimard, 1979.

Valensi, Lucette and Nathan Wachtel, *Jewish Memories*, Berkeley: University of California Press, 1991.

Varaut, Jean-Marc, *Le procès Pétain, 1945–1995*, Paris: Perrin, 1995.

Vergès, Jacques, *Pour en finir avec Ponce-Pilate*, Paris: Pré aux Clercs, 1983.

Veyrier, Henri, *La mémoire des français: recherches d'histoire culturelle*, Paris: Kronos, 1991.

Vidal-Naquet, Pierre, *Assassins of Memory*, New York: Columbia University Press, 1992.

——, *Les juifs, la mémoire et le présent*, 2 volumes, Paris: La Découverte, 1991.

Violet, Bernard, *Le dossier Papon*, Paris: Flammarion, 1997.

Wahl, Alfred (ed.), *Mémoire de la Seconde Guerre mondiale*, Metz: Centre de recherche histoire et civilisation de l'université de Metz, 1984.

Weber, Max, *The Methodology of the Social Sciences*, translated and edited by Edward A. Shils and Henry A. Finch, New York: The Free Press, 1949.

Weinberg, David H., "The Reconstruction of the French Jewish Community After World War II," *She'erit Hapletah, 1944–48*, 1990, 167–86.

——, *A Community on Trial: The Jews of Paris in the 1930s*, Chicago: The University of Chicago Press, 1977.

Weinberg, Henry, *The Myth of the Jew in France, 1967–1982*, New York: Mosaic Press, 1987.

Wellers, Georges (ed.), *La France et la question juive, 1940–1944*, Paris: Editions Sylvie Messinger, 1981.

White, Hayden, "Historical Emplotment and the Problem of Truth," in Friedlander (ed.), 1992, 37–53.

——, *The Content of the Form: Narrative Discourse and Historical Representation*, Baltimore: The Johns Hopkins University Press, 1987.

Wiedmer, Caroline, *The Claims of Memory: Representations of the Holocaust in Germany and France*, Ithaca: Cornell University Press, 1999.

Wieviorka, Annette, *Déportation et génocide: entre la mémoire et l'oubli*, Paris: Plon, 1992.

——, *Le procès Eichmann*, Brussels: Complexe, 1989.

——, "Un lieu de mémoire: le mémorial du martyr juif inconnu," *Pardès*, 2 (1985), 80–98.

Wieviorka, Olivier, *Nous entrerons dans la carrière*, Paris: Seuil, 1994.

Wilson, Stephen, *Ideology and Experience: Antisemitism in France at the Time of the Dreyfus Affair*, Rutherford, NJ: Fairleigh Dickinson University Press, 1982.

Winock, Michel (ed.), *Histoire de l'extrême droite en France*, Paris: Editions du Seuil, 1993.

——, *Nationalisme, antisémitisme, et fascisme en France*, Paris: Seuil, 1990.

Wolf, Joan B., "'Anne Frank is Dead, Long Live Anne Frank': The Six-Day War and the Holocaust in French Public Discourse," *History and Memory*, 11:1 (Summer 1999) 104–40.

Wolitz, Seth, "Imagining the Jew in France: From 1945 to the Present," *Yale French Studies*, 85 (1994), 119–34.

Wood, Nancy, *Vectors of Memory: Legacies of Trauma in Postwar Europe*, Oxford: Berg, 1999.

——, "Memory on Trial in Contemporary France: The Case of Maurice Papon," *History and Memory*, 11:1 (Spring/Summer 1999), 41–76.

Yerushalmi, Yosef Hayim, *Zakhor: Jewish History and Jewish Memory*, Seattle: University of Washington Press, 1982.

Yonnet, Paul, "La machine Carpentras: Histoire et sociologie d'un syndrome d'épuration," *Le débat*, 61 (September 1990), 18–34.

Young, James E., *Writing and Rewriting the Holocaust: Narrative and the Consequences of Interpretation*, Bloomington: Indiana University Press, 1988.

Zertal, Idith, "Du bon usage du souvenir: les Israéliens et la Shoa," *Le débat*, 58 (January–February 1990), 92–103.

Zerubavel, Yael, *Recovered Roots: Collective Memory and the Making of Israeli National Tradition*, Chicago: University of Chicago Press, 1995.

Zuccotti, Susan, *The Holocaust, the French, and the Jews*, New York: Basic Books, 1993.